The University of Southampton

An Illustrated History

The University of
Southampton

An Illustrated History

Sally Nash and Martin Sherwood

JAMES X JAMES

First published in 2002
© The University of Southampton
www.soton.ac.uk

ISBN hardback 0-907383-93-9
ISBN softback 0-907383-94-7

Project Editor and Designer: Susannah McSkimming
Picture Research Assistant: Nicholas Waddell

Published by James & James (Publishers) Ltd
Gordon House Business Centre
6 Lissenden Gardens
London NW5 1LX

Picture Acknowledgements

Dr Jim Andrews 234, 235; Associated Newspapers 36 (bottom); Alan D. Baker, Southampton 59 (top), 60 (top right); Baynard Press 38; Simon Blazquez 123 (middle, bottom middle, and bottom right); Steve Bottoms 118; Dr Ken Collins 242 (main picture); Debenham and Gould, Bournemouth 37 (top); Hulton Archive 272; Paul Joyce 91; Sally Loveday 30 (bottom); Fraser Lumsden 47; Barry Marsh 236; Dr Alexander Mustard 238 (top row); News Chronicle 56; Photo Studios, London 96; Steve Shrimpton 126 (top right) 179, 260; Nellie G. Smith 40 (bottom); University of Southampton Archives half-title page, 10 (top), 11, 12, 13, 15, 18, 19, 20, 21, 22, 23, 25, 26 (bottom), 27, 28, 29 (top), 30, 31, 32 (bottom), 33, 34, 35, 36, 37, 38, 40, 41, 44, 47, 55, 56, 57, 58 (bottom), 59, 60, 61, 62 (top), 69, 72, 73, 76, 84, 88, 91, 96, 97, 257, 261, 262 (top margin), 269; Staff and students of the University of Southampton 26 (top), 29 (bottom), 51 (bottom right), 54, 58 (bottom), 64, 65, 67, 70 (bottom), 82, 89, 102, 106, 110 (bottom), 113, 118, 122, 123 (middle left and middle right), 124, 126, 127, 130 (bottom left), 135, 138, 139, 142, 143, 144 (top right), 145, 147, 152, 154, 155, 157, 158, 159, 162, 166, 167, 170, 171, 186, 191, 197, 199, 202, 218, 219, 222, 223, 230, 231, 238 (bottom), 239, 242 (margin), 243, 246, 260, 262 (main, bottom margin), 271, 276 (bottom), 277, 282; *Southern Daily Echo* 58 (bottom right), 59 (bottom), 62 (top), 69, 72 (bottom), 73 (bottom), 76, 88, 269; Sportsphoto 115; R. G. Tulley 35 (top right), 36 (top middle, top right); Raymond V. Turley 123 (top); Vandyk 22 (top); Andy Vowles 224, 225, 226, 227; Arthur S. Young 26 (bottom left)

New photography by Joe Low
title page, 8, 10 (bottom), 32 (top), 39, 48, 51 (top, bottom left), 58 (top), 62-3, 66, 70 (top), 71, 74, 75, 78, 79, 94, 95, 98, 104, 107, 110 (top), 111, 114, 119, 123 (bottom left), 125, 130 (all but bottom left), 144 (top left, bottom), 175, 183, 190, 191, 194, 215, 250, 263, 266, 270, 273, 274, 275, 276 (margin), 278, 279

We are grateful to the people whose photographs have been reproduced but who could not be traced despite our best efforts, and are therefore unacknowledged.

Half-title page illustration: the mascot 'Kelly' in the care of a group of ex-service students, taken in the Engineering Block, *c*.1920.

Title page illustration: students on the lawn by the Hartley Library.

Foreword

On 29 April 1952, in the early weeks of the reign of HM Queen Elizabeth II, the University of Southampton was granted its Royal Charter, enabling it to award its own degrees and to determine its own future. The 50 years of the University celebrated in 2002 have therefore mirrored the reign of HM the Queen, and also witnessed a period of unique development for the UK's higher education sector.

Today there are many more universities and vastly increased numbers of students than in 1952, and the universities themselves are fulfilling new roles. In addition to the traditional emphasis on high-quality teaching, learning, and research, they are now also centres of enterprise and innovation, acting as catalysts for their regional economies, while increasingly involved in internationally co-ordinated research programmes to tackle global problems that affect us all.

As can be seen from this new history, the University of Southampton and its predecessor institutions have exemplified this process of adaptive change, responding with positive initiatives to national and international emergencies, government policies and funding regimes, and widespread changes in society. To survive and flourish against a background of dramatic and often rapid change is a great achievement in itself.

Since the early days of the University, over 100,000 students have graduated, and many thousands of staff have supported its aims and endeavours. It is their contribution that has made the University what it is today, and this is their story, full of character and incident, and set against the background of the evolution of the institution, which has been vividly brought to life by the authors of this book. It makes fascinating and compelling reading, fully demonstrating why the University can face its next 50 years with confidence.

The Earl of Selborne KBE FRS DL
Chancellor of the University of Southampton

Sir Basil Spence's staff refectory (right), the Nuffield Theatre (centre background), and Steel Forms *by Justin Knowles (centre foreground), seen through Barbara Hepworth's sculpture,* Two Figures, *on Highfield Campus.*

Contents

Authors' and Publishers' Acknowledgements

In the course of research for this work, many members of academic and administrative staff, past and present were interviewed and consulted. They willingly devoted valuable time to being interviewed, and reading and commenting on their sections. Any errors or inadequacies which remain, however, are exclusively our responsibility.

We are most grateful to Professor Sir Howard Newby who set the project in motion, and provided information about his period as Vice-Chancellor; also the project's advisory committee – who provided advice throughout – including Dr Peter Lanchester (former Deputy Vice-Chancellor), Bernard Naylor, (former University Librarian), Derek Schofield (former Secretary and Registrar), and Peter Reader (Director of External Relations, who chaired the advisory committee and contributed important revisions to the text). We received essential information and advice from John Lauwerys (Secretary and Registrar) and from heads of faculties and other departments or schools, including: Dr Jim Andrews (School of Ocean and Earth Science), Dr Barry Blott (Department of Physics and Astronomy), Professor Roger Briggs (Dean, Faculty of Medicine, Health, and Biological Sciences) Dr Bill Brooks (Dean, Faculty of Arts), Professor Paul Carling (Director, Environmental Sciences Centre), David Chettleburgh (Estates and Buildings) who contributed 'Building a Vision', Professor Paul Curran (Dean, Faculty of Science), Professor Ian Diamond (Dean, Faculty of Social Sciences), Professor Nick Foskett (Head, Research and Graduate School of Education), Professor Joe Hammond (Dean, Faculty of Engineering), Professor Geoffrey Luckhurst (Department of Chemistry), Karen Robson (University Archives), Professor Howard Roe (Director, Southampton Oceanography Centre), Dr David Rogers (Department of Chemistry), Professor Andrew Rutherford (Dean, Faculty of Law), Dawn Trenchard (Environmental Sciences Centre), and Dr Chris Woolgar (University Archives).

For the many others who contributed much important information for text and illustrations but are not mentioned here, we hope they will excuse the omission and accept our warm thanks.

Finally, we owe a particular debt to Joyce Lewis of External Relations who was a member of the project's advisory committee and devoted a great deal of time and expert knowledge to the project from beginning to end. Her contribution was pivotal.

I

INSTITUTION AND COLLEGE

1. Hartley's Good Deed, 1850–62

The University of Southampton was founded on port. Henry Robinson Hartley, who left the balance of his estate to the Corporation of Southampton for, among other things, the founding of the institution which eventually became the University, was the son of one Southampton wine merchant and the great nephew of another. At no time during his life did Henry Robinson Hartley follow his father into the wine business, or indeed go into any business. Instead he lived the life of a hypochondriac recluse, constantly looking for a place to which to escape from the modern world.

It was from Southampton especially that Hartley wanted to escape. In earlier centuries the town had experienced periods of decline followed by recovery and during Tudor times it had prospered. Italian merchants had built themselves luxurious houses here, some still standing, which English merchants had copied. By the early 1700s, however, visitors like Defoe agreed that it was in decline if not decay, 'the great houses of its merchants falling to the ground.'

During the rest of the century its fortunes began to improve. Although still small in 1801 with a population of only about 8,000, the town flourished in the last quarter of the eighteenth century. It was this newly flourishing and increasingly industrialised Southampton rather than the town of his childhood which Hartley disliked.

Apart from its smelliness, Wilkins's tannery typified the new Southampton. The end of the Napoleonic Wars in 1815 had at first brought an economic depression to the town, but from 1822 onwards there had been a strong

Susanna Hartley, mother of Henry Robinson Hartley.

Henry Robinson Hartley, 1777–1850, painted aged 9. This is the only known portrait of the University's founder.

recovery in its trade and above all in its passenger service to the Channel Islands and the Continent. In the early 1820s the town made a brief attempt to re-popularise itself as a spa, with a 'season', race meetings, regattas, balls, public lectures, balloon ascents and cruises. Between 1811 and 1831 its population doubled, growing from just over 9,000 to nearly 19,000. Even then its great expansion was still ahead and came only with the arrival of the railway in 1836, the opening of the docks in 1840 and the establishment in the town of P&O, the Royal Mail and other mail shipping lines. By 1851 its population had almost doubled again, rising to over 34,000.

By then Hartley was dead. First he had lived in Calais, then for 13 years in Southwark, then between 1846 and 1850 in Calais again. And the full terms of his bequest confirm that he had no love for the modern Southampton from which he had escaped but only a fondness for the town he had known long ago.

The funds were to be used in the first place to 'cause a small building to be erected on part of my Leasehold Estate, lying eastward of my Houses . . . to serve as a repository for my Household Furniture, Books, Manuscripts, and other moveables. The Corporation was to appoint a person with a salary, to have the care of the same.' Hartley's bequest may have seemed at first sight clear enough both in what it gave to the Corporation and what the Corporation should do with the money, but in practice it settled neither of these questions. The answers ultimately arrived at were to be of the greatest importance to the institution which eventually became the university. Hartley had died in 1850. It was not until 1858 that these problems were solved and another four years before the Hartley Institution was able to celebrate its opening.

Essentially, the court had to decide whether Hartley's next-of-kin, his supposed daughter and a remote Robinson relative, could claim all or part of Hartley's estate. The complex arguments, appeals, judgements and reversals of judgements which finally led to the Corporation's entitlement being confirmed are of less importance than the settlement to which the Corporation ultimately agreed. It was left with only £40,500, considerably less than half the amount it had hoped for. The result was the chronic shortage of money from which the Institution, when finally set up, was to suffer for the rest of the century.

The second matter now had to be settled: what precisely the Corporation should do with the bequest. It was a question which aroused in the town far fiercer controversy than the obscure proceedings in Chancery. The proposers fell into two groups: those who supported the establishment of a college, similar in character, for example, to Owens College, Manchester; and those who favoured the creation of an institute with a library and other features proposed by Hartley, to be used only by a select public.

The leader of the college party was the Revd Edmund Kell, the

Unitarian minister in Southampton. Essentially he wanted a college to be established in a new building where seven professors should teach traditional arts and science subjects. The institute party was led by Joseph Stebbing, a merchant who had come from Portsmouth and established himself in Southampton as an optician and maker of nautical instruments. He had already been much involved with the Literary and Philosophical Society and the Polytechnic. He had been a town councillor, later became an alderman and was altogether a much more influential figure than Kell.

Eventually, in July 1858 the Corporation arranged a public debate on the subject by which it might be guided. Kell and Stebbing were the chief speakers for the college and institute parties respectively. While Kell argued that a college would help a wider section of the population, Stebbing maintained that if Hartley had wanted to found a college he would have said so.

Stebbing's eloquence was successful. The meeting passed unanimously a motion urging the Hartley Bequest Committee to choose his proposals. The Committee therefore set about creating the sort of facilities which Hartley had wanted: a library, museum, and reading room together with a lecture hall and five classrooms. (An observatory and a botanical garden were to come later.)

On 15 October 1862 the Hartley Institution was ready for an opening which exceeded in splendour anything that anyone in the town could remember.

Henry Hartley, father of Henry Robinson Hartley.

Southampton High Street, mid-nineteenth century.

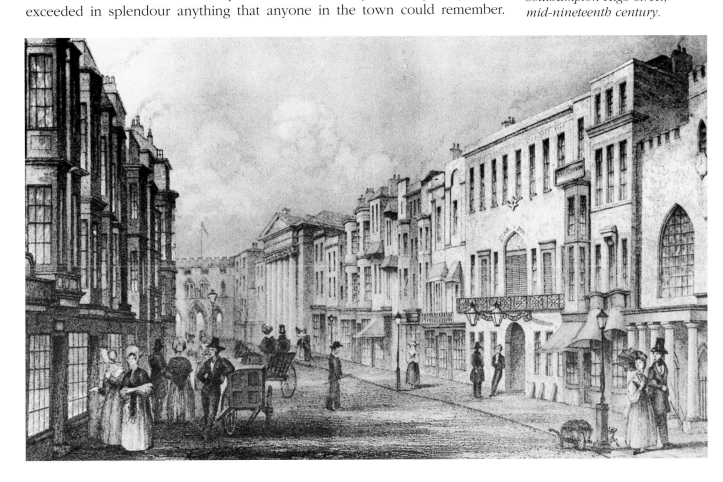

The opening of the Hartley Institution, 1862.

Main picture: *Lord Palmerston arrives at the front of the building.*

Below, left: *Lord Palmerston's procession through Southampton High Street (looking north to Bargate).*

Below, middle: *the interior of the Hartley Institution hall.*

Below, right: *the banquet in honour of the occasion.*

Lord Palmerston, the Prime Minister, performed the ceremony. Met by the mayor at the Common, he was led below triumphal arches in a procession which included eight bands, the crews of two naval vessels, contingents from three shipping companies, a fully crewed lifeboat on a wagon and representatives of the ancient companies of Oddfellows and Foresters. As he and a bevy of dignitaries reached the Institution they were welcomed by a 19-gun salute. Speeches came next, then a banquet at which, appropriately, the wines were abundant and 'of the best bouquet'. The ball which followed was attended by 500 and lasted till five in the morning.

2. Growing Pains, 1863–83

The Trials of Dr Bond

To those who favoured an institute, the grand opening of the Hartley Institution seemed to confirm their success. Underlying all that happened during the next 30 years was a relentless reversal of their victory and the effective transformation of their institute into a college.

After capital expenditure on the building, the Hartley Council was left with an annual income of £800. To face this and many other problems the Council had by now appointed as principal Dr Francis Bond. Bond, aged 28, was a medical doctor, but as Professor of Chemistry and Dean of Faculty at Queen's College, Birmingham, he had already been involved with education. He was a man of energy and intelligence. He did not mean to transform the Institution. On the contrary, he recommended that the Hartley Council retain the Institution's character.

Within a few years, however, reality began to impose itself. Though by 1865 the Institution had almost 700 members, thereafter its membership steadily declined, while its lectures and concerts were not successful. At first the classes which Bond began to arrange were no better supported. It was only when he managed to obtain the India Office's approval for courses which would train the telegraphists and engineers India needed, and the Hartley Council's agreement that they could be held at the Institution provided he and two other teachers took financial responsibility for them, that successful daytime classes began. By 1870, they had 70 students.

Evening classes also began to prosper when Bond obtained encouragement (and ultimately an annual grant) from the Science and Art Department, with 136 students attending in the 1870–1 session. The same department supported an arrangement by which the failing local School of Art became a branch of the Hartley Institution. To bring the School of Art to the Institution's site new classrooms were needed and again the Institution had to obtain the Charity Commissioners' permission to borrow from its capital. Nevertheless, by 1871 the Hartley Council was able to report 'a state of affairs which even the most sanguine person would hardly have anticipated two years ago'.

These had been Bond's eight successful years. They were followed by two years of frustration and failure. The most serious setback was a result of the India Office opening its own school at Cooper's Hill. Meanwhile Bond was being attacked by public petition, in the press and in committee – mainly unfairly – for his management of the Institution. Then a row blew up between Bond and the head of the School of Art. When the Hartley Council sided with Bond and recommended that Baker be dismissed, the Corporation refused to agree. Matters were only resolved when the Charity Commissioners suggested that a new Hartley Council be created. The importance of this was that for the first time it reduced the Corporation's hitherto total control of the Institution.

*Top: W. R. Bower, winner of a National Scholarship in Science, 1884.
Middle: F. V. Poole, gold medallist in Art, 1884.
Bottom: S. A. Sworn, Royal Exhibitioner and Silver Medallist of the Royal College of Science, 1884.*

The new Hartley Council sacked Baker and took over from Bond the financing of what remained of the daytime classes, but its support had come too late. In April 1873 Bond resigned, to spend the rest of his life as Gloucestershire's Medical Officer of Health.

Thomas Shore's Lengthy Interregnum

Bond was succeeded by a mathematician, Charles Blackadder, but after two years a scientist, Thomas Shore, was given charge of the Institution. He was named its Chief Executive Officer, not Principal, and this he remained for 20 years.

Shore, aged 34, came from Lancashire where he would probably have stayed but for the health of his family. Though physics and chemistry were his subjects, natural history was what really interested him. In 1885 he was to be one of the founders of the Hampshire Field Club and Archaeological Society. He would lead members on walks through the New Forest and elsewhere. In 1878 he was elected a Fellow of the Geographical Society and in 1892 he published a history of Hampshire.

It was likely, therefore, that Shore should persuade the Hartley Council to support the Institution's museum which he described as a collection of 'miscellaneous objects from all quarters and all climates, illustrative of anything in general and no special branch of knowledge in particular.' He reorganised it to illustrate his particular subject: the geology, archaeology and fauna of Hampshire. The Council also gave new support to the library, enabling it to expand to some 22,000 volumes.

Meanwhile most of the teachers whom Bond had appointed had left. One of the best to go was the chemist, A. W. Bickerton. When Bickerton died in 1929, aged 87, his old pupils still remembered how excellent his lectures had been. One of those to stay was not a teacher but the treasurer to the reformed Hartley Council, William Darwin, eldest son of Charles Darwin. He was to hold this position for 41 years, and also to make numerous donations to the Institution. Though a banker by profession, he was above all a gentleman. The picture of him given by his niece, Gwen Raverat, is also a picture of the sort of worthy Southampton citizen who supported the Institution during its early years.

In 1885 Shore secured for the Institution its most distinguished student of the century, Frederick William Lanchester, by pretending to Lanchester's father that what he saw through the frosted glass windows of a classroom was the line-shafting of a properly equipped engineering workshop. In fact it was merely a gas supply pipe. About Lanchester's later achievements his biographer wrote that he 'designed and made the first genuine automobile and laid bare the reasons for the flight of the aeroplane.'

He remembered his two years there, aged 14 to 16, with much gratitude. He lodged with Du Domaine, the Institution's tall, strong, iron-grey-bearded French teacher, and was taught mathematics by the newly arrived Irishman,

Jeffaires, whom he considered to have been the best teacher of mathematics he ever had. Less order was kept by the chemistry teacher, James Brierley, another Lancastrian, who remained convinced that the south of the country was intrinsically inferior to the north.

An advantage of the Institution for an independent-minded boy like Lanchester was that there were subjects which none of its staff was qualified to teach. In these the boys were merely encouraged to read for themselves. They included mathematics, heat, light and sound, electricity and magnetism, mechanics, steam engines, chemistry, metallurgy, machine drawing, building construction, descriptive geometry, animal physiology, agriculture and physiography, evidence of the breadth of scientific and technical subjects which the Institution at least encouraged its students to learn even if its staff could not teach them all. The standards to which it taught are harder to judge since each paper had three grades, between which candidates could choose. When Lanchester disliked the elementary chemistry paper he took the advanced one and scored full marks. His results put him seventh in the Arts and Science Department's list and earned him one of 20 national scholarships to the Normal School of Science at South Kensington.

The Hartley Institution, c.1908.

By 1885, as a result of a general lightening of the country's economic depression, the evening classes were being attended by 500 students. And though the daytime classes so diminished that at one time they were being held on only three days a week, after 1879 they too expanded. Now the *Southampton Times* considered that there was no reason why the Hartley should not soon 'do for the South of England what Owens College is doing for the North.'

Somewhat belatedly, during Shore's last ten years the Institution attempted to expand in a number of ways, the most important of them inspired by the recognition among educationalists and politicians that the country would soon trail behind if it did not provide better scientific and technical education.

In Shore's defence it must be said that it was he who often suggested ways in which the Institution might expand or improve its finances, and other people who ignored his suggestions or allowed them to fail. In 1885 he suggested that the Institution should join with similar establishments to ask the Government for regular direct aid. Four years and many meetings later, the Government gave £15,000 for this purpose. Of the 12 colleges and institutes which applied for a share, the Hartley Institution alone received nothing, on the grounds that it did not have adequate teachers and the Hartley Council was not a proper governing body.

The Council decided not to appeal, but to press the Corporation to take advantage of the Technical Instruction Act, passed the same year, which allowed it to raise a penny rate, to be spent on supporting technical education. To this the Corporation agreed but the Institution benefited less than it had hoped, receiving only £837 out of the £1,395 which the rate raised, the rest going to other Southampton establishments.

Shore had also, in order to qualify for a share of the penny rate, proposed a Technical Education Scheme, which would support the training of boys in skills connected with Southampton's industries and trades by offering 50 daytime and 150 evening scholarships in appropriate subjects. Unfortunately the new lecture hall, chemistry laboratory and classrooms could only be sited where they would deprive nearby houses of light. When the Corporation allowed building to continue, the executors of the tenants of these houses obtained an injunction against the Corporation which provoked the contractor to claim compensation for losses caused by the suspension of his work. Queen's College, Oxford, the freehold owner of the houses, eventually became the Corporation's chief opponent, and obtained virtually all it demanded, including legal costs and the removal of the top floor from the new teaching block.

More teachers were employed for the new projects and it was one of these, Halliday, who stirred up staff discontent. In November 1891 he persuaded four other staff members to join him in writing to the Hartley Council asking for direct access to the Council and the right to elect their own chairman to represent them. When the Council rejected this demand, Halliday and an outside supporter began to attack the Council in letters to the press.

Among other things they claimed that the Institution underpaid its staff, that Shore, in order to obtain a larger share of the penny rate, had exaggerated the number of the Institution's students, and that the share of the rate which it had received had not been spent on the Technical Education Scheme but on paying its debt to Queen's College.

There was enough truth in these accusations for the Corporation's Technical Instruction Committee to investigate them and for the Hartley Council to invite a general report on the Institution by Sir Philip Magnus, superintendent of the Department of Technology at the City and Guilds Institute. Magnus's report finally decided the Institution's future. It had done its best, he wrote, to be both an institute and to teach like a college, but this was no longer financially possible. To meet the 'increasing demands for popular and industrial education' it must decide to become primarily a college.

3. The London Connection, 1883–1913

Dr Stewart Has His Way

With the transformation of the Institution into a college Shore's influence declined. He was deprived of most of his responsibilities and two new parallel posts were created, the first to run the Institution's art school, the second to take charge of the teaching of all other subjects. In 1894 Dr R. W. Stewart was appointed to this second post.

Aged 35, Stewart had studied at Owens College, Manchester, and Aberystwyth University College. He had taught at an elementary school, becoming its headmaster, then became a lecturer in science at Bangor University College. He was thus not the widely experienced man Magnus had said should be chosen, but as usual shortage of money had prevented the Hartley Council from offering a salary which would have attracted more mature applicants. It was lucky in choosing a man whose energy and intelligence compensated for lack of experience. Bangor had obviously introduced him to university-level teaching, but it was probably as important that he had once been a headmaster and retained a taste for being in command, however much this sometimes irritated both Council and staff. He only stayed at the Institution until 1900 but the transformation he achieved in his few years was as important as any in its history.

Before he even left Bangor he sent the Hartley Council an outline of his proposals. The most significant of these set a minimum age of 16 for the Institution's students. It would thus become a place to which clever pupils at secondary schools could hope to progress, and at which they could take courses designed to lead to London University.

Stewart's vision was not entirely unlike those of his predecessors: to expand the Institution's activities and give it the extra staff and additional buildings which this would require. But it was based on a clear view of what he hoped the Institution would become. He wanted it to occupy a well-defined position in the educational arrangements for the town and county. To do so it needed a technical electrical laboratory, a new physics laboratory, equipment to complete the engineering laboratory, classrooms for teaching biology and geology, and a technology and science library. In total these would cost at least £3,000, while redecorating the existing premises would cost another £500 and additional staff another £800 a year.

The Hartley Council prevaricated. How was it to raise such a sum, and how to increase its income? In the 1894–5 academic year it had made a loss of £200. Stewart suggested a subscription list of the sort which had supported Aberystwyth for some years, but the Council had by then appealed for contributions to the building of the physics laboratory and was reluctant to ask for

The College Library,
c.1908.

more public support. He suggested asking for contributions from the Technical Instruction Committees of Hampshire and other counties. When this produced no worthwhile response he proposed asking the Corporation to raise another penny rate for the support of technical education.

Progress was made, with the physics laboratory an example. New scholarships were created, open to any student between the ages of 16 and 25. But the Council still would not authorise the appointment of half a dozen new full-time lecturers qualified to supervise courses for London degree candidates. And the Corporation still failed to raise a new rate which might have made these appointments affordable. As a result Stewart became exasperated, and in November 1895 demanded a meeting with the Hartley Council at which he could explain his difficulties. He was in a Catch-22 situation. Without more money the Institution could not pay for new teachers, but without more, well-qualified teachers to raise its standards it could not sell itself to bodies like County Councils which might provide the money.

Stewart's other complaint was that more was being spent on administration, still controlled by Shore, than was necessary. The outcome suggests that while the extravagant management of the Institution may have been Stewart's specific complaint, he also told the Council that it must choose between himself and Shore. The Council chose Stewart, appointing him Principal and raising his salary from £250 to £300. It invited Shore to retire within a few weeks, on 1 January 1896.

Stewart's difficulties were not over. His estimate that the deficit for the 1895–6 year would be larger than the previous year's was further alarming news. Now William Darwin, the Council's treasurer since the new Council had been formed in 1872, made a gesture which influenced events out of all proportion to its size. He persuaded two other Council members to join him in guaranteeing the deficit to the amount of £300. This, together with his reputation as a banker and his personal encouragement of the Council to risk making the new staff appointments, at last persuaded it to give Stewart what he wanted. By the start of the 1896–7 academic year the new staff had been appointed and the Institution was in a position to become a college in fact as well as intention. To emphasise this transformation it changed its name to Hartley College.

In July 1889 a Day Training Department to train adult teachers, a new venture which the Council, not Stewart, had proposed was sanctioned at the College. This was funded by the newly created Board of Education which gave 30 men and 30 women each year a maintenance allowance and paid their

College fees. They worked towards the London University matriculation examination after one year and a London intermediate degree after two years. But the Board would only support the Day Training Scheme if the College provided accommodation. It was thus forced to expand in a new way by arranging registered lodgings for men and hostel accommodation for women.

Stewart and the Council now considered that the College was ready to be promoted to a University College. While the Council set up a committee to devise ways to achieve this, Stewart took advice from other university colleges and drafted a charter. It was no help to the College's hopes or morale that in the autumn of 1898 the staff became discontented with Stewart's authoritarian regime and asked, as they had in Shore's time, to be allowed to form a staff council which would be independent of the Principal and enable them to take a larger part in running the college. This was by no means the sort of development which Stewart fancied, and the Council supported him. But in the autumn of 1900, Stewart unexpectedly resigned as an indirect result of the college having been forced to provide accommodation for women. This consisted of two houses in Avenue Place.

When Stewart cancelled this arrangement, their owner revenged herself by complaining to the Council that he had spent an unnecessary amount of time visiting the hostel's Lady Superintendent, Miss Blaxley, and that during a party there he and the lady had behaved improperly. The Council resolved that Stewart's behaviour had been 'extremely indiscreet' and accepted his resignation.

In November the following year, the University Council Grants Committee sent two inspectors to Southampton to report on the College. Though they wrote favourably about its teaching they were not satisfied with its finances. To simplify, the Treasury required it to have an income from local sources of £4,000, whereas it was only receiving a total of £3,198. Again William Darwin and other Council members made donations which covered the balance and promised to do so in future years. This satisfied the Treasury which gave the college a backdated grant of £1,000 a year, and on 23 November 1902 Hartley College became Hartley University College. Though Stewart had departed, there is little doubt that he should be given the credit for this success.

The Hartley Institution Museum with showcases, bookcases, two balconies wtih shields and mounted antlers, and skylights, c.1910.

Community

By now the new University College had developed into a very different institution from its predecessors. In short, it was becoming a community. Soon it would have most of the social and sporting features of other late Victorian and

Edwardian schools and colleges, from a debating society to games clubs, a rifle corps and a magazine.

The halls of residence (two women's hostels had now been opened, one at Bevois Mount House in Lodge Road, another at Windsor House in Cumberland Place) were important in this transformation. In the summer term the 30 women students at Bevois Mount Hostel would give garden parties, exciting occasions no doubt, when women students had to be in their halls by 6 p.m. in winter and 8.30 p.m. in summer, in bed by 10 p.m. and never speak to male students except on college premises.

Soon College societies proliferated. Professor F. J. C. Hearnshaw, Head of the History Department, became president of the Debating Society. In an early debate this showed itself properly patriotic by defeating the motion, 'That the British Empire will decay.' Soon afterwards, however, it carried 'by a large majority' the motion, 'That management of the Railways be in the hands of the state.'

There was also a Choral Society, a Camera Club, a Browning Society, a Christian Union with men's and women's branches, and an especially flourishing Engineering Society which made visits to local factories and the engine rooms of ships in the docks. Though there was no formal dramatic society, plays of a sort must have been staged at the various *soirées* because Richardson in 1906, in an attempt to improve academic standards, ordered that *soirées* must not include any dramatic performances which needed 'considerable preparation'.

As for games and sports, there was soon a Tennis Club, a Boat Club, and a Boxing and Gymnastic Club, the last two founded by H. E. Piggott, an assistant

The Football team, 1901–2.

in the Teacher Training Department. In spite of the College having no playing field, enthusiastic students also founded both a Cricket and a Football (soccer) Club.

An even more interesting arrival was a college magazine. This was suggested by Professor Hudson (mathematics) in 1900 and approved at a General College Meeting in February the following year. It was to have a member of staff as its editor, and Hudson was chosen.

Crisis

However, below the surface of the newly recognised University College with its talented staff, increasing number of students and growing sense of community, there lurked the causes of a disaster which in the next 11 years all but destroyed everything that Dr Stewart had achieved.

As usual money was the root of the problem. The College now had two patrons: the Treasury, and the Board of Education. But the Treasury's support depended not only on the College continuing to raise £4,000 a year locally, but also on it satisfying the University Commissioners that it was retaining university standards; and the Department of Education's support depended on the College providing a satisfactory Day Training Department. Within a few years it was doing none of these things.

The year after those worthy Council members had made it possible by personal contributions for the College to become a university college, one of them had died and others were unwilling to keep their promises to contribute

J. F. Hudson, Professor of Mathematics at the University College of Southampton, 1900–4.

The Art Room in the Hartley Institution, c.1908.

Claude Montefiore, Vice-President of University College 1908–10, 1934–8, and President of University College 1910–34, photographed c.1934.

again. The Council bridged the gap by re-stating as local support £300 of the money it received from the Department of Education in payment of the fees of the students in the Day Training Department. The Treasury, however, was advised by the University Commissioners that this was not satisfactory because most of these students were not doing university standard work. In practice the Treasury continued for three years to make grants to the College, but each time it warned the College that in future its grant might be reduced or discontinued.

Soon the Department of Education became equally dissatisfied. In 1906 one of its inspectors reported that many students in the Day Training Department were 'very ill-equipped to pursue a special course of study.' Far more disturbing, in 1907 the University Commissioners' inspectors made the same criticism of the College's students as a whole. They pointed out that where other university colleges only accepted students who had passed a matriculation examination, Hartley University College merely asked them to pass its own entrance exam.

Richardson attempted to do something about this problem, introducing stricter entry conditions, a tutorial system, periodic reports and monthly tests. Less easily solved was the problem of its buildings, a subject to which both its patrons returned again and again. In 1907 the University Commissioners' inspectors found them 'far from suitable for their purpose, as judged by modern standards, packed in the centre of the town . . . cramped, inconvenient and . . . ill-lighted.' The Department of Education inspectors wrote that they were 'of the rabbit-warren order'.

Finally the Treasury acted. It announced that its grant to the College (which had risen to £3,400 a year) would be reduced for each of the years 1907–8 and 1908–9 to £2,250. Two years later, in the autumn of 1909 the University Commissioners again sent inspectors who advised that the College should ultimately revert to being 'a local college under municipal management'. Meanwhile its grant should be cut to £1,500.

The High Street buildings, c.1910: the botany lab.

Rescue

At last the College was jolted into action. On becoming a university college it had acquired a top-heavy structure with a Court numbering 180 at its summit. It had retained its Council (in effect still its governing body) but now also had a Senate, consisting of the professors. From one point of view the most important feature of this new structure was that it continued the process of freeing the College from Southampton Borough Council. Where this had had 12 Borough Councillors, heavily outnumbering the three lay members, the new College Council of 53 only had to include ten Councillors of the Borough or its nominees.

The College now also had a President, the Duke of Wellington, and two Vice-Presidents, equivalents to today's Chancellor and Pro-Chancellors. In good times the President and Vice-Presidents left the running of the College to the Council, Senate and Principal. But these were not good times, and from another point of view the appointment of Claude Montefiore as one of the Vice-Presidents in 1908 and as Acting President in 1910 was to be more important for the College's future.

Montefiore was not a particularly likely man for the position. His first interest after leaving Oxford 30 years before had been Judaism and religious studies. He was now co-editor of the *Jewish Quarterly Review*. True, he had been involved in education for some years and had served on the London School Board, but he had had no particular connection with Southampton until he had come to live at Sarisbury on the Hamble River. It was only then that William Darwin among others interested him in the Hartley University College, persuading him in 1907 to agree to become a member of its Council. He was therefore well aware of the College's problems when appointed Vice-President.

The High Street buildings, c.1910: the chemistry lab.

In July 1910 Montefiore, with Richardson and the mayor of Southampton, visited the Chancellor of the Exchequer, Lloyd George, to appeal against the reduction of the College's grant, and persuaded him to continue the grant at its present level for a further year. But he attached a condition. The College must also help itself. By this time the Council had realised that nothing less than a move to a new site could satisfy the University Commissioners and had bought 11 acres of the Highfield Court Estate, on the town's outskirts. (Montefiore and William Darwin had each contributed £1,000 to the £5,000 this had cost.) But the cost of building a new college on this site was estimated by the architect at £100,000. Lloyd George told the delegation that the Treasury would not give the College any further grants unless it made a convincing effort to raise this amount. Within a fortnight of that meeting the Council was given another reason for urgent action when the Board of Education wrote to say that unless it received plans for new premises by the end of March 1911 it would cease to recognise the Day Training Department.

The full sum was impossibly large, and the Council therefore decided to start by building only a first stage at a cost of £31,000. It was found to be impossible to raise even this amount. Enough was done, however, in time to get a further extension of the grant for 1910–11. Subsequently contributions and promises from Hampshire County Council, and from a penny rate raised by Southampton Borough Council, when added to the estimated sale price of two of the High Street houses, made it possible to persuade the Board of Education (which had now taken over the Treasury's responsibilities, so giving the College one patron instead of two) that it would eventually be able to raise the full £31,000.

In 1912, Richardson resigned. By now he had alienated not only his staff but also students, Council and Court. Under him the College had declined until it was threatened with demotion if not collapse. Why he should have chosen to go just when rescue seemed possible is a mystery, but the Council's coolly worded gratitude for his past services suggests that it had made little effort to persuade him to stay.

4. War and the Years Between, 1913–39

Dr Hill Arrives

Dr Alexander Hill, Richardson's successor, became Principal in January 1913. Aged 57, he was older than any of his predecessors (apart from Blackadder who had stayed less than two years). He was also more experienced. As a medical doctor he had been a Professor at the Royal College of Surgeons in his twenties, then, aged 32, had become Master of Downing College, Cambridge. After holding this position for 19 years he had disagreed with its governing body, resigned and since 1907 been pursuing his other hobbies – gardening and farming – near Cambridge. Montefiore and Darwin had gone to see him there and with difficulty persuaded him to abandon his early retirement.

Dr Hill already knew the College which he had twice visited as one of the University Commissioners' inspectors, and he, like Montefiore, was therefore aware of its problems. The progress it made during his first two years in solving them was steady rather than dramatic. Not so the transformation he produced in the College's morale. 'In that short period,' Montefiore remembered, 'Dr Hill changed the whole situation . . . the aspect of the place changed completely, the tone changed . . . confidence grew . . . feelings of hope inspired us.'

Dr Alexander Hill, Principal of University College of Southampton 1912–20, c.1914.

Members of the Society of Old Hartleyans in costume, 1913.

25

Lord Haldane opening the new college buildings at Highfield, 20 June 1914.

University College in use as a military hospital in the First World War.

Below left: *the view from the South Wing, with staff and patients in wheel chairs, 1915.*

Below right: *inside a ward, decorated for Christmas, 1917.*

Most of his (and Council's) efforts were aimed at moving the College to the new Highfield site. Progress in this direction, however, often took the form of one step forward, one step back. An early step forward was the renting of Highfield Manor as a combined residence for the Principal and hall for staff and students. This had become necessary when Bevois Mount Hostel had to be closed. A step back followed when the Board of Education refused to allow the cost of conversion to be borrowed from the College's remaining endowment.

The Board did agree, however (step forward), to allow borrowing to pay for engineering and science laboratories on the new site. These had become necessary when (step back) the College had found that it could not continue temporarily to use the High Street laboratories. Meanwhile building on the new site went ahead steadily, but not of the planned administrative block since there turned out to be insufficient money for this (step forward, step back).

At last, on 20 June 1914 came the grand opening by Viscount Haldane, the Lord Chancellor, of the renamed Southampton University College. This consisted of the arts building, its two sections containing 28 large and many smaller lecture rooms; between the sections came a gap which the administration block should have filled; behind, to the north stood a row of single-storey brick-built laboratories for biology, chemistry, physics and, beyond a gravel road, engineering.

In celebration the students performed their war dance known as the Gobli, already a tradition though dating only from the early years of the century. It had been invented by Rugby enthusiasts in imitation of a dance they had seen performed on the dockside by the departing All Blacks and took the form of concentric circles of students rotating in opposite directions while giving ritual yells (for example, 'Bravo Hartley, Hartley Bravissimo, Bravo Hartley, Hartley Bravo'). The College mascot, a skeleton named Kelly (originally kept in a locked cupboard in the ladies' cloakroom of the old Hartley museum), was usually placed on a chair at the circle's centre and the performance ended with the singing of 'Has anybody here seen Kelly?' At the grand opening of 1914 two students added to the fun by dressing as suffragettes and threatening to

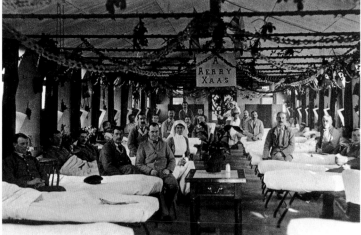

The women's hockey team, 1914–15.

attack the Lord Chancellor's car.

Six weeks later the country declared war on Germany, the move to Highfield was indefinitely postponed and the new buildings became a military hospital.

The First World War

Still in the High Street, the College suffered. By 1916–17 its pre-war 114 full-time students had declined to 29, and evening students from about 750 to about 500. Thereafter numbers began to recover but, while the war lasted, only slowly. More women students helped this recovery, but produced a new problem. Since Bevois Mount had been closed and Highfield Hall had been requisitioned there was no women's hall of residence.

Inevitably the College's community life declined. A new Stage Society was formed and gave combined entertainments with the old Choral Society, and the Engineering Society and science societies continued to meet and make appropriate visits, but for the last three war years the magazine was published annually instead of termly. And though hockey, tennis and soccer were still played, rugby and cricket disappeared.

Without grounds, the College could not contribute to the country's survival by growing vegetables. Instead, from 1915, Professor Eustice organised the manufacture of shells by volunteer staff and students in the engineering laboratory, and subsequently ran courses which taught men and women how to manufacture munitions. One of those who helped make shells was Jack

John Eustice, 1929, lecturer in engineering at the Hartley Institution 1892–1900, Professor of Engineering at the University College 1900–31.

27

Above: *the opening of the Highfield building in 1919.*

Above right: *Highfield Hall showing the Winter Garden, c.1918.*

Corbishley, an assistant in the biology department. He remembered being told off by the Registrar for skidding up the tiled entrance of the old Hartley building with a shell under his arm. With other volunteers he would collect lengths of steel on a cart from Parsons Engineering Co., and return them after machine work had been done on them at the College. His more normal duties included going with a box on his back to collect specimens for his department: frogs from Nursling, rabbits from Canal Walk and wild flowers from the New Forest. The Principal's contribution to the war was to work as a doctor at Highfield Hall, and during several vacations to join cross-channel hospital ships.

The missing students and staff were of course fighting. The College's volunteers, who by this time had become the 2nd company of the 5th (Territorial) Regiment, were some of them sent to India while others became NCOs or officers in various regiments. Most other students and staff who were of age and fit also volunteered. Of those who served in the armed forces, 40 died.

'November 11, 1918,' Madie Davies-Shiel (1918–22) remembered, 'saw the whole student body leave desks and books and rush into the streets Below

The Universtiy College orchestra, 1920.

The mascot 'Kelly' in the care of a group of ex-service students, taken in the Engineering Block, c.1920.

Bar, and form a crocodile which marched round the town, circumnavigated the Clock Tower and collected more and more people till it found itself at St Mary's Church.'

The 1920s

For the College the War had ended at an inconvenient time. By mid-November the 1918–19 academic year was well started, and to have moved to Highfield at once would have been impossible. This did not prevent new and returning students arriving in greater numbers than ever before. By May 1919 there were 215 of them and by October about 300. It was these who, for the 1919–20 academic year, moved to the new buildings, vacated at last, but so damaged that they had needed extensive repairs. In compensation the War Office gave the College a number of wooden huts it had erected in the grounds. Useful as this was (for the next 40 years) it is hard to imagine what else it could have done with them.

They descended the slope behind the main building in two rows. One was removed to be re-erected in the garden of Highfield Hall. Those in the hut were given 'tiny little cubicles' while the hut was "heated" by one old-fashioned stove of sorts,' Norah Hammond remembered, 'but where we hung our clothes I can't think . . . We got back to Hostel at about 4 p.m. and rushed to toast thick slices of bread at the one gas fire.'

Other huts became junior laboratories for chemistry and physics, the Botany Department's plant house, the Geology Department, the Music Department, the Arts and Woodwork Departments and a bookshop. At the bottom of the slope came the refectory, its door still marked 'DYSENTERY WARD' (or 'HUT

The university football team, 1920–1.

Students and staff outside the South Wing of the College, 1920–5.

Thomas Loveday, c.1920, Principal of University College 1920–2.

20 – DYSENTERY' – memories vary), while another opposite it was made the students' common room, where 'a group of dedicated musicians played daily for lunchtime dances' (Gilbert Hartley, 1931–4).

Two more huts were at first turned by ex-service students into a self-governing hall known as the Residential Club – an arrangement they enjoyed. But not all were contented. 'The cry of "We want our grants" was frequently heard when long files of hard-up ex-servicemen marched round the building' (Madie Davies-Shiel).

The move completed, Dr Hill told the Council, to its dismay, that he must resign, since his other interest – the Universities Bureau of the British Empire – needed his full attention. As Vice-President of the College, he remained a valuable adviser, living in a house at the bottom of Highfield Hall's garden where he grew peaches and chrysanthemums. 'One day when three of us [students] were walking on the lawn he came round the corner with three lovely large peaches in his hand, stopped and gave us one each, saying, "Three ladies and three peaches," with a courtly little bow' (Isabel Rendell, 1925–9).

To succeed him came Dr Thomas Loveday, previously Professor of Philosophy at Cape Town then Newcastle. Though Loveday set about solving the College's chronic financial problems by launching another appeal, his brief period in office (1920–2) only gave him time to make one significant contribution to its future. This was to acquire and open two new halls of residence: South Stoneham House for men and South Hill for women.

30

Ernest Holmes, one of the first to arrive at South Stoneham, remembered that the atmosphere of the hall was collegiate. Gowns had to be worn for dinner and for lectures. (As late as the 1940s, Professor Taylor (Physics) would enforce this rule with the cry, 'I will not lecture to the academically nude.') The South Stoneham regime was also 'distinctly paternalistic. A bell was rung at 5.45 each evening and everyone settled in silence to study until another bell two hours later released us for dinner. At 10 o'clock another bell called us to prayers. Half an hour later the warden came round to all the bedrooms to check that everyone was in bed.' Restrictions of this sort were not popular with ex-servicemen who had been moved from the Residential Club and one of them, Colonel Julian, was appointed Assistant Warden to help the Warden, Professor A. A. Cock (Education and Philosophy).

Throughout the 1920s and 1930s 'Joe' Cock was the most universally admired member of staff. 'A man before his time,' Allan Pike remembered, referring to Cock's sympathy with students and understanding of their psychology. 'You must go out and talk to people,' he told Pike who had been demoralised by a year with scarlet fever. 'The best advice I ever had. I've never stopped since.' When George Thomas, future Speaker of the House of Commons and ultimately Lord Tonypandy, told Cock that he was Labour and only read the *Daily Herald*, Cock asked if he was so narrow-minded that he wouldn't dare discover another point of view. It was advice Thomas never forgot.

When he lectured 'he did his best,' Michael Cotton remembered, 'in a flow of high academic rhetoric, to instil into us the true meaning of education. He was gentle and kind and was known to give financial aid to students at Stoneham.' 'He was a short, rather Pickwickian man,' Isabel Rendell remembered. 'At our request he gave some of us from Highfield tutorials in the nineteenth-century poets – his lectures were so much more illuminating than dear Miss Aubrey's. I'm afraid we led her to believe that we were taking tutorials in Education with Professor Cock.'

Cock's regime at Stoneham was emphatically Christian. 'A Latin Grace was said before meals. "Benedictus benedicat, per Jesum Christum Dominum Nostrum." Sunday services were held at Stoneham Church. Attendance was

A history lecture in the 1920s.

University College Southampton staff, 1921.

Front row: Principal Loveday is in the centre, Professor Eustice is on his right, and Dr Boyd on his left. Miss Aubrey is second from left, Professor Cock is third from right, and Professor Patchett is on the far right.
Middle row: Professor Forsey is second from left, and A. E. Clarence Smith is sixth from right.

Dr Kenneth Vickers, Principal of University College, 1922–46.

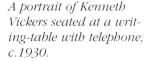

A portrait of Kenneth Vickers seated at a writing-table with telephone, c.1930.

voluntary, but we all went.' When Cock left to become Principal of York Training College and took holy orders, his best student followed him there and did the same.

It was Professor Cock who persuaded Nellie Carter (1923–7) to train at Southampton when he visited her sixth form in Poole. Like South Stoneham, the regime at the new women's hall, South Hill, was strict, with a book to sign if you left the hall at weekends, giving your destination and companions. It was also remote. 'I remember going to dances at the college – wearing Wellington boots down the muddy lane, carrying more suitable footwear. We hid our boots in the hedge and arrived properly shod.'

When Loveday departed, to become Vice-Chancellor of Bristol University, he was followed at Southampton by Kenneth Vickers, a historian, previously Professor at Armstrong College, Newcastle. Vickers was to remain Principal for 24 years, longer than any of his predecessors, only retiring at the end of the Second World War. At school at Oundle he had contracted poliomyelitis which left him with a limp and only the partial use of his left hand and right arm. Jim Smith, an office boy in the 1930s, could tell it was Vickers approaching by the uneven clump of his footsteps. The son of a clergyman and himself a committed Christian, the college Vickers hoped for would encourage students to 'play a proper part, with truth and righteousness, in the service of their fellow men' (Professor Forsey at Vickers's Memorial Service). To be that sort of college he believed it should be predominantly residential.

This was especially desirable in the early 1920s, when the sense of community which there had been in what Professor Cock remembered as that 'dear, damp, musty old pile in the High Street' had not survived the move to Highfield. Not surprisingly, only the students at the halls of residence felt that they belonged to any sort of a community. By 1924 providing more student residences had also become essential. The three which existed were full, with 93 men at South Stoneham House, 29 women at South Hill and 68 women at Highfield Hall. The following year the first two were extended, mainly by converting their outbuildings. By 1930 the third, Highfield Hall, was replaced with a new hall, the gift of Miss Charlotte Chamberlain, a member of the Council and a niece of the distinguished Victorian statesman, Joseph Chamberlain.

A building which did almost as much as the halls of residence to give students the sense that they belonged to a community was an assembly hall. This was created in 1925 out of the materials salvaged from two of the Army huts and a barn with seats for 600–700, a stage and good acoustics (provided the roaring under-floor gas heater was switched off and a rainstorm was not beating on its corrugated iron roof). For some 20 years it was used for plays, concerts, dances and many other formal and informal College occasions.

At about the same time, Mrs Montefiore, wife of Claude Montefiore (who since 1913 had been President of the College), bought and gave a piece of land opposite South

Stoneham House, for a playing field. Her husband paid for a pavilion. With adequate halls of residence, an assembly hall and a playing field, Highfield was at last acquiring the character of a campus.

In 1925 the College received another donation which transformed one department when George Moore, a one-time member of Council, left it a major contribution to the erection of the George Moore Botanical Building. This, sited alongside the engineering building to the north of the gravel road, was opened by the Duke of Connaught in 1928. By then Professor Sydney Mangham had held the chair of Botany for eight years, and he was to hold it until he retired in 1951. During this time members of the Department researched subjects as various as the respiration of barley and strawberry plants, the local mud-binding grass, *Spartinia townsendii*, and the diseases of larch trees at the Forestry Commission's Wareham nurseries. Mangham himself was more interested in teaching. In 1937 he and A. R. Hockley of the Zoology Department published *A Textbook for Pharmaceutical Students*. One of his final contributions to the College was to advise the Grounds Committee on the planting of the botanical garden across University Road in the old brickyard.

In these inter-war years the College began to teach economics and law. In 1919 a lecturer in economics was appointed, but it was Percy (Peter) Ford who arrived in 1926 who not only created the Faculty but was to extend its work far beyond economics into sociology. His first major work was to edit the Southampton Civic Survey of 1931. Three years later he published *Work and Wealth in a Modern Port*, and as a result was given a Leverhulme grant of £300 to study other parts of the country in a similar way. Soon he was researching the repercussions of the Depression on British industry, while other members of the Faculty of Economics and Commerce (as it was first named) were working on such subjects as the distribution of occupations in south-eastern

The Hartley Institution (that 'dear, damp, musty old pile in the High Street') up for sale in the 1930s.

The Prince of Wales (later Edward VIII) processes down University Road, 27 June 1924, on his visit to University College.

counties during the 1920s. In 1936 Ford was made Professor of Economics and also of Geography to fill a gap caused by the retirement of Professor Risbeth, but justified by the interest which geographers had in regional economics.

A Department of Legal Studies was formed in 1923, with one full-time member of staff. Its students, however, were mainly articled clerks, working for Law Society exams, and it was not for another 30 years that some began to work for law degrees.

Meanwhile the generous gifts of individual supporters of the College were not equalled by the people of Southampton as a whole. By the time of the 1931 financial crisis Loveday's post-war appeal had long been abandoned, and another, launched by Vickers with a target of £500,000, had collected a mere £110,000.

Above left: a group outside the winter garden of Highfield Hall, the women's hostel, 1928.

Above: a group of students, possibly in the garden of a hall of residence, c.1931.

Recession and Decline

The 1930s were a bad time for the College. However, the decade began hopefully. In the late 1920s the College had been trying to eliminate its two-year and three-year courses for trainee teachers and replace them with four-year courses. But as a result of the school-leaving age being raised the Department of Education had suddenly needed a large number of new primary school teachers and asked the College to accept 150 trainees who would take a two-year course. Only a new hall of residence could make this possible and Vickers persuaded Council to borrow £50,000 for building what was at first called New Hall (then Connaught Hall, at the Duke's request) on the site of South Stoneham's orchard.

The 1931 financial crisis followed, and the Department of Education withdrew from its agreement with the College, offering instead to support only an additional 11 a year who would take a four-year course – a change which reduced the College's income by £6,000 in 1933–4 and £4,000 the following year, as well as giving it a temporary surplus of accommodation.

There were compensations. In 1929 an anonymous benefactor gave £8,000 for a Zoology and Geology building which transformed the Department's

Facing page: the Duke of Connaught at the opening of the George Moore Laboratories (Botany), 14 June 1928.

A group of freshers in the early 1930s, apparently performing an extra-curricular initiation rite.

accommodation. After the war it had spent a dozen difficult years, first in a small room in the main building, then in two of the army huts. In 1926 a new chair of Zoology had been created and given to W. Rae Sheriffs (remembered as a keen philatelist). But the Department made little progress until its new building, sited below the army huts, opened in 1931.

This inspired confidence, Gilbert Hartley remembered, 'which the [1914] Chemistry and Physics labs, with their bouncy floors, certainly did not. Our floors were of polished maple wood, as smooth as glass, which in conjunction with the concrete stairs, led to the legend that everyone broke a leg in the long run. Zoology was on the upper floor. The Professor's room was at the top of the stairs, then the Zoo library, then the laboratory of Mr Stott the Demonstrator, a short-tempered man who wanted the Navy Estimates to be devoted to marine biology instead. Next along was a second lab/study occupied by John Berry, the Avon Research Officer, whose work was practical but not departmental.'

It was in fact John Berry who ran perhaps the College's most prestigious project of the 1930s. This began in 1932 when the Hampshire Rivers Board

Part of the realisation of Vickers' vision of a pre-dominantly residential college, Highfield Hall was opened by the Duke of York in 1930. It was the gift of Miss Charlotte Chamberlain, a member of the Council and a niece of the Victorian statesman, Joseph Chamberlain.

asked the College to report on ways of improving the stock of salmon In the Hampshire Avon. Gradually Berry's team began to study other freshwater and fishery problems and to extend its researches to other Wessex rivers. Now the Freshwater Biological Association helped the College to establish a laboratory beside the Itchen where it flowed past South Stoneham House, and Southampton was soon being asked for advice about freshwater matters by many countries. When Berry left in 1939 Vickers wrote that it was his enthusiasm, energy and ability which had made the project such a success. Unfortunately his departure was soon followed by the War and the withdrawal of the Treasury grant, with the result that the project closed.

Meanwhile in the late 1930s the Department of Zoology expanded its other research. By 1938 Rae Sheriff had published seven papers on the spiders of Hong Kong, while another member of the Department was researching *Corixidae* in ponds around Southampton. The new Zoology Building also provided space for zoological collections which the department was sometimes given, most notably the Cotton Collection of British Birds.

In 1932 a donation of £24,250 from the two daughters of the late Edward Turner Sims, one-time member of Council, made possible an adequate library, probably the College's most serious lack since its move to Highfield. The one room on the first floor of a wing of the main building had been totally inadequate for the 35,000 volumes brought from the old Hartley building. Although this had not prevented the librarian, Mrs Forsey, wife of the Professor of Classics, and Isabel Rendell who worked under her for five terms, considering their library one of the best of any university college, it meant that many volumes had to be placed on shelves in passages or stored, while one of Isabel's duties was to take books 'to the specialist libraries in each department. I soon developed the ability to carry large piles of books reaching from one hand stretched down up to my chin, along miles of corridor and up and down stone staircases without dropping any.'

The gap between the two wings of the main building had by now been partly filled with administration offices. These were moved elsewhere and the gap was finally closed by a library with shelves and stacks for 47,000 volumes. The main entrance to the library became in effect the College's front door. The Turner Sims Library was opened in 1935 by the Duke of York, the future

Edward Turner Sims, c.1900, a member of the Council. A generous donation from his daughters made possible an adequate library for the College.

Below: the framework of the Turner Sims Library, with the South wing of the original University College in the background, c.1930.

Below right: the completed Library from the north, floodlit at the time of its opening in 1935.

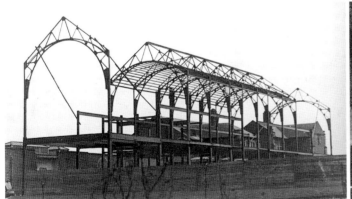

The interior of the Turner Sims Library, looking north, 1936.

Facing page, top: *the original buildings on the Highfield site.*

Facing page, bottom: *the Library today.*

George VI, an occasion somewhat marred by a mishap. Two explanations of this survive. Either too much time was allowed for the Duke's drive from the station and he arrived early, or the key broke in the lock. Whichever happened, he was kept waiting for some time stammering furiously on the doorstep.

Another development of the 1930s was an Extra-mural Department. Though a Board of Extra-mural Studies had been established in 1928–9, it only began to flourish in 1934 when John Parker came from Durham to be its secretary. Parker was lucky to arrive at the moment when the Board of Education restored half the cut it had made in 1931 in its grants for extra-mural courses. The following year it restored the rest, and Vickers reported 'a welcome change in its attitude to extra-mural work'.

The Department ran courses in Hampshire, East Dorset, West Sussex and the Isle of Wight. Typical of the lectures given by College staff were a series of ten by Professor Forsey on 'The Ancient World' which had average attendances of 45 to 50, and a series by Professor Pinto (English) on 'Modern English Writers' given both at Winchester and Southampton with average attendances of 80–90 and 120 respectively. In the year of Parker's arrival 852 students attended the Department's courses. Numbers rose steadily, reaching 2,453 in 1938, before fear of war led to a reduction when potential students deserted to rival First Aid and Air Raid Precautions classes.

In the same years the College developed a new venture: a School of Navigation. It had embarked on this in 1932 when it took over the Gilchrist Navigation School and moved it to South Hill – no longer needed as a hall of residence since the women had moved to the rebuilt Highfield Hall. At first the School ran courses for serving Merchant Navy officers studying for certificates of competency, but in 1935 it added courses in air navigation. In 1937 it opened a residential, one-year course for cadets which would count as six months of the four years service required for a Second Mate's Certificate. When the school continued to expand it was moved just before the war to South Stoneham House.

During the 1930s the Departments of the Faculty of Arts remained small, many of their students taking so-called General Degrees rather than honours degrees. Philosophy under Professor Cock became increasingly entangled with Theology. No fewer than 36 students of the inter-war years subsequently took holy orders. Cock and an assistant, F. F. Tindall, both wrote chapters of the Dean of Winchester's *History of Christian Thought* and Cock contributed a number of articles to the 1938 *Britannica Year Book*.

The chair of English was longest held by V. de Sola Pinto (1926–38). Pinto's most notable achievement was to edit *Wessex*, an annual founded in 1928 as 'a record of the movement for a University of Wessex', to which members of staff contributed learned articles. It survived for ten years, retaining a good standard, though the Wessex University plan foundered, and it also failed in another of its aims: to give effective support to Vickers's pre-war appeal.

In Pinto's time the English Association flourished, with town as well as College members. Audiences of as many as 100 heard such visiting speakers

*Ernest W. Patchett,
c.1930, Professor of
Modern Languages at
University College,
1920–36.*

*H. W. Lawton, c.1935,
Professor of French at
University College,
1928–50.*

as Arthur Bryant and L. A. G. Strong. Students in the English Honours class during the 1930s usually numbered around 25 while about the same number would be reading English as part of a General Degree course. The Department also catered for foreign students, often from as many as 17 countries, whose aim was to obtain the Cambridge Certificate for Proficiency in English.

From the Hartley Institution's earliest days modern languages were its most important non-science-based subjects. During the First World War the Department suffered two misfortunes, first when its lecturer, E. W. Patchett, was trapped in Germany and interned for the whole four years, then in 1915 when its Professor, V. G. Starkey, died. Released, Patchett became Professor in 1920 and held the chair for 16 years, making the Department one of the Faculty's most successful. By 1934–5, 30 students were reading for Honours degrees in some modern language. In 1937 Patchett was succeeded by Wilf Lawton, also fondly remembered, who held the chair even longer.

Though History, on the other hand, remained small, its Professor from 1934 to 1945, R. R. Betts, was a distinguished specialist in Eastern European matters. In 1937 he published *The Pre-Hussite Reformation in Bohemia and the Relations between England and Bohemia*. Next year he read a paper to the Royal Historical Society on 'English and Czech Influences on Huss'.

In 1921 George Leake, organist at St Mary's, became the College's first Professor of Music. When he died in 1928 no new professor was appointed, but Cecil Williams, also an organist, became Master of Music and kept the Department alive. In 1937 he was appointed Borough Organist. He had already begun summer orchestral concerts. From 1926, however, the musical event that attracted most support was the annual Gilbert and Sullivan opera in the old assembly hall.

Meanwhile the Faculties of Science and Engineering continued to be outstanding. Chemistry had begun to expand in 1919 when Boyd was joined by A. E. Clarence Smith. Photomicrography was his speciality, in which he became a leading authority. The high standard which the Chemistry Department reached during the 1920s and 1930s is confirmed by its exam successes. In 1925, out of nine candidates for the Special Honours London Degree, five were awarded firsts, in 1934 two out of five. By 1936 the department had a staff of six. Two of these, G. H. Jeffery and A. I. Vogel, went on to Woolwich Polytechnic, Vogel to become author of an outstandingly successful textbook on practical organic chemistry.

The Department's successes were the more remarkable considering its accommodation and equipment. Between the wars it had two single-storey brick buildings, first occupied in 1919, but its junior laboratory was still an army hut. Here Jeffery remembered that in winter the water frequently froze and in summer the ether nearly boiled, while the lecturer who used it most often considered it the worst chemical laboratory in the country.

In 1936 Clarence Smith died young, a serious loss, and next year Boyd retired. There was thus an important change of regime, but no deterioration in the Department's research. N. K. Adam, who succeeded Boyd, was a widely recognised chemist, the first member of any Faculty to be a Fellow of the Royal

Society. His research into surface films led to work on the mechanism of household detergents' action – and to a private interest in ducks, one of which he would lead about on a string. In vacation colleagues would send him postcards of rare species – and once of a mechanical DUKW (American army amphibious assault landing craft). A colleague who visited Adam at home, and was about to take a seat in his living room, was told, 'You can't sit there, that's Suzy's chair.' Suzy was the duck. Physics also prospered, at first under Professor Stansfield (1912–32), though, like Chemistry, it had only an army hut for its junior laboratory. In 1936, however, Miss Chamberlain made her second generous donation of £15,000 for a new physics laboratory. Professor A. C. Menzies, who had succeeded Stansfield, was largely responsible for its design. It was sited on the southern boundary of the College's land (opposite today's Chemistry Building) in an old gravel pit, thus making possible two ground floors on different levels – one at the back, one at the front – each with the stability which physics laboratories need.

R. C. J. Howland, c.1937, Professor of Mathematics at University College, 1931–7.

In the mid-1930s Geography and Mathematics each suffered a severe setback. In 1936 Geography was absorbed by Economics; the same year R. C. J. Howland, the brilliant young mathematician who had held the chair since 1930, died suddenly, aged only 40. He 'had taken particular care,' wrote Thomas Cave-Browne-Cave, the Professor of Engineering, 'to determine the engineers' requirements and therefore was able to give quite exceptional assistance in the education of engineering students.'

It was the Faculty of Engineering, however, which continued to give the College real distinction. Council recognised this in 1931 by agreeing to spend £10,000 on providing it with more equipment and accommodation. It also offered a higher salary for Eustice's successor and so was able to appoint the distinguished engineer, Wing-Commander Cave-Browne-Cave. Airship design was his speciality – he had helped design the ill-fated R101. To give him wider knowledge of engineering the College allowed him a year to tour the country's engineering businesses before replacing Eustice.

Under Cave-Browne-Cave, the Faculty's first wind tunnel was built, to be used for teaching and aeronautical research. The Faculty also researched many matters concerned with noise, from internal combustion engines' exhausts to silencers for concrete-breaking drills. And it became involved with Malcolm Campbell. In 1934–5 Campbell sent it a small racing car he was designing asking for suggestions about improving it. The same year the Faculty lent Campbell its experimental engineer, H. Leech, to become chief mechanic of the team preparing Bluebird for his (successful) attempt on the world land speed record.

Leech had previously worked with Cave-Browne-Cave at the Royal Aircraft works. He was a survivor of the crash of the R101, after which he had returned to the burning airship to try to rescue passengers. He was awarded the Albert Medal for his bravery. Students considered Leech 'an engineering wizard'.

In these years the College began negotiating with the local authorities and the Board of Education about the way in which it was sponsored by these bodies. Though it was primarily a university college with full-time students working for degrees, it was also providing evening classes in technical education. Kenneth Webb, who arrived to teach chemistry in 1939, remembered that he was also expected to start courses if required by some 2,000 part-time evening students in subjects which varied from boiler-making to laundry technology (important in Southampton because of its liners). The College believed that it should be properly rewarded for such teaching which was correctly the responsibility of the local authorities. The agreement finally reached was that these should make grants to the College for its university work, and should pay in addition for its technical classes according to their cost. The Board of Education would contribute half of the cost of this.

Though these changes did not at once transform the College's finances, they gave it sufficient confidence to add to its buildings. By September 1939 work had begun not only on the new engineering laboratory, a new chemistry building and a new assembly hall behind the library, but also (for the first time on the west side of University Road) on a building which would include new common rooms and a new refectory, to become known as West Building.

Life for students had meanwhile recovered many of the features of pre-war years. There were two Rugby XVs and David Morris (a Welshman) remembered 65 years later his disappointment at not being selected as No. 8 in the first-XV scrum. Morris also remembered keen rivalry between Faculties at the annual sports day, and a tug-of-war between Education and Engineering, for which the engineers had trained each lunchtime and which they seemed to win quite easily – until he pointed out that their team numbered nine instead of eight.

The Students' Union, besides distributing monies to clubs and societies, from time to time concerned itself with general matters affecting students. In the 1930s it suffered, like the College itself, from the fall in student numbers and consequent fall in its income. Nonetheless it continued to sponsor events like the annual inter-varsity debate, and to give lunch to the University Grants Committee on its five-yearly visits.

When the Turner Sims Library opened in 1935 the Union gained a group of rooms previously used by the library in one wing of the main building, and this area became, in the words of the president, 'a student quarter'. Next year it began to publish its own newspaper, *Wessex News*. Some of its proposals of these years seem ahead of their time. In 1938 the president recommended to Senate 'the provision of courses of general cultural interest,' their object to give 'the Science student an introduction to the appreciation of literature,' or 'the Engineering student some knowledge of the elements of Economic theory'. It stopped short of suggesting that arts students might benefit from learning something about science.

These were years of country-wide poverty during which students undertook various kinds of community service. On Sundays Morris and a few others would visit Winchester Prison and give talks to the prisoners. It didn't matter what they talked about 'as long as we could smuggle in the football scores for the previous day's matches.' The students were allowed 1/6d. (7.5p) for their train fares but would take the allowance and cycle the 25-mile round trip instead.

Despite the good work of some Faculties, the improved financial arrangements and the plans for new buildings, the number of full-time students steadily fell. In 1925 there had been over 400. Thirteen years later for the 1938–9 academic year there were only 269. The College's standards also declined. Kenneth Webb remembered that he 'set foot on what was felt to be a near-sinking ship academically.' By 1939 these problems were being discussed by Senate, the Development Committee, meetings of staff and a committee specially formed for the purpose. Decline in numbers and standards were the result of a decline in reputation, this caused by the poor results many students were getting. Poor results were the result of poor intake caused in turn by a declining reputation. On 3 September 1939, before anyone could think how to break this vicious circle, the country went to war again.

5. War and the Years After, 1939–52

There were similarities between the effects of the two World Wars on the College. In the Second as in the First many staff and students went to fight. As before, the College made valuable contributions to the war effort. But this time the College itself was in a war zone and it spent much time debating whether to move somewhere safer.

It considered evacuation as soon as war was declared, and again in the summer of 1940 after the fall of France, but each time decided against. Serious bombing began that autumn. Southampton was more heavily attacked for its size than any town in England except Plymouth, and though the attacks were largely on the town and docks, the College did not escape entirely. Bombs fell on and around the campus on the nights of 30 November and 1 December that year. Incendiaries set alight one of the army huts and high explosives blew out windows at South Stoneham House. The College sent its resident students home and moved evening classes to Saturday and Sunday afternoons, but again decided against evacuation.

Bomb damage to Westminster Bank, Southampton.

On 21 June 1941 a number of land mines fell in a road close to Highfield Hall, blowing all its doors off their hinges and doing £3,000 worth of damage. It was on this occasion that the Warden, Miss Lightbody, suffered the only wartime injury on campus, cutting her hand when picking up broken glass. Still in her early thirties, Miss Lightbody was remembered by Iris Oades as 'a wonderful person, very decorative, with a Scottish accent, who ran Highfield like a lady of the manor, providing a regime of gracious living, with everything appropriate from silver spoons upwards.' When Miss Oades herself became Chamberlain Hall's first warden she felt that she could never quite live up to Miss Lightbody's standards.

On 20 September 1941 Highfield Hall was bracketed by five bombs, one of them making a 20-foot crater outside its front door. Almost three years later on 15 May 1944 the Zoology and Geology Building was badly damaged, and lesser damage done to the physics, chemistry and engineering buildings, but now D-Day was only three weeks ahead and evacuation was no longer seriously considered. Despite these attacks the College afterwards claimed that it had never cancelled a lecture or practical. 'We used to say of the main College,' Webb remembered, that 'with its many tottering ramshackle huts, Hitler thought it had been bombed already.'

As the war progressed the College's war work became an argument against evacuation. This was of a far more sophisticated kind than the manufacture of shells and included research into matters as various as water-recovery for vehicles in the desert, rocket projectors, assault bridges and defence against poison gas. To facilitate the projects which the Engineering Department carried out, the Government allowed the new engineering building to be completed. More surprisingly, work was also allowed to continue on West Building, enabling the refectory to open in September 1940.

The College also provided courses for men in the forces, in skills they would need for mechanised warfare. By the autumn of 1942, 2,150 servicemen had taken such courses. It also provided courses for merchant seamen, engineers and wireless operators in the School of Navigation, and in a new School of Radio Telegraphy. Meanwhile the cadets at the School of Navigation became so numerous that some had to move from South Stoneham to Connaught Hall. 'Skirting quietly' along the back of a parade there, Webb remembered that he was 'stopped by a specially dispatched cadet with the words (and salute!), "Commander's orders, Sir, please do not walk on the deck during parade!" I felt suitably sea-sick and hastily withdrew.' In 1941 the Air Ministry began to send men on six-month courses to prepare them for joining the RAF.

Various groups in need were also given accommodation by the College. Polish sub-lieutenants were housed at South Hill, and in 1940 many French troops rescued from Dunkirk were given shelter. They included 40 army officers who were temporarily received at Highfield Hall where 'their morale was considerably raised by the sympathetic welcome which the women students gave them' (Temple Patterson). French Naval officers followed them, and later American officers and members of the American WASC. At other times Highfield sheltered evacuated students from University College, London, these allowing it to claim to be the only mixed-sex hall in the country.

Throughout the war the College continued to teach science and engineering students who were allowed to postpone their call-up for two years. From the 1941–2 academic year onwards the Government positively encouraged science and engineering students by offering them bursaries. As a result it was these Faculties which retained most students and continued to prosper.

Engineering, however, lost its Professor, Cave-Browne-Cave, who became Director of Camouflage under the Ministry of Home Security, his brief including the ships of the navy. And the Faculty's research, organised by Leech, became almost entirely concerned with the war. By 1944–5, however, there were 84 full-time students in the Faculty.

The same year, in the different Departments of the Faculty of Science there were 83 full-time students. Chemistry's research was similarly concerned for the most part with chemical warfare, undertaken by Professor Adam, who also served on the Ministry of Supply's Propellants sub-committee.

By this time Zoology and Geology were recovering from the bomb damage to their building, which had not only destroyed most of Professor Sheriff's oriental spiders but badly damaged the geological museum. For the time being (so the story goes) its exhibits were swept into a heap with other rubble, since the only geologist who could separate them was away at the war (Webb). The number of students reading Zoology had recovered since 1942 when the Government belatedly agreed that they, like other science students, could defer their call-up for two years.

In contrast to the science-based Faculties, others had suffered. Education's particular problem was a shortage of schools to which to send one-year-course students for their term of teaching practice, since many Southampton and south-coast schools had been evacuated. Eventually a scheme was devised which included schools as far away as North Staffordshire. Numbers held up for a while (114 in 1939–40) but then fell steadily, averaging about 50 from 1942 onwards.

By 1943 students in law, still mainly articled clerks, were so few that the Law Society withdrew its financial support and the Department closed. Students in the Faculty of Economics and Commerce (deprived of Professor Ford who went to the Ministry of Supply) were reduced to 19 when the war began and continued to decline. The Faculty continued, however, to collect statistics, including a series for the Oxford Institute of Statistics which was inquiring into the way the war had affected working-class consumers.

As for the Faculty of Arts, total numbers in its several Departments had fallen by 1944–5 to 51. In 1941 Philosophy had a single student, and he was reading Theology. By the end of the war the Department had closed. Staff were hard worked since many were away on war work. These included Professor Betts (History) who went to the BBC to broadcast in Czech. Vickers took his place as Acting Head of History. But there were new developments. Appropriately, when Russia became an ally, Dr Neuschaffer, an escaped German social democrat, began to teach Russian. And though lectures in music appreciation, given by Williams, continued to be one of the main activities of the Music Department, by 1942–3 four students were reading for BAs in the subject.

Staff of the Arts Faculty made a vital contribution to the Extra-mural Department which, above all others, expanded in the war years. During the Battle of Britain this Department had abandoned all its normal lectures and courses. But already it had begun to organise lectures and courses for service-men in the region. In its first year it arranged 32 single lectures, 12 short courses and 13 classes in French. In 1943–4 it arranged 4,949 lectures, 1,690 talks to small units, 92 short courses and 80 classes. These activities were not always appreciated. Philistine commanding officers considered them no way to win the war and other ranks, when compelled to attend, resented the inter-ference with their spare time. But it can be argued that education for the forces during the War, often conducted by teachers with radical opinions, trans-formed British society, and was partly responsible, for example, for the Labour Party's 1945 election victory.

As the war ended the Extra-mural Department used South Hill to run residen-tial courses for pre-demobilised troops. 'Students have been almost embarrassing,' Parker wrote, 'in their appreciation of the opportunity to leave service conditions for a while and begin attuning themselves anew to civil life.'

Wartime students were compelled to join the College's Senior Training Corps

The University College Senior Training Corps, c.1941.

as a condition of the deferment of their call-up. Each lunchtime they paraded. If a student missed more than four parades a year he would find himself within a few weeks in the army. In 1940 the STC became the Home Guard, and began more realistic training; the old brickfield behind West Building would echo to the detonation of thunder-flashes. Though its weapons were as primitive as those of all early Home Guard units, the War Office wrote to Vickers to congratulate him on its efficiency.

The War was a difficult time for the Students' Union. The Senior Training Corps and the Air Squadron took time which students might otherwise have given to clubs and societies. By 1941–2 only 15 of these were still functioning (though a Communist Group had been formed). The average age of students fell sharply, depriving the Union of the responsible lead which four- and five-year students had previously given.

Perhaps the most important event of the War was Senate's creation in 1941 of a Development Committee. Vickers, Professor Lawton (modern languages), Captain H. Teare Harry (Executive Officer of Technical Courses) and Miss Chamberlain (Council) were influential members of this committee. In 1944 it produced a statement, *The Needs of University College, Southampton, in the Post-War Period*, which divided the future into three five-year periods and made proposals for each. The details of these are not important – they were soon overtaken by events (it proposed an ultimate student population of between 1,000 and 1,500). Its importance was that it established a habit of forward planning which was to prove invaluable in the years ahead.

For the year 1946–7 student numbers rose to 835, already more than three times as many as in the last pre-war year. There was another contrast with 1939. The College's morale had been transformed. Again it had survived a crisis, if this time fortuitously.

Post-War Problems

*Sir Robert Wood,
Principal 1946–52,
Vice-Chancellor 1952.*

Sir Robert Wood, who succeeded Vickers in 1946, had spent 35 years in the Department (later Ministry) of Education. In the 1930s he had played an important part in gaining for the College proper payment for its technical instruction courses. He was pre-eminently a Civil Servant, not a man to whom the average student warmed, but an adept negotiator, perfect for finding ways and means to solve the College's post-war problems. These were not new. For 100 years it had suffered from inadequate buildings. For 50 years it had been hoping to become a university.

Just how inadequate its buildings were, Tony Manser discovered when he arrived as assistant lecturer in Philosophy in 1950. 'For five years I led a peripatetic existence in all corners of the campus. At first I was housed in the Zoology building. This was at least brick built, though it suffered from other disadvantages, such as the smell from the carcass of a very dead ostrich being boiled in acid so that its skeleton could be mounted for the museum.' From there he was moved to 'a very small room on the left of the refectory' where other people had unfortunately 'not been told of the new occupant, so I sometimes arrived to find meetings taking place there.' Next he was given part of one of the army huts before finally being found a place in the bathing huts, 'so-called because they were not much more roomy'. Admittedly Philosophy was still 'the sort of one-man-and-a-dog unit characteristic of post-war years, with Tony (of course) the dog' (from his obituary), but his experiences were typical.

A year later little had changed. Now the Government considered that science graduates were most urgently needed. In his first annual report Wood explained that the smaller universities and colleges would have to make a disproportionate contribution to the Government's proposed doubling of the country's output of these. He had therefore submitted to the University Grants Committee plans for a student body by 1951–2 of between 1,000 and 1,100. In no way could the College by that time provide the halls of residence for so many. Already in 1946–7, the Lodgings Officer had had to approve rooms for 90 students in the town. The following year almost 300 were needed, and were only found after an appeal in the press. By 1949–50 the number had risen to 328, almost as many as the 377 living in halls of residence.

The remainder lived at home, in the town or near by. Gilbert Hartley remembered coming daily from the New Forest, using the Hythe Ferry. 'This meant leaving home at 7.20 every morning to catch the 8 a.m. ferry, and not failing to catch the 5.30 p.m. ferry back from the Town Quay. The crossing was the high point of the day, with views of all the liners. The journey up the Avenue was by tram, swinging and swooping across the Common, to the corner of University Road.'

In 1948 the College took a major step towards increasing its halls of residence by buying the 18-acre Glen Eyre estate, lying north of Highfield, not far from South Hill. Gradually a new hall was built there. In October 1949, 44 students were able to move into its first three blocks. By the 1953–4 session the remaining three living blocks had been occupied, bringing the total of Glen Eyre students to 101. G and H blocks, still being built, would accommodate another 46. Glen Eyre was designed by Colonel R. F. Gutteridge, for many years the College's architect, and built 'like a fortress, with bricks of amazing hardness'.

Students lived four or five to a flat, each flat with its kitchen – a new and much-favoured arrangement. Here they catered for themselves until the dining hall was opened and 'the Domestic Bursar, the spirited Margaret Lywood, organised excellent meals for us' (John Discombe, 1949–52).

Glen Eyre students of the early days remembered it to have had a special atmosphere. On the one hand there was 'a good deal of civilised and responsible behaviour' by students who wanted 'to work and succeed,' on the other were such ventures as the creation of the Glen Eyre Elephant, which appeared, life-size, on a float for one Rag procession (perhaps inspired by two fine wooden elephants about two feet high, brought from India by Major Harold Mead, the first warden, which stood at either end of the dais in the dining hall) and the occasion when 'twelve able-bodied students from Glen Eyre' lifted an Austin 7 over the wall and deposited it on Highfield Hall's tennis court (Stefan Pietrusewicz). Most were ex-servicemen, and in 1952 when Discombe left he sensed that 'an era was ending and that this new expanding university would never be the same again.'

Space Race – the Sciences Win

By now the College had also bought 16 acres of land which fell away behind the new refectory – still the only completed building west of University Road. These consisted mainly of a derelict brickworks, strangely beautiful, a mass of syringa in summer, full of butterflies, where lizards sat on old bricks and not a sound could be heard. In future they would provide space for many new buildings. Meanwhile, however, it was on the old site that expansion began again. By 1947 a start had been made on new accommodation for Chemistry, Zoology and Physics. The following year a simple assembly hall (to replace the old one made from army hut material was nearly complete. It would seat 400–500, be equipped with a stage and serve among other things as a gymnasium and examination hall.

Of all the Departments demanding space, Chemistry was in a sense the most deserving since it had spent much time planning a new building between 1937 and 1939 which was never built because of the war. In Webb's opinion (and Adam's – in 1956 they published a joint article on the Department's history) this was fortunate because it would have been quite inadequate for post-war numbers. The building which was eventually opened in stages between 1948 and 1952 was magnificent compared with those it replaced, consisting of two blocks measuring 236 by 126 feet, each capable of being built up to three storeys and of eventually providing 45,000 square feet of laboratory and lecture room space.

When the War ended the arrival of many more zoology students made that Department's need for space as urgent as Chemistry's. In 1951 a new building was at last ready for use and next year there was space for its museum. The building stood parallel to the old one, but at first not connected to it, so creating a courtyard between at the bottom of the slope below the army huts.

The arrival of post-war servicemen, many studying science, also resulted in Physics being short of space, but plans for completing the Physics building with a third storey had to be abandoned and it was merely given a single-storey extension. By 1949 lack of space had become so serious that the Department was unable to accept all those who applied otherwise success-fully, but it was another ten years before it was at last given a new building.

The single-storey extension was in fact used by Electronics, Telecommun-ications and Radio Engineering. During the next 50 years Electronics was to become one of the University's most prestigious departments. Responsible for this was Eric Zepler, who returned in 1946 from war work at Cambridge to become its head.

In 1950 Geography emerged from its 14-year association with Economics. During this time Miss Miller had been its acting head, a remarkable lady who is believed to have taught navigation to members of the RAF on six-month courses. Many of its post-war students were ex-servicemen who brought a bonus to the Department. Joyce Gifford, a new assistant lecturer, remembered particularly 'those who had been in South East Asia . . . [as] soldiers in the jungle or flown over the forests.'

Engineering Waits its Turn

The Engineering Faculty was also short of space but its needs were not consid-ered so acute and Professor Cave-Browne-Cave's retirement was the most significant event in Wood's time. He was never the success with students that his predecessor, Professor Eustice, had been. 'He was a showman' (Allan Pike). 'Dour and opinionated, but interesting to talk to if you could put up with this' (A. Samuels, Law). It was an indication of his self-assurance (or perhaps of the College's broad-mindedness) that he never tried to hide his close relationship with Miss Ricks (physical education), whom he eventually married when his wife died. He also knew his rights. 'I'd arrived early with the idea of inter-viewing students,' his successor, Archie Black, remembered, 'but he sat at his desk till the last minute that his contract allowed.' At about the same time that Black became Professor of Mechanical Engineering, a new Chair of Aeronautical Engineering was given to Elfyn Richards, a Welshman, described by Black as 'a very live wire'. Richards had been responsible for the aerody-namic design of the highly successful Vickers Viscount turbo-prop airliner. His inspiration led to the foundation of the Institute of Sound and Vibration Research, which was to bring as much credit to the University as Zepler's Electronics Department.

The Glen Eyre site today. The site was acquired in 1948 and the first students moved in 1949.

Left: *students relax in the Glen Eyre grounds.*

Below: *the Glen Eyre domestic staff.*

Also Ran

Other Faculties and Departments expanded no less rapidly, but had similar space problems. Arts did not even have a building of its own. Eventually (1954) a so-called Tutorial Block was built behind the library to give 23 staff a (temporary) home, but until then all remained spread about the campus wherever there was a spare office or classroom. Nevertheless the numbers of full-time students rose to 247 by 1947–8, compared with 94 two years earlier.

In 1945 History had acquired Professor H. Rothwell, a medievalist, as Betts's successor, 'a nice man, but a less than inspiring lecturer' (Derek Schofield). H. W. Lawton, who remained Professor of Modern Languages, was also well liked. Roddy Urquhart (Admin), who knew him well when both of them went to Sheffield, thought him 'a gentle soul', who 'liked the limelight and was a good university politician, but in a very nice way'.

B. A. Wright remained Professor of English and continued his work on Milton. D. C. Williams, still Director of Music, was rewarded in 1946 for his many courses on music appreciation by being appointed Secretary of the Hampshire County Music Committee. These lectures and the annual concerts of the Choral Society, rather than the study of music as an academic subject, were the Department's main activities.

Philosophy, when eventually revived in 1948 with Arthur MacIver as Senior Lecturer, expanded least. It was still entangled with Theology. The latter, revived a year earlier, now had subtly changed aims. It was to be studied, not for its own sake, but because, in Wood's words, 'it is believed that a number of intending teachers wish to qualify as teachers of Divinity.'

And though the study of law was revived in 1950 – some of its students still articled clerks working for law examinations, others now for the first time for law degress – it was at first a small department. Economics and Commerce, on the other hand, grew quickly, with 113 full-time students by 1949. Professor Ford, returned with new energy from the Ministry of Supply, soon resumed what had become his major work: the study and publication of summaries of the Faculty's great collection of Parliamentary Papers.

The Department of Education expanded as dramatically, student numbers rising in 1946–7 to 130. Its professor was now G. G. Dudley, who had succeeded Cock (after an interlude) and was also well liked if not quite so extravagantly. 'A little man, as round as a football,' Iris Oades remembered, who would lecture with one hand on his hip, the other raised to the black-board – but advise his class when *they* lectured 'not to adopt this teapot attitude'. About the year 1946–7 Dudley wrote that it 'had been one of the most satisfactory and happy sessions within memory. The graduates who came from National Service set an example of zeal, industry and interest in all that pertains to teaching which has stimulated the others, and been a source of inspiration to the tutors.'

The same year an Institute of Education was established and given a building on the campus. Though the College's Department of Education took part in this, it was not a College body, but composed of representatives from the surrounding local education authorities and from other teacher-training establishments in the area. It was a response to the McNair Report, which had recommended that universities become the centres for the training of local teachers. The first of the Institute's activities to affect the College's Department of Education was the development of its own Certificate of Education, and from 1950–1 teacher trainees at the College sat for the Institute's certificate instead of the Cambridge certificate. Soon the Institute extended its activities, running courses on all manner of subjects in which qualified teachers might be interested, some obviously so, like 'General Studies in the Sixth Form', some less obviously so, like 'From School to Work'.

Meanwhile the Adult Education Department (as the Department of Extramural Studies was renamed in 1947) expanded its pre-war activities. By 1952 it was running 253 classes a year for a total of 4,285 students.

Rag Time

Looking back 40 years to the College which he joined in 1947 as a lecturer in English, John Swannell remembered 'the curious contrast of red-brick splendour and the shanty-town squalor of decrepit wooden huts; little metal notices urging us not to walk on the grass (and we didn't); men students with short-back-and-sides haircuts; the occasional newly demobilised RAF moustache; very few beards; duffle-coats; college scarves wrapped in endless coils round their wearers, like serpents; college blazers with brass buttons and breast-pocket badges; women students also in scarves and blazers – but not so many of them, if I remember rightly, in slacks, which the upper echelons of the College hierarchy saw as a threat to civilisation as we knew it; and everywhere, of course, people in gowns.' Swannell's memories give a fair picture of a College which was still small enough for most people to know most others and so retain a sense of community. Like many colleges of the time, the most spectacular communal event of the year was the Rag.

There had been rags, part philanthropic, part processional, part riotous, since early years, but by 1930 they had become too riotous and were suspended. In 1947 some 58 students met one lunch hour and voted for a revival. Committees were formed to arrange details and, on 10 February 1948, 700 students took part in the first post-war Rag. Central to it was the procession, which reminded *Wessex News*'s reporter of a South American Fiesta in Technicolor. Despite the absence of the King's Royal Rifle Corps band (booked accidentally for the wrong day) it was considered a spectacular success. Other Rag features included 'Gaslight Gaieties', an old time music-hall-style show, a Rag ball, a Silly Soccer match, and a Rag Magazine, *The Gobli*. About £1,000 was raised for charitable causes.

During the following years the Rag became a regular event. In 1951 a hailstorm left Shirley High Street a quarter-inch deep in ice and curtailed the procession. In 1952 the procession was cancelled because of the death of George VI. Otherwise, Rag collected annually a largish sum for charity, and

A chemistry Rag float, 1950s.

brought the University into closer contact with the town than on any other day of the year.

In the revived Rag Kelly, skeleton and mascot, rode the engineers' float, since this Faculty now claimed him. Anne Charlesworth (1951–5) however, remembered him as the mascot of the Students' Union and when certain freshers stole him and brought him to Highfield Hall, she and other third-year students recaptured him. Anne volunteered to keep him for the night. 'It was just a bit nerve-racking to see a glass topped coffin lying in one's room in the small hours, and I confess that after a while I spread a blanket over the top.' Unlike London Colleges which in post-war years regularly stole and recaptured each other's mascots, Southampton had no very near neighbours, but nevertheless managed to lose Kelly to Portsmouth Municipal College, so making necessary a successful recovery expedition.

End Game

Symbolising the passing of an era, 1951 was the year in which two of the College's most memorable characters retired. Before joining the Mathematics Department Miss A. M. Trout had worked during the First World War for A. V. Roe Aircraft Co. by the Hamble, where she was said to have been 'the only person who could cope with the calculations associated with the wing struts of the biplanes the firm was turning out' (Michael Cotton). Her interests lay well beyond mathematics. In Webb's words, she was 'a colossus of erudition, able to discourse instanter on anything from music to rare plants.' 'On many occasions,' Isabel Rendell remembered, 'I have walked round the gardens with her while she named the plants, particularly one favourite bush, *Buddleia Loganiacae*.' When she retired she gave the College £200 to be spent on the

gardens which Professor Mangham was laying out in the old brick works.

Charlie Taylor, the College Beadle, had first been employed in the 1890s, aged 16, as an assistant janitor. Before the First World War one of his duties was looking after the Hartley Museum, hence his control over Kelly, resident of the ladies' toilet. After the war he was given a cottage close to the library where he lived with his mother till she died, then on his own. Soon he had a team of juniors in brown coats, to clean and maintain the College's grounds and buildings.

George Grant, Registrar in the 1930s, remembered that after he had been interviewed for the job he called at The Stile pub. Here he was politely told that he had sat in the Professor's chair. Grant moved, but waited and watched,

Presentation of books to the Library by CARE, 1949/50.

Sir Robert Wood (Principal) accepts the first shipment (left) *and then examines the books with the help of students* (right).

The History Study Room in the Library, c.1950. This later became South Stack, and later still Terminal Room.

Students sitting on the grass, 1950s.

presently to see Charlie arrive to take the chair and 'be served with the deference paid to regular customers' – only to discover with amazement when he joined the College the real nature of Charlie's job.

'He was the first member of staff you met as a fresher,' Jack Taylor (1931–5) remembered, 'standing in the porch of the Assembly Hall calling "Science to the left, Arts to the right".' He appears regularly in the background of photographs of College ceremonial occasions, in his blue and yellow uniform, tall and upright, as he remained till his retirement, despite the loss of an eye.

Professor Black believed that Wood's official enthusiasm for the College's transformation into a University hid doubt and anxiety. On the one hand Black believed that Wood had a low opinion of the College's academic standards and doubted whether it would be allowed to make the change, on the other hand that he was afraid a Southampton degree would seem much less valuable than a London one and the quality and quantity of student applicants would decline. Wood's doubts did not prevent him encouraging the College to work steadily towards the change. The first encouraging result came in 1948–9 in the form of a 'special relationship' with London University. Southampton's staff would be appointed by London to co-operate in the setting and marking of Final examinations. The following year examinations for all Faculties except Engineering and Economics were set and marked in this way.

Staff experienced one, perhaps unforeseen, change. Until now they and their students had been on the same side. 'We were aligned against a common foe, the irresistible might of the London University examiners,' Swannell remembered. 'I must confess that I missed the excitement of the old embattled days when we began to set and mark our own Finals papers.'

During 1951 and 1952 'much anxious thought' (Wood) was given to new statutes for the University which the College hoped to become, and preparing the required petition to the King. It was his successor, the Queen, who on 29 April 1952 founded the University of Southampton by granting it a Royal Charter.

This was not quite the end of the affair. For another year students were allowed to choose to take either Southampton or London papers. And in 1953 the University College of Southampton had to be formally closed and its assets handed to the new University. But 1952 was effectively the year when the Hartley Institution, exactly 50 years after it had become a university college, became at last a fully independent university.

II

UNIVERSITY, 1952–2002

1. The Pre-Robbins Years, 1952–65

University in Name, College in Nature

In October 1952 David Gwilym James succeeded Sir Robert Wood as Vice-Chancellor. For the previous ten years James had been Professor of English at Bristol University. He was a mild-mannered man with Christian convictions, ideal for a small institution. He behaved like the master of an Oxbridge college, still possible when the University had only about 1,000 students and 100 staff. Staff and students would be invited to his house for sherry.

'He was formal – I was always "Miss Evans",' Sheila Evans remembered. She was secretary to James and to his four successors. 'And very Welsh.' So were Professor Richards (Engineering), Professor Davies (Mathematics) and subsequently Professor Phillips (Law). Paranoid members of staff spoke of the Welsh Mafia.

James's years were ones to which staff and students look back with nostalgia. They enjoyed the relaxed flavour of the 1950s – when 'it was not at all uncommon to see staff playing tennis during the afternoon' (Derek Schofield, 1952–8).

James's first year ended with a grand occasion: the installation of the Duke of Wellington as the University's first Chancellor. Among those on whom the Duke conferred the honorary degree of Doctor of Laws were Kenneth Vickers, Sir Samuel Gurney-Dixon and Sir Robert Wood. There followed the lunches, garden parties, dinners and congratulatory addresses which form part of such occasions.

A dinner held at South Stoneham House on the occasion of Dr James (seated in the middle of the left side of the table) succeeding Sir Robert Wood as Vice-Chancellor, 1952.

Dr David Gwilym James, Vice-Chancellor 1952–65.

Below right: *The Gurney-Dixon Building and Link during construction, with workmen's sheds and cars in the foreground. The long hut in the middle ground, though, was part of the University.*

Below: *Sir Samuel Gurney-Dixon, Chairman of University College Council 1936–57, Vice-President of University College 1947–52, and Pro-Chancellor of the University 1952–66. Photographed in the 1960s.*

The University's new charter and statutes were not very different from those of the College. The Duke of Wellington, previously the College's President, became the University's Chancellor. James, who would have been the College's Principal, was the University's Vice-Chancellor. Professor Forsey, previously the Vice-Principal, became the University's Deputy Vice-Chancellor. Like the College, the University had a Visitor, the Queen replacing Lord Mountbatten.

Similarly, the College's Court of Governors became the University's Court, and retained its status as 'supreme governing body'. In practice Council remained the real governing body. This was reduced in size from 57 to 33 members, of whom 25 were day members. The University's Senate differed less from the College's Senate, its size merely increased from 23 to 26. As before it included all the (15) Professors, the Deans and other representatives of Faculties. The Vice-Chancellor, like the College's Principal, became its chairman.

The new charter introduced one new body: Convocation. All graduates of the University (or College) could belong to this and its purpose was to give them a voice in its future. This they could exercise through Convocation's five members of Court, and its right to 'enter into communication' with Council or Senate on any University matter it chose. Convocation invited old graduates to an annual Convocation Day at the University.

James's arrival coincided with the University Grants Committee's report on the previous five years and proposals for its grants for the next five. There was to be a significant change in the nature of these grants. No longer would certain portions of them be earmarked for specific purposes, but universities would be free to spend what they received as they pleased, provided what

The University Senate at Glen Eyre, 1953.

they did was in the national interest. This was welcomed by James as 'a re-assertion by the State that it is anxious to preserve the autonomy of the universities.' Less welcome was a check on capital expenditure which meant that most of Southampton's plans for new buildings had to be postponed.

From this freeze the most important building slowly to emerge was an expanded library. In 1951 Senate had approved an outline plan for an extension. Three years later this was submitted to the University Grants Committee and Colonel Gutteridge appointed architect. Building finally began in 1957 and the new extension was opened on 4 December 1959 by Sir Samuel Gurney-Dixon in a speech 'packed with apt quotations and original humour' (Curators' report). He had been Chairman of Council for 21 years and the extension was named after him.

The Faculties

Engineering was the first Faculty to benefit from the relaxation of the building freeze. In June 1954 it obtained approval for a plan to complete the Engineering Building, and so give the Departments of Aeronautics, Electrical Engineering and Electronics adequate accommodation. Work began in 1957 and the building was ready for occupation by October 1959. Teaching rather than research remained Engineering's main activity. Its best-known work in these years, however, was in research when it constructed an enormous hydraulic model of Southampton Water and the Solent to determine the consequences of a deep water channel for tankers supplying a proposed oil refinery on the Solent's east side. Twenty years later, long after it had served its purpose, the model was demolished and its building became the John Hansard Gallery, hence the gallery's odd shape.

Professor Archie Black's important contribution to the country's universities as a whole was the national scheme he helped to devise for systematising the granting of university places to students. Until this was put in place and UCCA (University Central Council on Admissions) established, a university would

The Duke of Wellington inspecting the guard, 1953.

Right: *the Turner Sims Library in the early 1950s. Portraits of the Hartley family hang on the wall.*

Above: *Library staff examining books in the Library, 1958.*

Guests at a dinner held in 1972, in honour of Archie Black, Professor of Mechanical Engineering 1950–67, Professor of Engineering 1968–72, Deputy Vice-Chancellor of the University 1959–61. Archie Black is third from the right.

have little idea at the start of a new year whether the students to whom it had offered places would arrive or would have gone elsewhere. Southampton's Engineering Faculty took part in a pilot scheme before the full national scheme was launched in 1964–5 and Black was to become Vice-Chairman of UCCA.

In 1957 the Faculty of Engineering acquired a new chair in Civil Engineering, and a Professor of the subject, Peter Morice. Civil Engineering of a sort had been taught during the War by Ernie Mann, a memorable campus figure, riding a bicycle in plus fours, but until now its students had remained the smallest group in the Faculty. An expansion of the Faculty to prove even more important was the Institute of Sound and Vibration Research, established by Professor Richards in 1963 (see pages 153–6). Some of the earliest Faculty research had concerned noise, but it was Richards who saw how important this was to become.

There were significant changes to the staff of the Science Faculty. In 1953 Geography (still also part of Arts) lost Miss Miller, a character as memorable as Miss Trout, who had been head of the Department during its 14-year eclipse. She was succeeded by Professor F. J. Monkhouse who came from the University of Liverpool and was a regional geographer. In 1964 he was to edit *A Survey of Southampton and its Region*. In 1956 Professor Adam retired, working to the end on surface films and detergents, to be succeeded by Richard Cookson. Eric Zepler was working on microwave spectroscopy with Herman Jahn, recently appointed Professor of Applied Mathematics. Jahn had an established reputation in theoretical physics and had worked during the War at the Royal Aircraft Establishment.

In 1957 Alec Gambling joined Electronics where he was to have a significant influence on the development of optical fibres (see pages 163–4). As significant for the University's future was the research which Zoology under Professor John Raymont was now carrying out into the marine biology of coastal waters, using the Department's first boat, *Aurelia*. Within 15 years the Department of Oceanography to which those early beginnings led was exploring the world's oceans; within a further 25 it was operating from a £50m. waterfront campus (see page 239). In all the Faculty's Departments, with the possible exception of Geography, research was becoming ever more important.

Throughout the pre-Robbins years the Arts Faculty continued to suffer from the lack of its own building. As soon as the Gurney-Dixon Library was finished it lost its Tutorial Building and was given the library's ground floor, but many of its staff were still spread about the campus. Katy Hall, who arrived in the French Department in the late 1950s, had to share an army hut with a male colleague. 'Up through the floor sprouted a two-foot nettle which we called the Separating Sword.' Nevertheless the Faculty expanded in numbers as far as it could without upsetting the University's science/arts balance. And it improved its academic standards by replacing its General Degree with a new honours Combined Degree, to be taken in no more than three subjects.

Philosophy under MacIver and Tony Manser grew from almost nothing to a sizeable Department with an honours school from 1953–4. The Chair of English passed from Wright to Frank Prince, a poet, author of one of the most admired poems of the Second World War, 'Soldiers Bathing'. C. A. Hackett succeeded Lawton as Professor of Modern Languages, his chief interest Rimbaud. Besides French and German, the Department now included Spanish with Nigel Glendinning as Professor. In 1959 John Bromley was given a new Chair of Modern History. Glendinning and Professor Baldry (Classics), together with Morice and Janusz Rydzewski of Civil Engineering, were all to campaign for University support of the arts. The last two persuaded James to underwrite a concert society, Glendinning and Baldry organised the University's first art exhibitions and Morice was one of the committee which appointed Peter Evans as the first Professor of Music since 1928. This was to prove the most important appointment in the Arts Faculty during the pre-Robbins years. Only in 1963 was the Arts 1 Building completed as part of the Nuffield complex and the Faculty at last became united.

Level four of the Gurney-Dixon link, 1964.

Law also prospered, becoming a Faculty in 1953, with students working for law degrees. Three years later a Chair of Law was given to Arthur Philips, a man learned in ecclesiastical law, whose previous experience had been as a law officer in East Africa.

An equally important development was the transformation in 1962 of Economics into the Faculty of Social Sciences, by now a better description of much of the work in which Ford and his colleagues had been engaged since the 1930s. The new Faculty was divided into five Departments: Economics, Sociology and Social Studies, Politics, Economic Statistics, and Commerce and

A group at the last ever Hartley dinner, April 1963. Dr D. G. James, Vice-Chancellor, is on the left.

Accounting.

In 1950 Professor Wagner had succeeded Dudley as Head of the Department of Education. For 17 years Wagner was to run a department which was in many ways successful. Soon most of its students were taking the one-year courses which led to a Certificate of Education, and all but a few regularly obtained this. Under Wagner, however, the Department was not a happy one, and the appointment of Professor Jack Wrigley, to be responsible for research, led to conflict.

Music

It was James's opinion – at the time – that a university should not only enable students to get degrees in their subjects but support a broad range of cultural activities which they could experience or in which they could take part. Among these music was one of the most important.

It had not been entirely neglected. Before the war, Cecil Williams, as Master of Music, had started summer concerts. There had also been annual Gilbert and Sullivan performances, and these were revived in the early 1950s, Dr Kenneth Brooks (English) playing the entire accompaniment, rescored for solo piano. (He was remembered as a very dry lecturer in the history of language who, on stage in braces and bowler, became transformed into an inspired pub pianist.) In 1952 the Choral and Music Societies staged *Dido and Aeneas*, the first opera, as opposed to operetta, to be produced. In the following years the University Concert Society brought professional soloists and ensembles to the

University for subscription concerts, these proving so successful that the financial underwriting offered by James and the Students' Union was never needed. Peter Evans's appointment in 1961 as the first Professor of Music since 1928 brought a dramatic change. Though he would probably consider the virtual creation of a Music Department involved in the academic study of music his most important achievement, he also brought a huge expansion of live performance.

When the Nuffield Theatre opened in 1963 it provided a venue for most performances by visitors. These began with 'a splendid week of Britten chamber operas'. Inevitably there was residual philistinism. After one of these a Professor from another Department introduced Evans to the celebrated journalist Katharine Whitehorn as 'the man who has just lost the University a thousand pounds.' He referred to the hiring of the English Opera Group. Soon the BBC Third Programme was bringing its Invitation Concerts – 'by the day's standards daring'. Town as well as gown needed converting. Evans remembered 'an uncomfortable evening on which Southampton's mayor arrived unexpectedly for one of these. Though we could manipulate the seating to give him an appropriate placing, I could not too boldly suggest that the programme, ending with a vast avant-garde piano sonata, was unlikely to conform to his own well-developed taste for Welsh male-voice choirs; I fear he suspected an elaborate practical joke.'

In 1967 the Music Department was to pioneer a scheme sponsored by its major benefactor, the Radcliffe Trust, which each year brought the Allegri String Quartet to the University for short periods of residence. Besides this the University gave contracts to a succession of distinguished young players and

The Rothenstein Mural which hangs in the University's Senate Room was painted by Sir William Rothenstein in 1916 and presented to the University of Southampton by his son John Rothenstein in 1959. Designed as a memorial to members of the British universities who served in the First World War, it includes full-length portraits of chancellors, vice-chancellors and eminent scholars of the time, from the poet laureate Robert Bridges, to the author of The Golden Bough, *J. G. Frazer.*

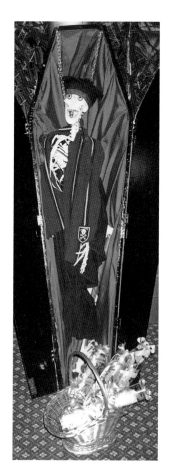

Kelly, the Engineering Faculty's mascot.

Facing page, top to bottom:

D. M. Boggett, one of the University's star foot-ballers in the 1950s.

M. W. A. Hannam, Black Belt, member of the University Judo Club 1955–9.

Fencing became the University's outstanding sport after the Second World War.

ensembles to enable them to reside for a number of years, giving regular performances and teaching their instruments to students. So professionals and students each presented weekly lunchtime recital series, while the madrigal choir (under David Brown for more than two decades), the chamber orchestra and the symphony orchestra gave regular concerts. At the same time the Choral Society joined forces with the Bournemouth Symphony Orchestra in Guildhall performances which included Southampton premières of such twentieth-century masterpieces as Stravinsky's *Symphony of Psalms* and Britten's *War Requiem*, but also of Beethoven's *Missa Solemnis* and the Berlioz *Requiem*. For these the University provided rehearsal facilities, Peter Evans's musical direction and the young voices of students, the result a quarter-century of town-and-gown collaboration.

Students and the Union

Although the disappearance of ex-servicemen meant that from about 1952 students were mostly younger, the flavour of campus life changed little in the 1950s, remaining that of a college rather than a university. Already, however, the Students' Union was beginning to acquire the political preoccupations which were to excite it for the next 40 years. This did not prevent it from taking an interest in campus matters. In 1952 it organised an Installation Ball at the Guildhall during which the newly installed Chancellor unveiled the newly restored mascot, Kelly. (Three years later the Union was to 'disestablish' Kelly and present him to the Engineering Faculty – but this did not prevent him disrupting the 1963 presentation of the Union's accounts by the Senior Treasurer, when lights went out and Kelly paraded through the meeting.)

In 1953–4 came a much appreciated agreement with the University that it would help fund a Union bar in the West Building. This was also the year in which, after a long and fierce debate, the Union disaffiliated itself from the National Union of Students by six votes. It considered that it was getting poor value for what it paid the NUS. The matter was still being fiercely debated the next year, and the year after Southampton rejoined the NUS. Meanwhile in 1955–6 the Union for the first time employed staff.

In 1958 the President reported that 'bitterness and hostility' was driving freshers away from Union meetings, but in 1959 his successor complained that 'meetings have become possibly too placid.' Relationships with the University had also become 'very happy'. The Vice-Chancellor in particular had been 'willing to assist in every way,' and give the Union 'sympathetic consideration'.

By 1960–1 the Union had expanded into almost the whole of the West Building, something it had been wanting to do for five years, but it had also since 1959 been discussing a new Union building which would be adequate for 4,000 students. Two issues preoccupied the Union in these years: the Rag and the Union Dinner. In 1959 the University threatened disciplinary action against the Rag and rules of conduct were drawn up. Probably as a result the Union itself cancelled the 1960 Rag, though in 1963 it was resurrected. The annual Union dinner, though regularly criticised as elitist, also remained an annual event. In 1963 there was conflict of a similar sort between the Union Council and the Athletic Union about the latter's gift of a wine decanter to the Duke of Wellington. The AU had its way.

Meanwhile the Suez Crisis, the Soviet Union's crushing of the Hungarian rising and apartheid in South Africa gave the Union plenty of causes to back. In 1957, for example, it voted by a large majority that it supported the South African Union in its opposition to the closing of Cape Town and Johannesburg Universities to coloured students. The same year it funded a scholarship for a refugee Hungarian student.

In October 1963 student discontent with the quantity and quality of refectory food caused the Union to call for a boycott of the refectory unless it was given representation on the Refectory Committee. It had been campaigning for representation on University committees for several years, but it was probably the threat of a boycott which produced results. In 1963–4 Council agreed to student representatives on the Refectory and Lodgings Committee among others. Gratifying as this was, it proved far from adequate and lack of student representation was to be an underlying grievance of the militant protests that began five years later.

Increasingly the Union became involved with the arts, sponsoring drama in particular, though the University still had only the post-war assembly hall for a theatre. In the early 1950s the University Theatre Group (as the Dramatic Society had been renamed) was producing, besides straight plays, an annual melodrama. In 1953 *Maria Marten* was received with 'tumultuous applause'. In 1962–3 the Theatre Group's *Volpone* was one of five finalists in *The Sunday Times* drama festival, and the following year *Dr Maccabre* was a finalist in the NUS Drama Festival. In 1952 and again in 1959 staff staged a Staff Revue, devised by Professor Williams (Botany) with the assistance of Tony Manser, Nancy Walls, David Cook and (for the music) Kenneth Brooks. Topical sketches included 'Space will not Permit' (a Senate meeting in a spaceship) and 'Portrait in Oils' (a trio of oil-rich sheikhs). In 1958–9 the Union supported a new Arts Club, and an annual Art Competition. Two years later it organised the first Arts Festival, opened in March 1961 by Sir Basil Spence. Though the Union itself criticised the result as being 'dull, unimaginative, and completely lacking in any form of aggression or adventure,' it claimed that the festival had nevertheless been a landmark event, and commented favourably on the following year's festival.

The Union continued to exercise one of its central functions by supporting the University's athletic clubs. In the first year of peace (1945–6) the Athletic Union set about raising its standards 'to the high pre-war level'. College teams, in particular rugby, soccer, men's hockey and women's hockey, were soon doing well, and by 1950 there were 17 athletic clubs, with four more – golf, squash, basketball and archery – soon to emerge. That year fencing became the College's outstanding sport, the Captain fencing for England and the team defeating both Oxford and London Universities.

Fencing continued to be successful, the team reaching the University Athletics Union (UAU) final in 1953–4. That year Ursula Smith won the WIVAB badminton singles for the third year in succession. 1954–6 was a period of decline, attributed to the final disappearance of ex-servicemen, though the women's athetics club won the WIVAB athletics championship in 1956. In the following two years there was a dramatic revival, the Union's President describing 1957–8 as the best year so far. The ladies' badminton and men's basketball teams were UAU champions. Two runners, Bruce Tulloh and Martin Hyman, however, were the stars. In 1958 Hyman came second in both the three and the six miles at the British Games and was the UAU cross-country champion. In 1959 Tulloh won the three miles and the six miles at the British Games. When Hyman was chosen to represent England in the six miles at Cardiff he was the first athlete to gain an English vest since the College became a University. In 1963 Tulloh broke the British two-, three- and six-mile records and won a gold medal at the World Games. In 1969 he was to run from Los Angeles to New York in 64 days 20 hours, breaking the previous record by eight days.

In the 1950s cricket had a number of successful seasons, reaching the UAU finals four times. Outstanding games player in 1959–60 was D'Souza, captain of hockey and tennis. Next year both the rifle club and the men's first VIII won all their fixtures. In 1963 the VIII went to Henley – where it did not distinguish itself but considered the experience useful.

Expansion

Sir James Matthews, Vice-Chair of Council, 1958–79.

Vice-Chancellor James never favoured expansion. In the 12 years between his arrival and 1963–4, however, student numbers more than doubled, from 933 to 2,094. Furthermore, in 1960 the University accepted that it would continue to grow and probably reach 4,000 by 1980.

One consequence of the growth so far was that the percentage of students living in halls of residence had fallen from 46 per cent to 37 per cent, and had only been kept at that level by a succession of extensions at South Stoneham, South Hill and Connaught. In 1959–60 the University began to benefit from a new hall, built with the third and most generous gift (£100,000) of the Chamberlain sisters, Charlotte and Mary. Charlotte had been a member of Council since 1928 and for 17 years had chaired the Halls and Refectory Committee. Her new donation, together with her funding of the 1930 rebuilding of Highfield Hall, suggest a special interest in women's education.

Charlotte died in 1956 and it was Mary who laid the foundation stone of what was to be named Chamberlain Hall. Built in the grounds of South Hill, it was traditional in plan, with common rooms and a dining hall. Iris Oades, the first warden, remembered going round London buying nice furniture (with part of the donation) for her new hall. October 1959, when the first 50 girls arrived, she thought of as 'the beginning of a golden age'. Eventually Chamberlain Hall was to accommodate 210 students and to become mixed.

A student body of 4,000, however, would need more than additional halls of residence and from 1960 onwards the Council, largely persuaded by a long-standing member, James Matthews, who was also for many years leader of the Labour group on the Borough and City Councils, set about acquiring the first essential: more land.

Connaught Hall today.

In July 1961 the University submitted proposals to the Borough Council, which led to a Public Enquiry in February 1963. The proposals were modified and the University withdrew its plan for a graduate hall of residence at Highfield, but they were essentially approved. To compensate for the modifications, it was allowed to buy 4 acres of land at the junction of Burgess Road and the Avenue. The most important effect of the Minister's approval was that it gave the University the right to acquire some 200 houses on or near the campus. Although some were for temporary use, they were all for subsequent demolition to release their sites. Matthews's persuasion of James to support planning on this scale was probably the most important event thus far in the independent University's history.

Meanwhile the University had either already completed, was now erecting, or was planning, a remarkable number of buildings on sites it already possessed. They included a Mathematics Building, a new Physics Building, an extension to the Chemistry Building, a third Engineering Building, new buildings for Geology, Botany and Oceanography and further extensions to Connaught, South Stoneham and Glen Eyre. It was thus that, when the Robbins Report was published in 1963, Southampton was better prepared than any other university to take advantage of the great expansion the report proposed.

2. Years of Plenty, 1966–71

After Robbins

The Robbins Report proposed that the number of students at English universities should rise from 150,000 to 170,000. Southampton's response, out of proportion to its size, was to offer to increase its students to 4,000, not by 1980 as planned, but by 1967.

During James's last two years the University set about making such growth possible. In addition to the buildings and extensions already under construction or planned, it now planned Arts 2, into which the Arts and Law Faculties could expand, a Geography Building, additional storeys to the Tizard Engineering Building, a further storey for the Gurney-Dixon Library, a new Animal House for Physiology and Biochemistry, a further expansion at Glen Eyre, the opening of a hall of residence at the newly purchased Chilworth Manor and the building of a new hall on part of the playing field given to the College by Mrs Montefiore. The latter would house 300 students in two blocks, their accommodation to consist for the first time, of study-bedrooms, without a dining hall or common rooms. In the cautious opinion of the Secretary and Registrar, this was financially attractive, but raised administrative and discipline problems.

In 1963–4 seven new Chairs were created and about 50 new appointments made, against 15 departures. The following year, including professors, about 135 appointments were made against four departures. Other developments of these two years were the gift to the University of the Parkes Library (its subject Judaism's relations with other peoples) the establishment of a student health centre with sick bay at Chamberlain Hall, and the formal opening of the Nuffield Theatre on 2 March 1964 by Dame Sybil Thorndike.

James's successor, Kenneth Mather, took office in August 1965. 'None of them knew what they were coming to,' Sheila Evans remembered, about the five Vice-Chancellors to whom she was secretary. In general it is probably true that all underestimated the job, and that both Mather and his successor Roberts remained much involved with their own work. Mather was a Fellow of the Royal Society and a highly regarded geneticist. 'On Monday mornings,' Sheila remembered, 'it wasn't University business he thought about when he arrived at the office. First he had to visit his fruit flies.' But Mather had been Pro-Vice-Chancellor of the University of Birmingham and must have had a fair idea of what a Vice-Chancellor's job required.

It was Mather's misfortune that his six years included those of early student unrest, with which he did not deal skilfully. On the other hand they also included the emergence of a Faculty and a Department which were to become of the greatest importance to the University: Medicine and Oceanography. Mather should have credit for the encouragement he gave, especially to Medicine. Furthermore the University faced early discouragement. At the start of Mather's second term (January 1966) the chairman of the University Grants Committee, Sir John Wolfenden, made it clear that development of this sort was not what the Committee expected. The Robbins Report, Wolfenden said, 'still formed the basis of national policy' but there would be very little expansion in the universities during the next five years and Southampton should 'build on established strengths rather than branch out'. In 1966 Oceanography was far from an established strength and Medicine did not exist.

Oceanography, it is true, was already an embryonic department. To promote it Mather had mainly to support Professor Raymont's enormous enthusiasm for the subject. Medicine was another matter. Though the University had a medicine-related Department of Physiology and Biochemistry, James had never favoured a medical school, and many staff were also opposed to one. It was against them that Mather had to argue. The Medical School was planned throughout Mather's time and its first students arrived in October 1971, the term after he had left.

Third only to Oceanography and Medicine as a new venture was a Department of Archaeology, established in 1966. The Chair was given to Barry Cunliffe who, aged 26, was believed to be the youngest professor the University or College had ever appointed. Under Cunliffe, then Colin Renfrew, then Peter Ucko, each with a different approach to the subject, the Department was to increase in size and reputation during the next 30 years until, in the 1990s, it had over 100 students and the Higher Education Funding Council was awarding it the highest rating (5) for its research.

Other Departments behaved more in the way Wolfenden had suggested, by building on their strengths. Mathematics devised and promoted the School Mathematics Project (SMP), a new way to teach Mathematics. The Modern Languages Department transferred its teaching of languages for non-specialists to a new language centre under Tom Carter, with two language laboratories.

The official opening of the Parkes Library, 23 June, 1965 – an exhibition in the Turner Sims Library. Speaking is Mr Rothschild; Mr Bland to his right and Professor Baldry is to his left. Lord Perth consults his notes, and Dr Parkes is on the far right of the picture.

Professor Sir Kenneth Mather, Vice-Chancellor 1965–71.

Science Week, March 1998. The University has been concerned to raise the profile of science and engineering in schools since the 1970s, and this work continues today, with students visiting local schools.

Physics became increasingly interested in cryogenics, while the Institute of Sound and Vibration Research worked on an expanding range of problems, some to the layman not obviously connected with sound or vibration, for example using lasers to predict failure in heavy machinery of the sort used in ships or drilling rigs.

Despite the growth in student numbers during its first dozen years, the Engineering Faculty was unable at this time to find enough good applicants to expand as fast as other Faculties. To help to remedy this, it founded the Southampton Engineering and Applied Science Forum in 1967 with Bob Gammon, then Head of Science at Richard Taunton's College, as the first Director and Professor Ron Bell as the first Chairman. This brought together representatives of schools, universities and industry, its aim to devise ways of persuading more young people to choose careers in applied science. Once established the Forum gained general recognition from Local Education Authorities, schools and colleges, regional industry and the University. Funds became available from many sources and the value placed on this activity by central government was reflected in a pump-priming grant from the Department of Trade and Industry. Bob Gammon was appointed as full-time Director in 1971 and the name was changed to Southern Science and Technology Forum to include the wider involvement of Hampshire, Dorset, Isle of Wight and South Wiltshire.

The need to make young children more aware of the needs of the country in science and engineering and the attractiveness of careers in engineering was to be an increasingly important theme of the 1970s and 1980s. A highlight was the publication of the Finniston Report which emphasised what the government should do to prevent the further destruction of many of the country's traditional manufacturing industries. Finniston argued that, without strong manufacturing industries, the wealth and position of the UK in the world would decline. Bob Gammon, together with Professor Geoffrey Lilley and colleagues from Portsmouth Polytechnic, decided on an initiative to aid in stopping this decline. The aim of this was to get all children in primary and secondary schools more aware of the world around them and to understand the importance of engineering and applied science both in the world and the development of the nation, and as an important choice of future career. This, they argued, could only be done if children built and then performed carefully selected experiments to gain hands-on experience of engineering and applied science. In partnership with the Hampshire Education Committee, and the Hampshire Technology Centre, an interactive exhibition centre called INTECH was set up in Winchester. Most of the schoolchildren in Hampshire today attend classes at INTECH, which recently received a £10 million grant from the Millennium Commission for a new purpose-made building together with a planetarium.

In addition, following the Finniston Report, a National Steering Committee was established under Bob Gammon's

The Nuffield Theatre today. In the foreground is F. E. McWilliams's Puy de Dome Figure (Bronze, 1962).

Luke Graves Hansard, 1783–1841, ancestor of John Hansard.

Chairmanship to carry out a pilot project into 'Preformation of undergraduate engineers'. The principal aim of this was to provide full-time, paid industrial employment for high-quality undergraduates during a gap year before starting their courses. The value to employers and students alike exceeded expectations and the Committee was able to make a submission to the Manpower Services Commission to expand the project into two further regions. Subsequently it amalgamated with other, similar activities to produce the present, nationwide 'Year in Industry' scheme.

Fine Art

A further consequence of 'the Robbins Cornucopia' was John Sweetman's appointment in 1967 to be the University's first lecturer in Fine Art. As such he had three responsibilities: to organise art exhibitions, to manage the University's permanent art collection and to lecture on the history of art.

Since 1964 there had been a Fine Art Committee which arranged exhibitions in a gallery in the Nuffield Theatre. These had been organised by Nigel Glendinning, Professor of Spanish, an authority on Goya. The gallery in the Nuffield was far from satisfactory, with windows on three sides which had to be blacked out, but it was here that Sweetman organised three exhibitions a term. From 1972, when a new gallery was opened at Boldrewood, he organised a further three a term there. Between 1967 and 1980 the University's galleries held a total of 192 exhibitions (all hung at weekends with an opening on Sunday evenings). These did not include a large number held in a Photographic Gallery, which had opened in 1973 on the initiative of Leo Stable (Administration).

In 1978 an unrelated event – the University's decision to demolish the Civil Engineering Department's tidal model of Southampton Water and the Solent – brought a dramatic change. Its building was transformed into the John Hansard Gallery.

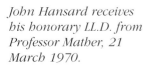

John Hansard receives his honorary LL.D. from Professor Mather, 21 March 1970.

The late John Hansard had been the last lineal descendent of Luke Hansard who in the final year of the eighteenth century became Printer to the House of Commons, and after whom records of parliamentary proceedings have since been named. John Hansard, on retiring as an executive director of Lever Bros, had started a second career as a merchant banker, and at the same time began searching for somewhere to lodge his family papers. He chose Southampton because of Professor Ford's work on parliamentary papers. During this time John Hansard had been a member of the Parliamentary Papers Research Committee and had financed additions to the Ford collection. He had also helped the University to secure the 1st Duke of Wellington's papers, one part of which consisted of the Duke's set of Hansard from 1801 to 1826 (213 volumes).

Despite Hansard's donations, more money was needed for converting the tidal model's building and an appeal for £150,000 was launched. To supervise all three galleries a new committee was formed, on which the Arts Council,

Southern Arts, Hampshire County Council and Southampton City Council were represented. A staff for the three galleries was appointed, Leo Stable was given charge and the John Hansard Gallery was formally opened on 22 September 1980.

Meanwhile Sweetman had been using a small budget to add to the University's permanent collection, and devising a scheme for making it better known. Departments and Halls of Residence were encouraged to have paintings and prints from the collection on temporary loan. The scheme was strongly supported.

A University collection of sculpture was a different matter. If its items were to be seen they had to be found sites around the campus. Apprehensive about the reception of 'Steel Tubes' by Justin Knowles (sponsored by British Steel), Sweetman had a maquette of this 55-foot erection displayed in the library, but Senate was not converted and summoned him to defend it. Only when he got the support of Basil Spence and the Tate Gallery was it accepted, and sited close to the Senior Common Room. Knowles, however, wished his steel girders to rise directly from the ground while the Works and Buildings Officer complained that this would become worn or boggy, depending on the weather, and suggested a dense, low planting of berberis and heather. Several months of correspondence and meetings followed before the dense planting was imposed, but a small central area of grass was permitted.

Sweetman's third responsibility, the teaching of the history of art, he undertook in the History Department, where he found Professor Bromley a great ally. The number of his students rose from eight taking the ancillary course in 1967 to 90 taking the subject as part of their honours courses. Mostly these were History or English students, but a few, whom he specially valued, came from science departments. One history student, Stephen Deuchar, was to publish *Sporting Art in the Eighteenth Century* (1988) and subsequently become Director of the Tate's Millbank Gallery.

From 1967 a succession of Fine Arts Fellows (among them Ned Hoskins and Ray Smith) spent periods at the University where they were given studios and provided general support to its cultural life. Some gave classes or lectures, some invited leading artists to visit the campus. Sweetman himself invited among others Ernst Gombrich and Anthony Blunt.

No more Fine Arts Fellows came after 1981. When Sweetman retired in 1990 he was not replaced and the teaching of the history of art was abandoned until 1996 when Winchester School of Art merged with the University.

The opening of the Parliamentary Papers Library. Professor and Mrs Ford talking to Lord Maybray-King, 7 July 1971.

The official opening of the Wellington Suite, 14 May 1983. Dr Woolgar shows a bound volume of papers to the Duke and Duchess of Wellington.

Students and the Union

Between 1965 and 1971 the Students' Union supported parochial, national and international causes with increasing vigour, this culminating in 'direct action' such as sit-ins and boycotts. It also sometimes supported student enterprise, for example a visit to Spain by Toastrack, a vintage bus bought for £25 by the Engineering Faculty to use as a minibus. In Spain Toastrack became stranded and had to be brought back to England 'at considerable expense'. 'It is hoped', the Union President wrote, 'that the new back axle will receive a regular supply of the appropriate lubricant.' Toastrack was to make more successful continental expeditions. In 1988, ten engineering students took it to Russia to attend the opening of the first national motor museum behind the Iron Curtain.

International causes the Union expressed support for were protesting students in Berlin (June 1967), French students and workers opposing the Gaullist regime (May 1968), and imprisoned Russian intellectuals (June 1968). Among ruling bodies it deplored were the Greek Military Junta, the Malayan and Singapore Governments and the USA for its Vietnam campaign. British causes it supported were the right of Sikhs to wear turbans when employed by Wolverhampton Corporation, Vickers apprentices in their dispute with the company at Barrow-in-Furness and Ford workers in their strike at Wide Lane. In 1969 it voted to ban Enoch Powell from Union premises.

Its parochial campaigns were for more representation on committees, for sabbatical years for its presidents and for more student accommodation. In November 1968 it secured agreement that there should be staff/student committees in all Departments and that students should have representation on an increased number of Senate and Council committees. In 1970, however, the President was still hoping for 'even more' representation. Meanwhile in April 1965 the Vice-Chancellor had agreed to reduce the academic commitments of Union presidents, but they were not given sabbatical years until 1967–8. In 1971 the Union, in protest against the shortage of University accom-

Two sculptures in bronze by Barbara Hepworth.

Right: Two Forms in Echelon, *1961.*

Far right: Two Figures, *1968.*

modation, voted for the organisation of three indefinite squats in derelict or vacant houses in the centre of Southampton.

Meanwhile on campus there had been four sit-ins. The first, an unofficial one, occurred on 3–4 February 1968 when about 50 students occupied the Administration's offices in the main building for 24 hours in support of London School of Economics students. No damage was done, though the occupation put the University's telephone exchange out of action. Seventeen months later (30 June–2 July 1969) there was a 48-hour official occupation of the same offices by about 60 students, protesting at the number of students required to resit examinations that year. Again no damage was done. That October the Union's *Wessex News* commented, 'If we are to win our case for automatic re-sits . . . it is Reason which will prove to be a better ally to our cause than passion.'

On 26–7 February 1970 there was a second official sit-in, this time at the new Administration Building, by about 200 students in support of Warwick University students. £650 worth of damage was done, mainly in searching for students' personal files to discover comments on their political beliefs or activities. This event was taken more seriously and the University set up a fact-finding committee, chaired by Professor Baldry (Classics). The Students' Union was invited to send two members, but by the time the committee met

Steel Forms *by Justin Knowles, 1973, situated on the Highfield campus by Sir Basil Spence's staff refectory* (above) *and the Nuffield Theatre* (below).

The Royal visit to the University in 1966.

The Chancellor and the Mace on the stairs of Southampton Civic Centre, 10 July 1970.

on 10 March 1970 it had not decided whether to do so. Six days later it voted (175 to 160) to send only two observers.

Eventually the committee published a 23-page report describing in detail the events of the sit-in including the critical vote of 10.30 p.m. of 26 February in favour of searching for files, passed by 101 to 97 after three counts. No student's records were found, but various documents including personal records of staff were taken away or photocopied. Mostly they consisted of contracts made with outside organisations, these intended (as at Warwick) to prove that the University was under the influence of big business. All had in fact been reported to Senate and Council during meetings at which student representatives were present.

Most important of the committee's conclusions was that the Students' Union, in theory a democratic body, had in practice ceased to be so. Its procedures, designed for a university of about 1,000 students, no longer suited one of 4,300. The debating chamber in the Union building would only seat 375, yet the Union was still taking important decisions at mass meetings. Only 5.2 per cent of students had voted on 26 February for the sit-in. Furthermore the Union was in the habit of publicising its meetings inadequately, of holding meetings during the lunch hour which would continue long into the afternoon, so forcing students who remained to miss lectures, of accepting for discussion composite and thus confusing motions, and of taking votes by a show of hands. Such conditions made it easy for a small but determined minority to manipulate a placid majority.

A further and much longer sit-in occurred in March 1971. This concerned the appointment of Dr W. A. Coupe to succeed Wilf Lucas as Professor of German. At Birmingham University Coupe had recently been appointed Professor of German but, as a result of student protests that he was not a 'modernist' and might not continue the department's 'liberal staff–student relations', had withdrawn before his appointment was ratified. At Southampton members of the German Department had similar worries, and four staff and 99 students signed a memorandum to Senate, pointing out that 'in his published work at least, Dr Coupe does not appear to see the critical evaluation of works of literature as his primary task . . . It was Professor Lucas who established the prevailing critical tradition and it would be tragic if his retirement should be the prelude to its disruption or even reversal.'

Senate nevertheless ratified Coupe's appointment, and in protest on 15 February 1971 students of the German Department occupied Arts 1 for 24 hours. A week later a delegation from the Department met the Vice-Chancellor and was promised a mass meeting with Dr Coupe. The meeting took place on 28 February, but Coupe failed to reassure his audience and next day students, having first tried the Administrative Building but found it locked, occupied the Nuffield Theatre. It was only ten days later that Mather announced that he would 'visit' the Nuffield and address the occupiers, but this event never took place as the Union voted to end the sit-in soon afterwards.

Dr Coupe's appointment was confirmed by Council and the University authorities were able to claim that they had successfully defended the procedures which governed (and should govern) the making of appointments. In 1972 Senate and Council amplified these procedures, ruling that students would not serve on appointment committees, that the University, not a Department, was responsible for changes in the direction of a Department's activities and that departmental representatives on appointment committees should not form a majority.

Though many students supported the protests of these times, a fair number continued to do what interested them more – play games or practise athletics. These were encouraged by the sports hall in the new Union building, with its six squash courts, judo, billiards and table tennis rooms. Men's table tennis certainly benefited. For four years in succession the team were UAU champions (1968–71). In three of these the men's cricket eleven were also champions. During the same period the rowing tank and ramp into the river were installed at the Boat Yard, developments which were to lead to impressive results in future.

Mather retired at the end of the 1970–1 session. His unpopularity with students has tainted his reputation, overshadowing the good he did the University. Alongside his support for the establishment of the School of Medicine, he contributed to the research and teaching of genetics, his special subject, and was warmly thanked for this by the Dean of Science. More generally, he worked with persistence to raise the University's reputation. This was evident to all who attended Appointment Committee meetings which he chaired. Always he wanted to appoint someone who was a high flier. Those whom the committee appointed are evidence of his success.

They brought him a problem. Many were young and full of expectations for themselves and their disciplines. The form their expectations often took was competition for increases in their intake of students. It was on student numbers that additional staff, buildings and equipment depended. With this he coped tactfully but firmly, being 'fundamentally opposed to the establishment of mini-empires' (John Smith, Deputy Vice-Chancellor). He was, Smith considered, 'absolutely straight (in the old fashioned sense). Whenever he said he would do something he did it, come what may,' a characteristic which 'gave him an exceptional authority with Senate.'

3. Hard Times, 1971–9

Jim Gower – Completely Unstuffy

Some Vice-Chancellors are background figures – in retrospect it seems that the University over which they presided would have developed in much the same way with another Vice-Chancellor. Lawrence Cecil Bartlett (Jim) Gower was of a different sort. In half a dozen ways he played a central part in making the University a different place by the time he left it.

As an articled clerk in the 1930s, Gower had already begun to take part-time law classes at University College London. His interest in legal education led to him being appointed Cassel Professor of Commercial Law at the London School of Economics in 1950, spending three years in Nigeria advising its government on legal education and serving both on the Denning Committee on Legal Education for Students from Africa, and on the Government's Committee on Legal Education. He was also a Fellow of the British Academy.

'Do you think a lawyer has any special qualifications as a Vice-Chancellor?' the editor of *Viewpoint* (the periodical of the Staff Consultative Group) asked him.

'One is alive to things like not disciplining students without giving them an opportunity of defending themselves,' he answered.

'Some would say that a Vice-Chancellor should maintain a certain aloofness,' the editor suggested.

'To those who appointed me I made it quite clear,' Gower said, 'that if they wanted someone who would be aloof they certainly should not appoint me.'

Before he had been at the University for 24 hours he had demonstrated his dislike of aloofness by touring the campus, asking everyone he met who they were and what they did, from professors and students to laboratory assistants and gardeners.

Though Gower had not been involved in founding the Medical School, which opened a month after the start of his first term, it was still a young Faculty in need of support. It had been clear from the start that 'by no means all staff welcomed the creation of a powerful competitor for scarce resources' (S. M. Cretney). As late as 1981, when the ten years during which government funds had been earmarked for the Medical School were about to end, Professor Howell remembered colleagues telling him how pleased they would be to have the chance to collect some of its money for their own Faculties. In Cretney's opinion Gower was able to persuade 'doubters that Medicine was an addition to the University's strengths rather than a cuckoo in the nest.' He demonstrated his personal support for the school by becoming one of the University's two representatives on the Wessex Regional Hospital Board, and the University's support by arranging for Kingsley Williams, Chairman of the Board, and John Revans, its Senior Administrative Medical Officer, to become members of Council.

Lawrence Cecil Bartlett (Jim) Gower, Vice-Chancellor 1971–9.

Facing page: *the Gower building, the University's 'entrance' building at Highfield. Built in the 1990s under the Vice-Chancellorship of Howard Newby, its name fittingly reflects the pride in the University that Gower wanted to instil in the residents of Southampton.*

Gower was also keen to establish a better relationship with the people of Southampton in general and with its political establishment in particular. 'All newcomers to the university,' he wrote, 'seem to be struck by the lack of pride which the inhabitants of Southampton take in their university. The attitude of many seems to be one of apathy or positive hostility.' He understood why this was so: resentment by 'the deprived majority' of what it saw as the privileged life of 'the lucky few'. But the arguments used to support this envy were mostly unjustified by the facts and ignored the material benefits which the University brought to the city. 'My postbag contains a steady stream of letters from irate ratepayers, drawing attention to the amount which the local authorities spend on education and implying that most of this goes to the University.' In fact the University spent about £13 million in and about Southampton (including the wages of 3,000 citizens) to which the local authorities contributed only £26,000, the city's share of this a mere £3,100. 'These statistics . . . shock those who hear them (as well they may).' 'In the eyes of some members of the City Council students are not regarded as citizens of Southampton either in relation to pedestrian crossings or residential accommodation.'

Gower's general influence on the University's morale was of even greater importance. Towards the end of his first year the editor of *Viewpoint* wrote, 'the new Vice-Chancellor has more than lived up to his desire to be accessible to all sections of the University. Perhaps this more than any other single factor explains the more harmonious atmosphere which has prevailed of late.'

Halls and Lodgings – a Desperate Shortage

Overhanging the whole of Gower's time were the country's financial troubles, these amplified by the 1973 oil crisis and taking the form of high inflation, high interest rates and a steady reduction in government funding of higher education. On the one hand Southampton was expected to increase the number of its students by a further 2,000 before 1980, on the other there was a virtual freeze on government money for new buildings.

Most seriously affected was student accommodation. Gower recognised the importance of this. 'I don't see how you can expect students not to be agitators if you give them cast-iron things to agitate against like inadequate living conditions.' But nor was he in favour of trying to increase the number who lived at home. 'I hope we shall not get to a situation where a large proportion of our students just come in for the day and go back to Bournemouth, Poole or Portsmouth at five o'clock. Students learn much more from their fellow students and the sort of things that go on in the evenings than they do from attending lectures and classes.'

For most students a place in a hall of residence or some university property was their first choice, but the steady rise in student numbers meant that there were too few of these. In 1976 the University calculated that it needed to create 1,350 new residential places. It continued to attempt this by enlarging existing halls and by building or renting a variety of fresh accommodation. One property which it had bought in 1964 was Chilworth Manor, lying some two miles north-west of Highfield. This it had made into a hall of residence for about 60 first-year students. Besides the Manor House, Chilworth had a modern, single-storey factory building and, more importantly, 100 acres of land. Now, in 1972, the University applied for outline planning permission to build accommodation for 1,420 students on this land. Its application was rejected by Test Valley District Council, and by the time this decision was reversed four years later the University had partly solved its problem by building earlier than planned on the Montefiore site. In 1978 the Chilworth hall was closed as uneconomic and for another six years the only parts of Chilworth of benefit to the University were a wing of the manor in which a dozen postgraduates lived, the factory building into which the Engineering Faculty expanded and the walled garden with greenhouses which the University's garden staff and the Botany Department found useful.

In 1971 the financing of new student accommodation was helped by a gift of £136,000 from the Brunei Government, nominally to commemorate the first royal visit to Brunei, but also because the first Brunei graduate, Pehin Isa Bin Ibrahim, the first Brunei Government Scholar, had been a student in Southampton's Faculty of Law. Other funding for accommodation had to be borrowed and here Gower proved an able negotiator. During the renegotiation of one loan, when the bank manager who had provided it told him that the terms the University was offering meant that it would never repay what it owed, Gower observed that he could think of no arrangement which would suit the University so well.

There were two changes at the halls of residence during the 1970s. First one, then all began to take both men and women. The other change, first made in 1975, gave all freshers the opportunity to spend their first year in a hall. This allowed them to get to know Southampton and become more successful when they needed to find their own accommodation. A year later the new policy was proving a success when, for the first time for many years, the session started with no homeless students. But it also meant that halls had to recreate their traditions at the start of each academic year.

Students who could not be accommodated in the University's halls or properties had to look for their own places to live. Once most of these had been provided by landladies who served meals, but in the 1970s more and more students wanted to find flats or houses with kitchens, and such accommodation was particularly scarce. Even when lodgings with landladies were available, homeless students would reject them. Some helped themselves by negotiating the right to occupy condemned Council properties, but the 100 accommodated in these by the autumn of 1973 could not solve the problem. Nor did a subsequent squat in Overdell Court make a significant difference. In 1972 the president of the Union wrote that the shortage was the fault of 'successive governments not putting their money where their White Papers were.' But he also blamed universities for taking more students than they had accommodation for. The ability of the University to help was, however, limited, since it was not permitted to spend money given it for teaching or research on accommodation.

In spite of difficulties the University did manage to increase student accommodation during Gower's time by 32 per cent, the same percentage by which student numbers rose. The last large expansion, mentioned above, was of Montefiore House where 420 new rooms were added. Over half its students were now in their first year and as a consequence it was given some of the features of the older halls, including a common room, with bar, games rooms and television room. Though it remained a self-catering hall, instead of 20 students sharing a kitchen as in the earlier blocks, the new block consisted of so-called flats shared by seven.

In January 1979 a different accommodation block opened: Clarkson House. This small two-storey building, sited just south of the Administration Building, was designed to take 25 students, including some with disabilities. It had been funded jointly by the British Council for the Disabled and the Clarkson Foundation, with the Department of Health and Social Security paying (indirectly) for losses made in its running and the University Grants Committee contributing to the installing of ramps to enable disabled students to use other buildings. Two years later the University received a Commendation under the Building for the Disabled 1981 Scheme.

Chilworth Manor, bought by the University in 1964.

Our Own Miseries

Government funding reductions affected not only student accommodation but the whole range of the University's activities. Even when appeals had modified the cuts proposed by the UGC for 1973, the University calculated that in the following year the Medical Faculty would be in deficit by £400,000 and the rest of the University by £500,000. The Government suggested that it could recover these amounts by increasing the proportion of Arts to Science students, by reducing its postgraduates and by economies resulting from 'increasing the scale' of certain activities.

One Southampton response was to devolve responsibility for spending to Faculties, in the hope that this would produce 'flexibility' if not economies. The change was proposed by a committee set up by Gower to consider the implications of the ending of quinquennial funding, consisting of himself and the two Deputy Vice-Chancellors with four attendant members of the Administration. The setting up of this committee was almost as important as its first proposal. As the Budgets and Development Sub-Committee, for some 20 years it made the most important proposals (commonly in effect decisions) on all University matters.

Budgetary devolution was welcomed by the Faculties though it hardly filled them with optimism. Professor Manser, Dean of Arts, noted that 94 per cent of the money which came to the Arts Faculty was already committed to academic salaries. 'Consequently the margin for flexibility depends chiefly on resignations and retirements and these are unlikely to be many.' Professor Gambling, Dean of Engineering and Applied Science, noted that 'we have now, to some extent at least, the privilege of choosing our own miseries instead of having more arbitrary ones forced upon us.'

In December 1973 Gower wrote: 'We were resigned to a period of gradually reducing unit costs and of worsening staff/student ratios. Now, in addition, we face severe cutbacks on maintenance of buildings and equipment and on essential furniture for existing buildings and new buildings.' Like the rest of the country, the University was also affected by rising fuel, electricity and telephone costs and an increased bill for wages and National Insurance contributions. That autumn a moratorium had been imposed on tendering for new buildings. The total effect was to 'change the prospect of small but steady growth over the rest of the quinquennium into one of halting development and inadequate resources. Sensible long-term planning is not possible in these conditions and the effect on morale need not be laboured.'

It was hardly surprising that the University continued to turn increasingly to research which would bring direct grants from research councils, foundations and government departments, and to industry which would pay for what the University provided. It was right, Gower wrote in 1973, 'to show that we are not concerned here solely with research conducted with the aim of the advancement of knowledge for itself. Much of our research effort is in fields directly concerned with industry, business and public services.' The idea was not new. In 1969–70, for example, different departments had carried out work

The Fawley Foundation lecture delivered by Professor Ralf Dahrendorf (middle), 8 November 1973. On the left is Dr A. W. Pearce, Chairman of Esso Petroleum Co., and on the right is Mr R. L. Pincott, Managing Director of Esso.

for British Aircraft Corporation, British Leyland, Esso, Ford, General Motors, Hawker Siddeley, ICI, Lucas, Monsanto, Rolls-Royce and Shell as well as many less well-known companies. Official or semi-official benefactors or customers had been many times more numerous and varied from the British Egg Marketing Board to the Ministry of Defence. Foundations and trusts which had given support included Courtaulds Educational Trust, the Leverhulme Trust, the Nuffield Foundation, the Radcliffe Trust and the Wellcome Trust.

The Wolfson Trust was a special case. Since the mid-1960s it had been supporting the establishment of units to carry out industry-related or industry-commissioned research which would eventually make them self-supporting. In 1967–8, for example, it had enabled the Industrial Noise Unit to expand its activities with a grant of £30,000. The following year it had provided funds to enable an Electronics Unit to be set up. In 1975–6 it funded a new building which would provide accommodation for such units.

Drama and Music

The Nuffield Theatre did not escape the problems of the time. By 1974, ten years after it had opened with so much optimism, it was in trouble. During those years it had provided a venue not only for University drama and music but also for performances by visiting companies, both professional and amateur. In a typical year (1966–7) 113 dramatic performances were staged by professional companies, 44 by University societies and 28 by amateur groups. There were 13 concerts and 18 film programmes.

The Nuffield had been recognised for the contribution it was making to drama in the south of the country by grants from Southampton City Council, the Arts Council and most generously from Southern Arts (£2,750 a year from 1971–2), while the Leverhulme Trust had supported a Fellow of Drama. The first of these, Roger Warren, concluded his three-year term by producing *Idomeneo* and *Cymbeline* (in which visitors, staff and students all performed).

The first sign of trouble came in 1974 when the City of Southampton and Southern Arts both failed to raise their grants in line with inflation. The following year, by which time the running costs of the Nuffield had doubled, it made its first loss. In May 1975 an open meeting was held to consider the situation. For some years members of staff had been considering this. In 1971 Professor Manser had argued that unless the Nuffield had an academic purpose it should become a lecture room, used occasionally for student drama. In reply Professor Baldry, chairman of the Nuffield Theatre Committee, argued that from the start the Nuffield had never been meant to serve only the University, but also the town (which had no theatre of its own). And Adrian Vinson observed that 'some of us may still be sufficiently old-fashioned to believe that academics in the narrow sense form only a part of the educational role of a university.'

The Nuffield struggled on. The year 1975–6 it described as 'testing', the next year as its 'most testing' and the year after as the one in which it reached 'the edge of disaster'. It survived financially only by drawing on its depreciation fund and persuading the University to make it an increased grant. Meanwhile it set about saving itself by starting a Theatre Club and establishing a resident professional company.

Sue Wilson, previously with Manchester University's resident company, was appointed its director. Within four months most of these problems were solved, and in its second year the new company played for 24 weeks. It had early encouragement when its production of *Fat Harold* transferred to the Shaw Theatre in London. It also began to gain a local following. *Paddington Bear*, its 1977 Christmas show, played to full houses. Meanwhile the Theatre Club had devised a fresh form of support (reported somewhat apologetically in those innocent days) when it arranged that Ladbroke's would run a lottery for the Nuffield's benefit. In March 1979 its future seemed more firmly secured when the funding bodies (still the University, the City, the Arts Council and Southern Arts) recommended the formation of a fully independent Nuffield Theatre Trust.

Though the Nuffield Theatre had been for Music a huge improvement on what had existed before, it had disadvantages, one of which might have been tolerated ('its acoustics, so good for speech, were too dry for music') but one which could not be: the demands on its space being made by drama. Within a few years Evans began to write memos 'on what was becoming increasingly obvious – the impossibility of squeezing the quart of drama-plus-music into the theatre's pint pot. What was needed was a second auditorium, expressly designed for the performance of music.'

Fortunately in 1967 Miss Margaret Grassam Sims left the University a bequest of about £30,000, to be used specifically for a hall, theatre or building of like purpose. After much discussion it was agreed that a small hall should be built (to be named the Turner Sims Concert Hall), but with a 'crippling condition: that, in order to house University examinations, it should have a flat floor.' The advisory committee, however, refused to proceed on this brief, and 'after innumerable revisions of the project (each managing to increase the rake slightly)' plans were agreed for building, at an amazingly low budget, 'what we now know to be a most effective and attractive auditorium for music' (Evans).

Another hurdle had first to be overcome. Though the hall would be relatively inexpensive, the controllers of the University finances held that the additional monies required were beyond its means. At first Jim Gower, newly appointed Vice-Chancellor, agreed, but soon 'this enthusiastic and knowledgeable music-lover' changed his mind and negotiated a loan from the City Council. 'As has often been said,' Evans wrote, 'the Turner Sims Hall is above all a memorial to Jim Gower.' It can also be seen as a memorial to Peter Evans, for it was the Music Department which he had created which changed Gower's mind. The acoustics for the new hall, much valued by the BBC for recording, were designed by staff from the Institution of Sound and Vibration research (see pages 153–6).

University Road – a Closure Too Far

A project which failed to survive the financial problems of the decade was the closure of University Road. When Gower arrived one of his great ambitions had been to leave the campus looking nicer. Though some of the architecture was superb, its general appearance was a mess. 'We have this wretched road running right through the middle with a rash of ribbon development along it.'

In 1971–2 the University set aside £80,000 towards the first stage of University Road's closure. And though in 1973–4 the City Council abandoned the Hartley Avenue–Broadlands Road link (essential for the project), it still in principle favoured the closure. Three years later Gower hoped that it would come about in 1978–9, using as an argument the arrival of students with disabilities, and in that year discussions with the City continued, but thereafter the project was allowed to fade away as City and University both realised that they could not afford it.

Farewell to Navigation

The decision by the University to give up responsibility for the School of Navigation was unconnected with the financial crisis of the mid-1970s since it had already become effective in April 1972. By then it was 40 years since the University had acquired the School and moved it to South Hill. Its time at Southampton had ended in September 1946 when it moved to Warsash on the Hamble River. There, with better facilities for boat work and sailing, it continued to run residential courses for cadets who, as part of their course, made voyages in the sailing vessel *Moyana*. By 1949 over 800 cadets from the British Isles and 162 from other parts of the world had taken this course. Each year applicants for the course exceeded by hundreds the 120 it could take.

The School also continued to run courses for serving officers in the merchant navy studying for Certificates of Competency, these usually numbering some 300. By now it was acquiring an international reputation (in the future it was to train officers from Belgium, Burma, the Sudan, Bahrain and Ghana). In 1949 it was recognised by the Ministry of Education as a Direct Grant School and given its own governing body in the form of a committee of Council.

The same year it acquired a new sea-going training ship, the *South Hill*. The whole of *South Hill's* reconstruction, including the fitting of radar, was carried out by staff and cadets. In 1950, as well as running courses for 112 cadets and 400 serving officers, it was providing correspondence teaching for a further 145 students. Soon those taking the senior courses included many who had once been cadets at the School.

1956 was a year of success and disaster. The *Moyana* won the International Sail Training-ship trophy in the race from Torbay to Lisbon, despite being the oldest ship competing, but while returning to England met exceptionally bad weather in the Bay of Biscay and sank. No one drowned and the Mayor of Southampton launched an appeal for a replacement.

In 1962 a new, 27-week intermediate course was launched to provide merchant-navy apprentices sent by their companies with 'intellectual stimulus' when about halfway through their apprenticeships. This, like the cadet course, would count as six months of the four years sea service required before a candidate could be examined for a Second Mate's Certificate.

By the end of the 1960s the pattern of nautical education was changing and with it the composition of the School. In the Senior Department there were now often as many as 1,250 serving officers, half of them taking Tanker Safety courses. In the cadet departments a scheme of sandwich courses lasting three years was being introduced, designed to provide a thorough training scheme from cadet to second mate, which would replace the traditional one-year course. At the government's Department of Education there was also growing concern about its direct funding of what it regarded as a 'monotechnic' institution.

When the University relinquished responsibility for the School in 1972 it passed to the Southampton Local Education Authority, this being a first step towards combining it with Southampton College of Technology's School of Marine Engineering. No account of the School of Navigation should omit the contribution made to its success by Captain G. W. Wakeford, its director for 25 years – a disciplinarian and a traditionalist under whose regime cadets were taught ballroom dancing.

Twenty-five Years On

In 1977 the University celebrated its silver jubilee. Twenty-five years earlier in 1952 Vice-Chancellor James had observed that the current quinquennium was unlikely 'to be notable for any major expansions'. In 1966 Sir John Wolfenden, chairman of the University Grants Committee, had warned that there would be very little expansion at universities during the next quinquennium. Such warnings make the University of Southampton's growth during its first 25 years the more remarkable. In 1952 it had been a college-size establishment of 1,000 students with an income of £274,000. In 1977 it was a university of 5,700 students with an income of £17m.

The explanation for such expansion must lie partly in the energy of a young institution and the continual willingness of its staff to urge it forward but, at the same time, to question where it was going; and partly its practice of planning ahead, both for the space it would need and for the academic activities it should foster.

The Staff Consultative Group and its periodical, *Viewpoint*, were other products of the University's forward-looking, but at the same time self-examining culture. They were established in 1971, soon after the ten-day Nuffield sit-in, to remedy what *Viewpoint's* first editor, Robert Grime (Law), described as 'a good many misconceptions and some sheer factual ignorance about the structures and procedures of the university' – for example, how appointment committees worked. But *Viewpoint* had the wider aim of allowing

A presentation in 1974 to Lord Murray of Newhaven, Chancellor of the University 1964–74.

Left to right: Sir Hugh Tett, Pro-Chancellor 1967–79; Professor Gower; Lord Murray; Sir Alan Lubbock, Pro-Chancellor 1967–75, Chairman of the University Council 1957–69; Professor Mather, Vice-Chancellor 1965–71.

Vice-Chancellor Gower conferring an honorary LL.D. on Professor F. Ford, 27 April 1974.

staff to express opinions about any university matter they liked *before* decisions were taken by Senate or Council. These bodies would thus know about such opinions and staff would no longer feel that they were ill-informed and remote. Few universities funded a periodical the purpose of which was to allow staff to question its policies.

Looking back 25 years, Gower noted that James had had an advantage which the University of 1977 did not have. At that time the quinquennial system had still been in operation, giving the University a financial basis on which to plan for the following five years. The demise of this arrangement and substitution of annual grants for only the year ahead was, in Gower's opinion, almost as serious an impediment to the sensible running of the University as the steady decline in the actual size of these grants. 'Few items in a university budget can be turned on and off on an annual basis,' he wrote. 'The lead-time for new courses is very much longer than that, and research programmes take many years to complete.'

Southampton celebrated its jubilee with a Festival Week, an Anniversary Ball and numerous awards. Among those given honorary degrees were Eric Zepler, founder of the Electronics Department, and George Thomas, pre-war pupil of Professor Cock, now Speaker of the House of Commons. 1977 was also the Queen's Jubilee year and Silver Jubilee medals were awarded to B. M. Bland, the University Librarian from 1961, Bill Conway, boatman then chief technician of the Oceanography Department, and Sir Kenneth Mather, knighted for his services to higher education. In the jubilee year the Chemistry Department had particular reason to celebrate. The previous year one of the first six Senior Research Fellowships (the most prestigious awards of the Science Research Council) had been given to Professor Carrington for his research into photo-ionisation molecular spectroscopy. Now Professor Martin Fleischmann was awarded a similar SRC Senior Fellowship for his research into electrochemistry.

The most curious of Gower's comments on the University's jubilee (which he began by noting how wrong James had been to forecast little expansion) was a near repetition of James's forecast. 'The coming year,' Gower wrote, 'must be regarded primarily as a period of consolidation and constructive thinking.' Certainly there was to be more than one difficult year ahead, but during its second 25 years seen as a whole Southampton was to undergo at least as remarkable an expansion as in its first.

Direct Action

Gower had been warned before he came to Southampton that he 'would find scarred battlefields occupied by destructive hordes of students with no interest in their studies, and beleaguered bands of intimidated teachers and administrators intent only on survival.' He had in fact found 'students who were still the friendly, knowledgeable, eager and maddening creatures that they always were, differing only in that they were considerably less immature and better informed than my generation was.' Nevertheless, after two years he was faced

with direct action when students occupied the Administration Building for 48 hours on 14–15 November 1973. They were supporting the National Union of Students' campaign for grants which kept pace with inflation, a cause with which most staff were in sympathy but which the University had no power to rectify.

At the end of the year Gower described it as a 'very mild affair' compared with events at other universities, only undertaken after the national campaign had failed to make much impression on the Government. 'At least the demonstrators cleaned up afterwards and paid for the minimal damage done.' A week later students barricaded the room at Boldrewood in which 'our distinguished visitors' (the University Grants Committee) were meeting Senate. The police were called but Gower, in order to speak to them, was forced by student pickets blocking the doorway, to climb out of a window. He was less amused, describing it as 'a demonstration which can have done little if anything to further a cause for which sympathy, within and without the University, had already been secured.'

When the Government relented and raised grants by 25 per cent for 1974–5 this was welcomed both by the University and the Union though both pointed out that it left students poorer than they had previously been. The 22 per cent rise for 1975–6 was no better. Since students had to pay for accommodation, the cost of which rose at a higher rate than inflation, the University calculated that to maintain support for students at the previous level grants should have been increased by 33 per cent.

In early 1975 the main student grievance shifted from inadequate grants to refectory prices. These had been increased for the 1974–5 session by 26 per cent, provoking a campaign of boycotts (along with a less well supported rent strike). Now the Union called a mass meeting to ratify a resolution in favour of a campaign of 'occupations' in support of a reduction of 15 per cent in refectory prices. Before the mass meeting the Union president held various

Above left: *the Women's Hockey Club in the 1970s.*

Above: *the University Archery Club, 1977.*

meetings with University committees, then finally with the Vice-Chancellor. This resulted in an offer from the Vice-Chancellor to reduce prices from their new level by an average of 7.2 per cent, which was overwhelmingly accepted by the mass meeting.

That August Gower took the president of the Union with him to meet the Minister for Higher Education, Lord Crowther-Hunt. 'The Minister had with him half-a-dozen of his senior civil servants and the Secretary of the University Grants Committee,' Gower reported 'and they listened to us for over an hour . . . The operation was, we think, worthwhile as a means of making an impact on the powers-that-be . . . But we felt that it will not, alas, result in any immediate increase in student grants.'

On 28 October 1975 the Union held another mass meeting. Government cuts in spending on education were now the target, and the purpose of the meeting was to decide how to protest against them. 'A mass meeting *par excellence* it was too,' Cassandra wrote in *Viewpoint*. 'Posters were plastered around like wallpaper. Cuts Bulletins, handouts and tannoy announcements had made it impossible not to be aware of the importance of the issue, and well over a thousand students were shoe-horned into the Debating Chamber and its overspill, the Sports Hall.' The meeting eventually passed overwhelmingly a motion calling for a national campaign against the cuts, but rejected a sit-in by 909 votes to 351.

The motion also included a demand for a forum where all members of the University could discuss the cuts. At the resulting open forums held on 6 and 13 November there was much discussion of the latest Union (and NUS) proposal for solving the University's financial problems: deficit financing, i.e. that the University should bankrupt itself, so forcing the Government to rescue it. Against this Gower argued that 'it would lead the Government, if not to close the University, at least to take greater control of it, by . . . placing it under the direction of the Hampshire County Council.' Nor would he 'relish going to the Government seeking help with a large debt deliberately and irresponsibly acquired.'

In the years 1973 to 1978, Union resolutions in support of left-wing causes were noticeably fewer. In 1978 it even withdrew its support for the pro-Irish nationalist 'Troops out Movement'. Direct action also declined and the final sit-in of Gower's time had a certain ritualistic flavour. First came a number of meetings between the Vice-Chancellor and the Union President to discuss the new issue: the Government's plan to increase tuition fees, thereby causing great hardship to privately funded, overseas, mature and postgraduate students. There followed the President's letter to the Vice-Chancellor (starting 'Dear Friend'), announcing a Union meeting to discuss an occupation, and the Vice-Chancellor's answer earnestly suggesting that it would do more harm than good to a cause which virtually the whole university considered just.

Nevertheless the 48-hour occupation of the Administration Building duly took place (1–3 March 1977). Most bizarre, according to the *Echo*, was that the uninvited guests, arriving with sleeping bags, found the Administration Building unlocked with tea and biscuits waiting for them. When they left the

Vice-Chancellor agreed to inspect the building for damage and found none.

Gower was therefore right when he said in 1978 that, since the 1973 sit-in, exchanges between the University authorities and students had 'generally been sensible and constructive, due in large part to the fact that we have had a succession of Union Presidents who have had at heart the interests of the University as a whole and who have not sought to make their reputations by strife and confrontation.' He might justifiably have added that he personally had played an important part in this change.

Jim Gower photographed in 1979.

So it was somewhat late in the day when, in 1979, the Union devised a way to make political donations which, as an educational charity, it was forbidden to make. It formed a Union Club to which it let a room in the Union Building for £1 a year. There the club installed pinball tables, football machines and a jukebox which raised large sums of money. Since it was an independent body the club was entitled to spend these as it chose. In November 1979 it invited members to propose to a club meeting how it should spend £900, a decent sum at the time. The club survives, but now uses its funds mainly for loans to needy students.

As always, sports and athletics preoccupied some students. Though fewer individuals or teams were successful in Gower's time, there were exceptions. For three years in succession the ladies' badminton team were UAU champions (1975–7). The ladies' lawn tennis team were champions for two years. The ladies' and men's ten-pin bowling teams were each champions for one year. In 1974 Mike Beresford (Commonwealth gold medallist) began to coach at the University Boat Club and continued to do so for the rest of the century.

Gower retired at the end of the 1979 summer term. He was not quite everybody's favourite Vice-Chancellor but many admired and trusted him, considering him to have been 'the first democratic Vice-Chancellor'.

The report on his last year (1978–9), written by his successor, John Roberts, was if possible more pessimistic and more critical of the treatment by government of higher education than any of Gower's had been. 'The unresponsiveness of officials in the Department of Education and Science,' Roberts wrote, 'has begun to make some of us wonder whether the usual methods of presenting our case and the rational arguments which uphold it are still sufficient.' The warning of what might lie ahead was clear.

4. Who Pays the Piper, 1979–85

John Roberts, World Historian

John Roberts, the new Vice-Chancellor, aged 50, came from Merton College, Oxford, to which he was to return six years later as Warden. He was a historian, currently preparing a history of the world for television entitled *The Triumph of the West*. His report on his own first year in office set Southampton's problems in the context of a general history of the country's universities. In doing so he provided ample clues to the part he was to play in the crisis of a year later – a crisis described by long-serving members of staff as the most dramatic of their time.

British universities, in Roberts's opinion, were partly what they were as a result of inertia, which in its extreme manifestation took the form of 'parrot-like repetition of the cry "no cuts" (not even it seems, cuts of the manifestly wasteful, inadequate and inefficient).' Cuts imposed from outside were undesirable, it was claimed, because they deprived a university of its autonomy. But the truth was that universities had never been independent of society.

It was 'surely not deplorable that the public authorities should seek to satisfy themselves that the public interest is properly secured in the expenditure of over £1,000 millions per year (which is roughly the cost of the recurrent funding of our universities).' The problems which universities today faced were that the public authorities, in the form of the Government and the University Grants Committee, were requiring change at a far more rapid rate than ever before, were using the single weapon of finance to impose it, and, most important, were being 'imprecise' about the sort of change they wanted.

The solution wasn't 'more money all round'. It was 'not credible that everything which now goes on in universities should continue.' What was wanted was guidance about the 'sort of university provision the country wanted'. In the absence of guidance it had been only sensible of Southampton to set up a working party to make proposals about the University's academic goals.

This working party, chaired by Roberts, reported in July 1980. It recommended that Theology should be closed, that Italian should be reviewed in three or four years' time and that Russian should be reduced as rapidly as possible. Members of the Arts Faculty already felt threatened. Some had formed an unofficial Arts Faculty Cuts Action Group, which had issued its own report, drawing attention to what it regarded as insufficient funding and opposing further cuts of any kind. A large proportion of the Faculty's academic staff had put their signatures to this report.

Roberts did not apologise for what he had done. Issuing the working party's Academic Goals report had removed 'a psychological restraint on debate which appeared to me as a newcomer to be inhibiting frank discussion of our problems . . . The working party thus, far from bypassing our democracy . . . has actually offered it new scope.' So events were to prove.

1981

The crisis of 1981 should not have been unexpected. The University had by then experienced a decade of government parsimony and the Vice-Chancellor had shown that he foresaw more of the same when he set up the Academic Goals working party. Furthermore, the University Grants Committee had written to all universities on 30 December 1980 warning them that severe cuts were likely. Nevertheless the UGC's letter of 1 July 1981 to Southampton was a shock. 'The lifting of the fog in which we have been moving for some years revealed a very bleak landscape,' Roberts wrote. The UGC would cut its grant by 3.2 per cent in 1981–2, 8.7 per cent in 1982–3, and by 6.2 per cent in 1983–4. Southampton calculated that the cumulative effect would be a cut of about 19 per cent. It had also to take into account the recent loss of overseas students' fees and the UGC's request for it to take more (more costly) students of science-based subjects. If nothing was done the University's deficit for the year 1983–4 would be £3.6 million. In order to eliminate such a deficit by reducing staff (whose salaries formed by far the largest part of the University's expenditure) over 200 jobs would have to go.

The Budgets and Development sub-committee considered what should be done. This six-man sub-committee was the most important in the University, responsible for all major policy proposals. It now consisted of the Vice-Chancellor, the two deputy Vice-Chancellors, two Professors representing Senate, and the Secretary and Registrar.

B & D 1 did not propose abandoning the arrangement made eight years earlier under which the different Faculties (and other so-called budgetary groups) were each given their own allocation of money to spend within broad guidelines as they chose. It took the view that it had too little information to suggest, for example, that particular Departments within Faculties should be reduced or closed. Instead it recommended the reduction of the allocations to the different Faculties. This led, as Roberts put it, 'to a report which discriminated very considerably between the Faculties'. Specifically, the funds of the Arts, Education and Social Sciences Faculties were to be reduced by almost three times as much as those of the Science, Engineering and Medicine Faculties. It suggested that Faculties, in order to balance their budgets, would need to dismiss staff.

B & D 1 had to be approved by Senate and Council, but well before this could happen it was made public, allowing time for other proposals (which the sub-committee had invited). The most important of these was prepared by six members of the Faculty of Social Sciences, among whom Professor Ken Hilton was probably the most influential. In the words of a colleague, 'Ken was outraged at what he saw as ineptitude, soon also seeing an admixture of cunning in the evident attempt to use the funding crisis to restructure the university' (Michael Bourn, Professor of Accountancy). Members of the sub-committee would deny this, claiming that they had no intention to destroy what was good in 'non-science' Faculties. Less easily denied is that this was the way many staff saw B & D 1.

Professor John Roberts, Vice-Chancellor 1979–85.

Facing page: *the staff social centre in the grounds of Highfield campus today.*

The Hilton proposal, created with his colleagues over a weekend and sub-titled 'A Viable Alternative Strategy', found fault with B & D 1 on five grounds. The most important of these were that it had been unnecessarily cautious in calculating the University's readily available reserves which amounted to £4 m., not £1.5m., and that it had failed to take account of the cost of imposing compulsory redundancies, which might be £4m. Nor had it considered the demoralisation of the staff, and reduction in public confidence and student recruitment which had occurred at other universities where compulsory redundancies had been proposed. Instead the Alternative Strategy document argued that 'the University has sufficient resources to undertake a balanced strategy which includes cutting non-wage expenditure, increasing revenue and allowing time for natural wastage and voluntary early retirement to take place.'

More fundamentally, it claimed that B & D 1 did not conform to the UGC's recommendations since it was seriously destructive of many activities which the UGC rated highly. These were also activities (often described as 'centres of excellence') of which the Academic Goals report had approved. By not backing them B & D 1 was failing to support the University's own convictions.

At the same time indignation grew and 'numerous General Staff Meetings were held which often filled Physics A to overflowing with people standing and sitting in the aisles.' And successive issues of *Viewpoint* were filled with mainly hostile comments on B & D 1.

Opposition to B & D 1 became more organised, and included the collection of signatures from over half the members of Senate saying they would under no circumstances support B & D 1. At the pre-Senate briefing a delegation led by David Rowan, a former Deputy Vice-Chancellor, presented itself uninvited to explain the strength of opposition to B & D 1's proposals.

About the events of 4 November Professor Butterfield (Civil Engineering) wrote, 'The whole University was so concerned at the measures being driven through that well over 100 staff, carrying placards and banners lined the road in front of the Administration building. Running a gauntlet to get to a Senate meeting must surely have been a unique event in the history of the University . . . The atmosphere in Senate was electric . . . The two sides of the debate were, as you might imagine, occupied by those justifying their smaller cuts and those deploring their excessive ones. The latter [Arts, Education and Social Sciences] were also at pains to point out that hardly any opportunities were available to them to improve their financial position via external funding from industry etc., in contrast to Science and Engineering.'

Early in the meeting a motion was passed by a show of hands which the Vice-Chancellor had known about and did not oppose. Its most important section recommended to Council that B & D 1's 'basis of differential allocation of resources across the University be reconsidered, utilising voluntary retirement and natural wastage as far as possible.' B & D 1 was therefore in effect rejected. Nevertheless, to clinch the matter, a further motion, 'Senate considers that the University should not base its strategy for the eighties on the B & D report', was proposed from the floor by Butterfield and seconded by Hilton. The 'fierce and emotional' debate which followed was what most of those

The presentation of a portrait of Lord Tonypandy to the University by Lord Hailsham in 1984.

present remember best, with the vote which followed as the meeting's dramatic climax. 'Tellers were appointed and voters actually exited the Senate Room to be counted, "Ayes to the left", "Noes to the right". The motion was carried 67–59; in my [Butterfield's] view, a turning point in the history of the University determined by only five votes.'

A second motion, carried by a show of hands, asked Council to reinforce the Budgets and Development sub-committee with an additional number of members. Council complied, adding Professors Acheson, Bourn, Cookson and Morris, and asking for new proposals.

The expanded sub-committee again went to work, eventually in January 1982 producing B & D 2. This differed most significantly from B & D 1 in the cuts it made of allocations to different Faculties, which now ranged from 14.7 per cent (Arts) to 10.3 per cent (Science), others at in-between levels. This, the sub-committee admitted, was a compromise, but added that it 'did not think it possible to devise a system that would ever meet with complete approval.' The allocations it recommended were 'a deliberate reduction in the range of differential cuts while seeking to take into account the UGC's advice.' More important in making B & D 2 acceptable was its recommendation that staff were not to be dismissed save in exceptional cases, but asked to retire voluntarily. In practice 51 did so and many of these remained employed part-time for up to three years.

The new proposals received almost 100 per cent approval. Nevertheless Faculty after Faculty found 1981–2 a depressing year. The events of 1981 – some might say the scars of battle – lasted a long time. Seventeen years later Roberts defended himself in the *Oxford Review of Education*. Again he offered a historical background against which to see Southampton's experience. The country's universities up to 1981 had been living in a 'pre-Revolutionary' era, a term by which he meant 'the immediate prelude to the [French] upheaval of 1789'. Their basic beliefs had been that public money was the only possible way to support British universities, and that all universities were equal in the sense that all should be allowed to continue to study and teach a full range of subjects.

Southampton, he claimed, had been early to recognise this and by setting up its Academic Goals working party had succeeded in 'getting ahead in the game'. The purpose of the game was to impress the University Grants Committee, not so much by what you did (in fact the Academic Goals report recommended some expansion, for example an additional chair of French, as well as the demolition of Theology, Italian and Russian), but by demonstrating the sort of things you were willing to do.

This view of events sees B & D 1 as forward-looking, its opponents as supporters of the *ancien régime*, and B & D 2 as an unfortunate compromise. Certainly the less severe treatment the University received in 1981 suggests that the University Grants Committee approved of Southampton. Favours to come were also a consequence, Roberts implied, including the selection of Oceanography for major expansion, though it would be closer to the truth to say that this Department earned its selection by the quality of its research.

It would make a tidy sequence of events if Budgets and Development sub-committee, as a result of the defeat Senate had inflicted on it, had set about reducing Senate's power. In his 1998 article Roberts wrote of the importance of Council (the sovereign body) having lay members who could 'save the University from its wilder academic staff' – a possible reference to Senate. But in fact a working party under Professor Fordham (set up by Senate) had made proposals for Senate's reform as early as 1977. The aim of these (finally implemented in 1982–3) was to reduce the influence of the University's Professors. To bring this about newly appointed Professors would no longer be automatic members of Senate and those who were already members would be invited to resign. Instead Faculties would be represented by their Deans plus one elected member for every six full-time members of academic staff. The Vice-Chancellor, Deputy Vice-Chancellors, Librarian and Director of Computer Services would be ex-officio members and student membership would be unchanged.

A New Scenario

The dramatic cuts of 1981 were not the first and were by no means the last of their kind. Further cuts continued year after year, most damagingly in 'per capita' funding, that is, increases in grants which did not take full account of increases in student numbers (nor of more students taking science-based courses). In retrospect the University's recovery during these years was remarkable and began remarkably quickly. As early as the autumn of 1983 Roberts was able to report that in one more year the University's income and expenditure would be in balance and suggested that 'a mild optimism [was] not out of order.' The next session he described as 'the most encouraging of the five years of my Vice-Chancellorship, so far.' It had been 'the year in which the University at last emerged from grappling with the consequences of the reduction in funding which had threatened to paralyse it.'

Nor had the University stood still. By then, for example, the University Grants Committee had agreed to provide £2 million for a major expansion of the Library, and the Leverhulme Trust £95,000 for work on the recently acquired Wellington papers. Other significant developments in the history of different Faculties and Departments between 1981 and 1985 were the commitment of £800,000 for new buildings for Music and Electronics, the latter to be subsequently given a substantial grant from the University Grants Committee; the establishment of an Institute of Maritime Law, a Department of Computer Studies and a Centre for Mathematics Education; the award in 1982 and 1983 of funding for 15 new staff under the 'New Blood' scheme, four of these in Information Technology; and above all the decision in 1984 that

The Adult Education Department, viewed from University Road, 1983.

Southampton's Oceanography Department was to be one of the two chosen out of the country's four to survive and be hugely expanded.

Among developments which affected the University more generally in these years the transformation of Chilworth was probably most important. From 1978 onwards, when the hall of residence in the manor house was closed, a number of possible uses for the estate had been discussed – among them that the manor should become a day conference centre or a centre for short courses. At the same time there had been informal discussions, encouraged in particular by Professor Graham Hills (Chemistry), about developing a science park at Chilworth. In July 1980 Roberts brought these to the attention of the Joint Policy Committee. As a result the University applied for outline planning permission for a cluster of buildings in Chilworth's grounds to be used by research companies, but at the same time applied for detailed planning permission for the building of student accommodation there, to keep this plan alive. Test Valley District Council liked neither alternative but chose the science park as the lesser evil, and granted it outline planning permission provided the University surrendered its outline permission for residential accommodation.

In February 1984 the University's Joint Policy and Finance Committee agreed that the project should go ahead. Southampton City Council had meanwhile promised to contribute £500,000. It would be built on two of Chilworth's fields and ultimately provide 150,000 square feet of office and laboratory accommodation. Work on the smaller field would begin first but a new access road would be needed and the University agreed to commission this. The Centre was to be run by a private company, Chilworth Centre Limited. This would have five shares, all of which would be held either by officers of the University or, when it was launched, by Southampton University Development Trust. Once established it would be self-supporting.

The Dean of Engineering, Professor John Large, was appointed Chairman of the new company. On his appointment, Large noted that roughly half the 30 science parks in the country were connected with universities, but that most of the companies using them had little contact with their universities. 'It is my belief,' he continued, 'that from the start Chilworth must seek tenants who are strongly linked with the University.'

Chilworth was soon successful. By the end of November 1984 one of the first three buildings was about to be taken over by Ferring Research Ltd, a pharmaceutical firm closely connected with the Faculty of Medicine, which planned research into products connected with cardiovascular diseases. Such research needed 'quiet surroundings', a Ferring director explained, since it involved 'synthesising in milligram quantities, novel peptides, purifying them and studying them by spectroscopic methods.' A firm researching optical fibres, a field in which the University's Electronics Department had from the start led the country, was negotiating for the second building. Another, working on medical ultrasonics, was discussing renting part of the third.

Roberts's years were also those in which the John Hansard Gallery, opened in September 1980, began to acquire a reputation. In 1981 the Staff Club was formed, to which all those employed by the University would belong, its

Facing page: *bikes on campus today.*

99

purpose to encourage social and recreational activities for its members. Professor Morice (Civil Engineering) was elected its first Chairman. The club secured for all staff access to all parts of the refectory building from dining room to John Arlott Room. Within five years it had 24 special interest groups, including a jazz and blues society, a film society, a theatre group, a travel club, a cycling club and a garden club; and was organising such activities as sailing courses, outings to historic gardens, wine tastings and coach rides through the New Forest.

In 1983 the Nuffield Theatre's future seemed finally secured when an independent Southampton Nuffield Theatre Trust was formed, of which Southern Arts, the City Council, the County Council and the University were to be the principal funders. The new trust was registered as a charity, and was granted a ten-year lease of the theatre. The Nuffield's first production as a trust, *Daisy Pulls It Off*, was named comedy of the year by the Society of West End Theatres.

Student Affairs

The Students' Union was only peripherally involved in the events of 1981. While the University's budgetary groups suffered, the Union's funds remained unaffected since they were provided by the Local Education Authority – a piece of good luck which aroused a certain amount of staff indignation. Students themselves, on the other hand, did not escape the consequences of the Government's miserly treatment of higher education. Jon Sopel, Union president for 1981–2 (and a future BBC Political Correspondent), calculated that the promised increase of 4 per cent in the student grant meant that in real terms the Government, since taking office in 1979, had cut the grant by 13.4 per cent.

In 1983–4 students were much excited by a local storm in a teacup provoked when Alec Samuels refused to lecture to law students wearing CND badges. But in general the political passions of students reverted to concern about national or international matters. The debating chamber was 'filled to the rafters', the overflow also filling the ballroom, to listen to Ken Livingstone, chairman of the Greater London Council. Other visitors who spoke about animal liberation and vivisection, the American invasion of Grenada and the miners' strike were also well received. The Union declared itself a 'Nuclear Free Zone'.

Next year the Union considered that it had been unfairly treated when its block grant was reduced by £15,000 (out of £449,000), and in protest reverted in a small way to the tactics of the 1970s by occupying the offices of the local Conservative Association. But it also encouraged a campaign of protest letters to local MPs, and on the whole negotiation rather than confrontation remained the pattern of student behaviour. Throughout these years the Rag continued to raise money for charities and remind the citizens of Southampton in a colourful way of the existence of their University. To this end the Union now had a

Community Interaction Department.

In 1980 P. Emery, Union President, wrote that 'whatever problems of economy and expenditure' the University faced it should remember that 'students wanted to come to Southampton . . . not because the course is so good but because the University offers a place in Hall for first years, or has a good reputation for sport or music or other leisure pursuits.' Even in the years of confrontation the Athletic Union had continued to support this important contribution to the University's reputation. To pick examples at random, in 1971 Jack Lane won a silver medal in the World Student Games 5,000 metres, and the University team retained the UAU table-tennis cup. 1976–7 was a notably successful year for the archery, badminton, swimming, water-polo, netball and women's hockey clubs. It was no doubt such a range of successes which, the following year, in the words of the President, transformed 'the "Sports Lobby" within the Union from a relatively small group of vocal protagonists into a huge, coherent band of determined activists.'

Women's lacrosse and men's squash were the outstanding clubs of 1979–80. 'One of its most successful seasons ever,' the president wrote of the Athletic Union in 1984–5, with achievements which included a Bronze Medal winner at hockey during the Los Angeles Olympics, a volleyball player at the World Student Games and a sculling champion. The women's volleyball and sailing teams and the archery club were particularly successful.

A Chapter Closes

For the University itself, meanwhile, the reduction of government funding overhung all else. One consequence was that it put still more emphasis on research, and as a result increased what it earned from research grants and the different sorts of services which it rendered from £5.4m. in 1980–1 to £11.4 m. in 1983–4 – over a quarter of its total income. Another was the establishment of a Development Office, its aim to raise much needed additional funds for the University.

It also revised the way in which it planned for three years ahead. This practice had been introduced soon after the UGC, in the mid-1970s, abolished the quinquennial system in favour of grants for only the next year. The University's so-called Triennial Plans had from the start been revisable for their second and third years. Besides allocating funds to different Faculties, they had set aside a reserve from which Faculties could draw or borrow to fund special initiatives. Budgets and Development sub-committee laboured at revising the Triennial Plan for two years, under the chairmanship of Deputy Vice-Chancellor Professor Charnock (his second important contribution to the University, his first being to gain recognition for Oceanography) and ultimately proposed cuts for the first year which fell on six Faculties and varied from 0.2 per cent to 4.9 per cent. It set aside £500,000 from reserves to be used to protect those which would suffer most.

This was a great improvement, Roberts wrote, 'given that the University does

Above: *Rag, 1998.*

Above right: *the money raised by Rag is presented to charities, 1998.*

not yet want to move further in that direction.' The direction in which he wanted it to move was towards a system which allowed more 'innovation and ordered change'. The current system preserved activities which should not be preserved, and failed to reward 'quality'.

In February 1984 Roberts announced his resignation. Unexpectedly the Wardenship of his old Oxford college, Merton, had been offered him and, after several weeks of anxious thought, he decided to accept an opportunity which was unlikely to recur. Many at Southampton, including some who had been

A student working for Mencap as part of the Students' Union's Community Interaction initiative.

his fierce critics in 1981, were sorry. Three years later he was recovering the confidence which the events of that autumn had damaged and becoming the sort of 'man of stature' the University needed.

In his last annual report (on the year 1983–4, when his final year in office was still ahead) he listed some of the difficulties which still faced the University. Significantly, he put first 'exaggeration of sectional interests' which could 'easily and quickly lead to misunderstanding, more slowly (but, if left unchecked, inexorably) to jealousy, and then to animosity between different sections of the University.' Here was an acknowledgement that the growing respect in which he personally was held had not yet healed the division in the university with scientists, engineers and medical staff on one side and the rest on the other. To heal it came his successor, Gordon Higginson, by happy chance among other things a Professor of Lubrication.

5. Winning the Obstacle Race, 1985–94

Sir Gordon Higginson, Vice-Chancellor 1985–94.

The new Vice-Chancellor, Gordon Higginson, aged 55, had been Professor of Engineering at Durham University. He had at the same time been Chairman for seven years of the University Grants Committee's Technology sub-committee, so had visited Southampton and was well acquainted with its Engineering Faculty.

He was aware that the 1981 crisis had left behind feelings of inter-Faculty rivalry. Many staff believed that his informal, friendly, north-country manner was important in reducing these. But his manner alone was not responsible. Though he thought well of the University's Engineering, Science and Medical Faculties, he considered that a number of Departments were poor, a view confirmed by their low assessment ratings. On the one hand he set about improving their morale by telling them that they were standard bearers for the country's intellectual life, on the other he pressed them to make good appointments – the key, he believed, to improvement. He discovered for example that the Chair of French had not been filled as an economy, and insisted that it must be filled, whatever the cost.

A notable success was a Leverhulme Trust grant in 1987 of £207,000 to enable members of the History Department to take part in a project entitled 'Government and the Defence of the Realm'. Arts departments by their nature rarely received such large grants.

Peter Ucko helped. For several years he was greatly preoccupied with organising the World Archaeological Congress, which took place at Southampton in 1987 and brought much credit to the University – confirming in the process his reputation for frenetic energy (he was believed often to sleep for only two hours a night and during this period sometimes for none). When this obsessive archaeologist became Dean of Arts there was much foreboding, but he revealed an unexpectedly businesslike approach, of much value to the Faculty. Under Ucko it was to launch the University's first graduate school (1994–5).

The 1985–6 session partly coincided with the country's Industry Year, so it was appropriate that the University's earnings from research grants, contracts and other services to industry reached £15m. – a third of its total income. To most people it was unimaginable, Roberts had said, that any source other than the Government should fund higher education. With each year Southampton was demonstrating that most people had been unimaginative. In 1986 the University showed how aware it was of its new financial situation by appointing Professor John Large (Chairman of Chilworth Research Centre) to the new post of Director of Industrial Affairs.

Large promoted co-operation between the University and industry, and was responsible for distributing the Innovation Fund, which the University had established, from a percentage of the royalties it received. But Large admitted that personal contact with members of industrial companies was in practice often 'the most profitable process'.

Chilworth, meanwhile, was expanding rapidly. By the time the Duke of Kent planted a tree to mark its official opening (June 1986), 12 firms were either occupying its new buildings or temporarily using accommodation in the manor house. The following year it was to be subdivided into two companies, both subsidiaries of the University. Chilworth Centre Ltd was to be responsible for the science park. Here Phase II was adding 100,000 sq.ft. of research buildings. This, together with British Satellite Broadcasting's nearby satellite transmitting centre, and Phase I's 46,000 sq.ft., would produce a total of 200,000 sq.ft. of space.

Chilworth Manor Ltd would develop the manor house as a conference centre and training centre, with 95 beds, most of them in a new annexe. Conferences, large and small, had long been a significant feature of the University's activities, with a conference office to organise them. Formerly these had usually been held during vacations at one or other of the halls of residence. In 1987 Chamberlain Hall was substantially improved to enable it to receive them more comfortably. Commenting on this, John Hiett, Conference Officer, explained that it would help the University to compete in 'the conference business', which had become highly competitive. Conferences were lucrative. That year the University made a profit, after deducting all expenses including the cost of the conference office, of £143,000. There had been 120 'residential events'. One large organisation to hold a conference was IBM. 750 visitors had come for an RAF ex-PoW reunion. University-generated events had included the International Cryogenic Engineering Council's conference. In 1990 the University was voted by the International Conference and Convention Association, 'Best Academic Conference Venue' for the third time in five years. Halls of residence continued to be the venues for many conferences, but from 1990 Chilworth Manor Conference Centre provided an alternative which was purpose converted, open at all times of the year and more commodious.

In 1986 another funding body was officially launched: Southampton University Development Trust. Its more active function was to raise funds for the benefit of the University by any means it thought effective, then distribute them appropriately. The trust was officially launched in April and at the same time received its first donation: £105,000 from Television South (TVS Trust), which it assigned to work on the Mountbatten papers. In the same way that Departments were encouraged by the Director of Industrial Affairs to publicise what they had to offer, they were encouraged by the new trust to tell it which of their projects were in financial need.

Despite these important contributions by the University to its own financial survival, the constriction in real terms of direct government funding remained an ever-present background to its development. Roberts's view that the UGC thought well of Southampton was supported in 1986 when its block grant was reduced by only 2 per cent, compared with an average for all the country's universities of 4 per cent. Higginson, with his UGC experience, considered that it anyway had less reason to complain than the majority of universities, since it was among the ten which had been least severely treated by the 1981 and subsequent cuts. But the 'unit of resource' (grant divided by number of students) was steadily reduced, and the obvious remedy, to expand, was not possible while Southampton's numbers were restricted to 8,000.

Nevertheless the University's submission to the UGC of its overall plans for the next five years (on which its 1986 grant had been based) had included a proposal to expand. It was the UGC's acceptance of expansion which was therefore of greater importance than the grant itself. Ultimately the targets set were student populations of 10,000 by the year 2000 and of 15,000 by 2030. Of the events of his time, Higginson rightly considered persuading the UGC and subsequently the University Funding Council that Southampton should expand to have been the most important, and took some credit for achieving this, but admitted that the Budgets and Development sub-committee (to be renamed the University Management Committee) deserved more. It was this small group which 'really ran the University', as indeed it had since the early 1970s.

From this time onwards it worked to devise a strategic plan which would make the agreed expansion possible. More space was essential. Some was already in prospect. In 1988 the Natural Environment Research Council (NERC) announced plans to create a national oceanographic centre at Southampton, bringing there its fleet of ocean-going research vessels from south Wales and the Institute of Oceanographic Sciences from Surrey. In the late summer of 1990 proposals for a dockside campus were agreed, the Universities Funding Council contributing £12.5m. and NERC the remainder, which ultimately amounted to over £40m. Here Departments of Oceanography and Geology would link with the Institute of Oceanography. But formal lectures in

Chamberlain Hall, 1998.

Oceanography and Geology would still be given at Highfield which was now hopelessly crowded, the new Mountbatten building for Electronics currently being erected on the last free space of any size. The University therefore looked for a site for another new campus. Some staff, including John Large, favoured creating this at Chilworth, but when outside professional planners were asked to choose between this and two other possible sites they chose one of the others, Lords Wood.

Lords Wood, however, lying on the fringe of Southampton, some two miles north of Highfield, consisting of coniferous woodland managed by the Forestry Commission, was a greenfield site, and so aroused much local hostility. And it would require the planning approval of Test Valley Borough Council, within whose area it lay, and of Southampton City Council, through which approach roads would run.

The University worked hard to suggest that its proposed development, with 'low-density' building occupying only 15 per cent of the area, the retention of woodland and planting of more broad-leaf species, together with cycle and

The Oceanography Building, Eastern Docks, Southampton.

Main picture: *with Discovery.*

Inset: *at sunset, from Arundel Towers roof.*

pedestrian access to minimise the intrusion of cars, would produce an ecologically acceptable result. In 1990 it staged two information fairs at Chilworth and an exhibition at Nursling to explain its plans. And that autumn it held a series of (inconclusive) meetings with the City Council and Hampshire County Council. At the same time, however, Southampton City Council announced plans for the building of a football stadium on the city's outskirts, so suggesting that in special circumstances it would allow development beyond its previous limits. This encouraged the University in June 1991 to submit three planning applications, one for Lords Wood, another for building on Wide Lane sports ground, a third for the more intensive use of Highfield campus, the last two both depending on the building of student accommodation elsewhere.

Throughout negotiations the University had been under the impression that Southampton City Council, in particular its leader, Alan Whitehead, would support the Lords Wood plan, but at the last moment Whitehead spoke against it, with the result that it was not accepted. In Higginson's opinion, it was perhaps to compensate for this failure to give the University the support it had expected that the City Council now suggested an alternative: that the University should acquire the site of one of two unwanted schools in Southampton. These belonged to Hampshire County Council, and the County Council agreed to offer for sale the old Richard Taunton's College in Highfield Lane, only a few hundred yards from the Highfield Campus. To summarise the subsequent negotiations, it asked £5m., the University offered £1m. And when the deal was finally done in December 1993 the price paid was £2m.

Subsequently it also bought Hampton Park School, by then reduced to little more than a site. But it was Richard Taunton's College which it meanwhile developed, renaming it Avenue Campus. All Departments considered this a splendid idea, Higginson remembered, 'so long as *they* didn't have to move there'. Arts and Social Sciences, the two most likely candidates, were firmly against such a move. By the time the decision was taken, however, they were competing to be chosen. This was a result of the 'wonderful persuasive powers' of Tim Holt, Professor of Social Statistics, Deputy Vice-Chancellor. 'How he managed it I have no idea' (Higginson). Arts was chosen – though Music was left behind at Highfield, not to be separated from the Turner Sims Concert Hall. The Faculty was in due course rewarded with light, airy, colourful premises which skilfully seem to avoid the usual indistinguishable corridors of office doors and must surely be a model for such conversions.

Among other events of these ten years were the graduation in 1986 of the first ten nurses from the School of Nursing Studies, established four years earlier at Southampton General Hospital; and the return to the Mathematics Faculty of the School Mathematics Project (SMP) which Professor Bryan Thwaites had taken with him when he left in 1966.

1986–7 saw the creation of the School of Biological Sciences, bringing together staff from several schools, to be designated as one of two such groups in the country; and the opening by the Secretary of State for Education and Science of the University's new IBM computer system.

The University meanwhile continued to contribute to the cultural life of campus and city with concerts, theatrical performances and exhibitions. Since 1980 the John Hansard Gallery had been acquiring a national, indeed an international reputation. To this Barry Barker, for some seven years the gallery's director, made an important contribution. He combined 'a professional, cool and elegant sense of style with an eye to the future,' his successor, Stephen Foster, wrote. Foster's own success from 1987 onwards he attributed in part to the University's 'stalwart and enthusiastic support', but also to the gallery's peculiar shape. While most galleries consisted of white square boxes in which exhibitions were 'laid out in sequence' the Hansard's shape, originally dictated by the tidal model's shape, meant that its exhibitions were hung 'as if in a kaleidoscope'. This, together with its low dark ceiling, provoked one Austrian art dealer to describe it as 'not a gallery at all, more a chapel of art'.

In the autumn of 1987 the University celebrated the 125th anniversary of the opening of the Hartley Institution. A special event of this jubilee was the opening of the rebuilt library, renamed the Hartley Library, by Countess Mountbatten of Burma, who at the same time formally handed over the vast Mountbatten collection of papers. That year Geology scored a similar success to Oceanography's of a few years earlier when the UGC agreed that it should double in size and be one of only 16 Geology departments from the country's 30 to continue to offer an Honours degree in the subject. In 1987–8 the University's total earned income rose to £20m., an increase of one-third in three years. To this the Institute of Sound and Vibration Research, celebrating its silver jubilee, contributed £3.2m.

In 1989, when the UGC, during its final months, published reviews of various subjects, it nominated Music as one of the University's outstanding Departments despite the fact that it still lacked a satisfactory building for its academic work. The UGC also recommended that both Philosophy and Archaeology should expand and recruit more staff. The Mountbatten Centre for International Studies in the Department of Politics, and the A. B. Wood Underwater Acoustic Laboratory, were both opened that year.

In the summer of 1989 the examinations boycott by academic staff in protest against their inadequate pay was settled just in time for the examinations to be held. The result for the staff was less satisfactory, the Government as usual taking advantage of their unwillingness in the last resort to harm their students. As a consequence they had a weak union and, in Higginson's opinion, before they were properly paid, 'there would have to be blood on the floor'.

In July 1991 the Optoelectronics Research Centre was opened, where, in co-operation with University College London, it continued its internationally famous research into optical communications. Two years later its Professors, Alec Gambling and David Payne, won the 1993 Computers and Communications Prize for their invention of the erbium-doped fibre amplifier which has transformed global telecommunications.

In 1992 the Electronics and Computer Science Departments, now merged into one department, were able to move from their previous accommodation scattered about the campus to the new Mountbatten Building. Two events of the session suggest the variety of the University's research. The Mechanical

The weather vane at Avenue Campus.

Avenue Campus.

Engineering Department won the Prince of Wales Award for Innovation with its 'Vortoil' hydrocyclone device for separating liquids, in particular oil and water around drilling platforms. And students of the Aeronautics and Astronautics Department built and flew a human-powered airship, ideal (because silent) for observing without terrifying the wildlife of rainforests.

Different groups in the Medical School were now working on glue ear, asthma, endometriosis and leukaemia, 'the new wave of professors and staff gaining the school the sort of reputation for research which the original wave had gained for its novel teaching curriculum,' wrote Higginson. The star event of 1992, however, was the week-long British Association Science Festival, jointly hosted by the city and the University. Five thousand visitors came to the campus and 400 lectures were delivered. Appropriately, with the new campus rising at the docks, the world's oceans were the festival's theme. The Royal Research Ship *Challenger* lay alongside and was open for guided tours. 'An illuminating, exciting and exhausting week,' Sir David Attenborough told its final meeting.

An important change introduced in 1992–3 was the extension of the so-called semester system to many Faculties. The pattern of three ten-week terms was retained, but on to this was imposed an academic year consisting of two semesters, each of 12 weeks, the first from October to mid-January, the second from February to May. Within reason, students would be able, on the American pattern, to accumulate credit towards their degrees with courses offered by different Faculties and Departments. The sort of combined degrees which became possible included Mathematics with Economics or with certain Modern Languages, Computer Sciences with Modern Languages, and Oceanography with Underwater Acoustics.

In 1993–4 the Royal Navy chose Southampton as the University to which it would transfer its 30 engineers who began their training each year, so adding a new feature to the education of members of the armed forces which the University's Defence Studies Unit had for many years been providing. That year IBM chose Southampton to be the only British university at that time to join its Shared University Research Programme. And Mark Roberts, an archaeology postgraduate, discovered the remains of Boxgrove Man, the oldest human being to be found in Britain, perhaps in Europe.

Shortly after his appointment to succeed Derek Schofield in 1992 the incoming Secretary and Registrar, John Lauwerys was asked by the Vice-Chancellor to undertake a full review of the University's Governance and Committee Structure. The subsequent report led to the most fundamental changes in these structures since the University received its Charter in 1952. The Founding Charter and Statutes had defined the Court with some 350 members as the supreme governing

Avenue Campus.

body of the University, a role it was clearly inappropriately constituted to perform. The Review Report recommended the abolition of the Court, a reduction in the size of Council and the establishment of a new Policy and Resources Committee as the key joint Committee of Council and Senate to act as the focus of decision-making in the University. The only recommendation which did not find favour was that three of the Deans should be brought into membership of the new University Management Committee, the renamed Budgets and Development Sub-Committee (B & D of old).

Council and Senate supported the proposed changes, almost without amendment, including the abolition of the Court. Preliminary consultation by the Chair of Council, Mr Kingsley Williams and the Secretary and Registrar with the Privy Council confirmed that they would have no objections to these radical changes. However, at the key meeting at which the Court was asked to vote on its own demise, the paucity of Council and Senate members attending (all of whom were ex-officio members of Court) resulted in the rejection of the proposal by the 'back bench' Court members. The Court survives therefore, although it is no longer the supreme governing body, has no role in the amendment of the Charter and Statutes and is confined to an annual meeting at which it receives a report from the Vice-Chancellor and Treasurer.

The change in role of the Court towards being a meeting of those who are interested and supportive of the University, rather than having a role in its governance anticipated the recommendation made some years later by the Dearing Report which has led to a similar change in governance in the other chartered universities. Likewise, the reduction in the size of the membership of the Council from 50 down to 37 members by removing the largely inactive local authority nominees predated the firm recommendation by Dearing that Council, as the University Governing Body, should have a membership of around 30.

Approval of these changes by the Privy Council also included the abolition of Convocation, the old alumni association created in 1952, and which had been given a small voice in the running of the University in the form of five seats in Court.

This might suggest that the University had become less interested in its past students, but the opposite was the truth. In July 1992 an Alumni Office had been created to foster the University's relations with all who had attended it. The following year this began the essential task of tracing the 35,000 former students for whom it did not have addresses. By 1997 the number for whom it did have addresses had risen from 27,000 to 36,000, by 2001 to 60,000.

At the same time (May 1993) a new alumni body, the University of Southampton Society, was launched. This in effect became Convocation's replacement, the social events and reunions it staged replacing Convocation Day.

Nor in these years did the world of Higher Education stand still. 'Each year,' Higginson began his 1993 report, 'Higher Education has to contend with ever more sweeping and wide-ranging changes.' In May 1991 the government White Paper on Higher Education had proposed that by the year 2000, instead

The Head of the River Race, 1989.

of one in five of the country's 18–19-year-olds beginning some form of higher education, the proportion should rise to one in three. Increasing its numbers was in any case a necessity, as Southampton had long realised. Fortunately it had no problem with the quality or quantity of its applicants. In October 1991 it admitted 2,020 new entrants out of approximately 21,840 applicants. Next October applicants rose by 11.6 per cent to 24,688, with Law, Arts and Social Sciences particularly oversubscribed.

In 1992–3 the number of the country's universities was doubled when polytechnics were given this title. As a consequence the replacement of the Universities Funding Council, after an existence of barely three years, was logical, since the new Higher Education Funding Council for England alone had around 100 institutions of higher education to fund. This number meant that it could no longer provide detailed guidance to universities and was more and more to resort to formula funding.

Students, like the University, were gradually forced to recognise that they would have to earn much of what they got, the difference being that the earning period was deferred. This essentially was the nature of student loans, something the Students' Union had been protesting against for 20 years. By 1986 students throughout the country were involved in a campaign against the change, and a number from Southampton took part in a mass lobby of Parliament that year. In 1988 the Union passed a motion which described top-up loans as 'merely the thin end of the wedge . . . eventually leading to a full loans system' and calling for direct action.

In fact there was only one serious threat of such action in these years, the result of a proposal to use one floor of the already overcrowded Students' Union building for teaching. Uncertain in his first year how to deal with this, Higginson was presented by his staff with 'The Gower Rules' for handling such disputes. He remembered it as 'a very civilised protest'. The threatened occupation never occurred (the administration building was locked) and the

proposal to take from the Union part of its building was abandoned.

Meanwhile students steadily increased their right to have at least a say in University affairs. In these ten years they were given representation on a further 13 committees or subcommittees of Council or Senate. And the Union continued to protest against lack of accommodation for students, both private and provided by the University. In October 1990 it resolved to support the NUS's 'day of action on housing', this to include a sleep-out. The Union was, however, less committed to the NUS and its policies than at one time, and resolved that December to reconsider its affiliation every three years.

At the same time the Union, as ever, supported political campaigns which were less concerned with student life (e.g. against racism, or in support of women), and promoted 'awareness weeks' on such subjects as prostitution, AIDS, deafness and drugs. It also continued to invite as speakers many of the better-known or more notorious political figures of the day (among them Shirley Williams and Arthur Scargill).

Student sportsmen and women had been encouraged in 1980 when the new Wellington Sports ground was opened by Bruce Tulloh, champion runner of the 1950s and 1960s, probably the greatest of the University's athletes. The Athletics Union continued to score many successes. 1986–7 was a particularly good year, with the University's sailing, gliding, football, hockey and ladies' volleyball clubs outstanding, the last of these the UAU champion for the second year running. Individual sportsmen who distinguished themselves included Jon Potter who won a gold as one of Britain's hockey team at the 1988 Olympics. The following year there were again many successes, the five-a-side soccer team and the ladies sailing team both UAU champions, while Adrian Stead and Richard Lott sailed for Britain. That year cricket matches with the MCC were introduced by Ian Geddes, former captain of the Cricket Club.

In 1990 Roger Black won the World Championships silver medal in the 400 metres. He had been in the School of Medicine for one term, but left to concentrate on athletics. At the 1992 Olympics Jon Potter again played hockey for Britain. Other representatives from the University were Adrian Stead (sailing), Miriam Batten (rowing – pairs) and Katy Brownlow (rowing – eights).

During Higginson's final year, 1993–4, the first members of the Faculty of Arts (the Faunal Remains Unit of the Department of Archaeology) moved into the new Avenue Campus. Just as appropriately, his final month coincided with a symbolic event for the Waterfront Campus when, in June 1994, the Mayor of Southampton, Eddie Read, helped hoist a four-tonne flue tower 26 metres on to the roof of the new building, so completing its main structure.

Roger Black at the European Championships in 1994.

Facing page: *students on campus.*

6. Into the Premier League, 1994–2001

Howard Newby, Vice-Chancellor, 1994–2001

The new Vice-Chancellor, Howard Newby, aged 46, came from Derby, had begun his education at a local grammar school and progressed via the prestigious Atlantic College in Wales to the University of Essex. There he wrote a PhD thesis on agricultural labourers which was published by Penguin as *The Deferential Worker*. He then became a lecturer and, after three years at Madison, Wisconsin, returned to Essex as a Professor (1983). Five years later he was appointed Chairman (later Chief Executive) of the Government's Economic and Social Research Council. Interviewed by *Viewpoint*, he made a favourable impression. 'I anticipated the usual "long on words, short on content" platitudes,' the editor wrote. 'In fact the reverse was the case . . . We have a young, energetic, personable Vice-Chancellor who insists that he won't turn the place upside down – but is definitely going to make us all sharpen up our image.'

He was appointed ten months before he took office, months which, together with his ESRC experience, enabled him to get to know Southampton and to form a clear view of the future it should aim for. In recent years it had not performed as well as its strengths should have made possible. Its results in the 1992 Research Assessment Exercise, though not disastrous, had been disappointing. This was a consequence of it not having made a firm decision about the sort of university it wanted to be. Taking such a decision had become essential since the number of the country's universities had increased dramatically with all polytechnics and some other institutions gaining university status and title. Many did not conform to the traditional pattern: they no longer all had predominantly high-grade A-level students and they were no longer all attempting both to research and teach a broad range of subjects. 'There is no way,' Newby told *Viewpoint*, 'that we will improve our status by teaching more undergraduates in better ways; the crucial gain must come in enhancing our reputation in research.' During the previous 43 years the transformation of the University's view of itself had been gradual. In 1952 there had been research but teaching had come first. In 1995 teaching remained important, but research had to come first.

The positive side of this was comparatively easy: to encourage and invest in more and better-quality research. The negative side was less easy: to continue to teach well but to abandon certain luxuries, most obviously tutorials. During the ten-month interlude before he took up office Newby spread his message, particularly from May 1994 when be became chairman of the University's new Research Strategy Committee. His visits to departments found support and some enthusiasm for a 'research-led' university; the problem, Newby told a colleague at the time, was that each department had its own definition of what was meant by a 'research-led' university.

Not all staff were enthralled, but given the University's ambitions, and its already good reputation for research, together with the Government's determination that universities should earn ever more of their income, the policy was inevitable. Furthermore, Southampton could demonstrate that quality research and good teaching were compatible. The teaching of the five Departments (English, Geography, Geology, Music and Oceanography) which submitted themselves for assessment in 1995 was judged excellent.

A second aim was to introduce more effective planning. Since 1952 and, in particular, since the early 1960s, the University had planned ahead with much success, but this had become an obligation and plans had tended to remain pieces of paper. The practice Newby wanted to introduce was 'management by objectives'. Only this would provide targets against which to judge success or failure. The University must also be prepared to take action more quickly. Works soon commenced on the University's first strategic plan. Newby was at pains that this should define the mission of the University and set challenging but achievable targets. Work on the first Strategic Plan shadowed the adoption of the University's first mission statement in which it was declared that Southampton was a research-led institution in which teaching and research took place in an active research environment. The mission statement committed the University to the advancement, communication and application of knowledge. The first Strategic Plan was published in autumn 1995 and widely promoted across the University and externally. Following the excellent results of the 1996 Research Assessment Exercise, a second strategic plan was agreed in 1997.

In part at Newby's instigation and in part in response to the requirements of the Funding Council a series of further strategies were agreed. These included an estates strategy, aiming to maintain a campus of the highest quality and to promote a safe working environment, an information strategy, a teaching and learning strategy and, of course, a research strategy. New procedures for resource allocation with emphasis on strategic planning followed, an annual planning cycle was created and a Strategic Developments Fund was set up.

One area of concern to the new Vice-Chancellor was the need to increase the amount of income to the University from non-government resources. He saw the potential of exploiting the University's intellectual property, and in 1996 the former Office of Industrial Affairs was re-established under new leadership as the Office of Innovation and Research Support to negotiate research contracts and to protect intellectual property. Southampton Innovations Limited set up alongside to exploit commercially promising research developments.

The University's success in innovation was acknowledged in the following years by the designation of no less than nine University inventions as Millennium Products, the best record of any university. The innovative, environmentally-friendly cockroach trap was awarded the Prince of Wales Prize for Innovation in 1997. It was the precursor of a series of inventions concerned with insect control that won Millennium status: the ecobiotic roach trap, the innovative fly trap, the ExoSex Bait Station and Smartseeker, a 'smart' fly-killer aerosol. Other innovations to be recognised as Millennium Products were the Tribopen,

The Synthetic Chemistry Building, 1998.

a hand-held instrument to sort plastics for recycling; PolyAna, a general plastics identification machine; a unique portable device for measuring cerebral and cochlear fluid; the stereo dipole; and Autosub 1, an intelligent underwater research vessel.

Growth continued too at the Chilworth Science Park which, by 1995, generated over 550 jobs. Two years later it was announced that the research and development facility of Merck KgaA, the German-based pharmaceutical, speciality chemical and laboratory supplies company, would relocate from Poole to the Science Park, critically to build on its existing strong links with the University. Merck opened in its new location, in a purpose built facility, in 2001, by which time the first of two incubator units for start-up enterprises had also opened on the Park.

The previous year the largest university spin-out ever achieved in the UK, the start-up of Southampton Photonics was announced, based on research in the Optoelectronics Research Centre. The start-up attracted first-round funding of some £37 million, one of the largest private investments in the industry to date. Southampton Photonics, set up to design and manufacture fibre-optic components and based on technology licensed from the University, was set to create 200 skilled jobs in the UK, many of which were due to be based on development and production facilities on the Science Park.

Planning aimed to remedy the University's weaknesses. One of these was its infrastructure. Like most of his predecessors, Newby was dismayed by the ramshackle, shabby appearance of the Highfield Campus. The Robbins Report had been followed by or coincided with a number of new buildings – Arts 1, Arts 2 and the Nuffield among them – but during the following 30 years (admittedly in part because of government restrictions) there had been only three new academic buildings at Highfield of any significance: Murray, Mountbatten and Boldrewood.

To deal with this problem the University had to transform its attitude to the funding of capital projects. Instead of waiting in a queue for a government grant it must itself find the money it needed by borrowing. In financial terms it was undergeared. John Lauwerys, who had succeeded Derek Schofield as Secretary and Registrar in 1992, had brought with him his experience of how Royal Holloway College had transformed itself by 'going for growth' in this way.

Southampton had expanded in numbers but not to the extent that similar universities had done, and this was a second problem – vital for its finances since roughly two-thirds of direct government funding depended on student numbers. Nor was it succeeding in attracting as many overseas students as it could, their fees also a significant contribution to its income.

Highfield Campus and the Arts 2 building (below) .

To finance an improved infrastructure the University borrowed £50m. The results gave the Highfield Campus something in the nature of an entrance. The Gower Building, facing Burgess Road, was of a new sort, self-financing and supplying many of a student's needs from a choice of banks to a much enlarged bookshop. To the south, facing Salisbury Road, the Zepler Building provided Electronics and Computer Science with much-needed, purpose-built accommodation, whilst on the opposite side of Salisbury Road, the new Social Sciences Graduate Centre also provided a link between the Murray Building and Building 2. At the south end of the campus, Chemistry was in even more serious need, its buildings barely passing health and safety regulations. It was given a six-storey, £12m. Synthetic Chemistry building.

During this period the University also acquired two further campuses, both connected with previously affiliated colleges. Most of these had at one time been teacher-training colleges, but now taught other subjects, mainly in the Arts and Social Sciences. The University validated their degrees but – here was the problem – had inadequate control of their courses and academic standards. In 1992 the Higher Education Quality Council issued a report which criticised such arrangements. Soon after he arrived Newby visited the four which survived: King Alfred's College (Winchester), West Sussex Institute (Chichester), Winchester School of Art and La Sainte Union College, Southampton. He returned less worried about their standards, but admitting that Southampton had failed to have a clear view of how it would like its relationship with them to develop. He suggested several possibilities, including one of a sort he had met at Madison, Wisconsin: the central university research-led, its attached satellite colleges mainly concerned with teaching.

Events then moved fast. In April 1995 Winchester School of Art was well on its way to becoming part of the University. The School had been founded in 1860 to teach cabinet-making, embroidery and leather work. Its big expansion had occurred after 1989 and it now had more than 1,000 students. It offered a one-year foundation course, as well as undergraduate and postgraduate degrees. Though it still specialised in textiles and fashion, among students its sculpture department had the best reputation. It was unique in offering all who took degree courses the chance to live and work for several months abroad, usually in Barcelona, but also in Seville.

Though the final amalgamation seemed rapid the possibility had been discussed for some 15 years. During the last ten of these Kingsley Williams had been both chairman of the University's Council and of the School's governing body. It was a development he favoured, but he had not 'pushed the idea, instead letting it quietly mature'. He considered that the School had the weakness of being monotechnic, and had become too cosy. It would benefit from exposure to a more rigorous intellectual climate.

Meanwhile, however, it considered various other possibilities, including amalgamation with King Alfred's College. This had foundered because King Alfred's, as a Church of England Foundation, and Winchester had not been able to reconcile their aims or statutes. Eventually the School had managed (with some difficulty because it was small) to get itself accepted by the Polytechnics and Colleges Funding Council. Though it was reasonably content with this arrangement, its dependence on state funding and ultimately on a Department of Education which often changed its policies, was less than satisfactory, and became even less so after it had spent £3.5m. in the early 1990s on extensive new buildings. Joining the University would not only cut its overheads but enable it to borrow for further expansion.

For the University the School was an example (in practice if not technically) of a satellite institution mainly concerned with teaching. The School also had a campus, full at the moment, but perhaps expandable in the future. It also reintroduced to the University the study of the history of art, abandoned when it lost its lecturer in fine art in 1990. In August 1996 the School officially joined the University as a Department of the Arts Faculty, its deputy head becoming deputy Dean of Arts. Within a year, it was announced that the Winchester campus, as the School site had become known, was to be the new home of the Textile Conservation Centre, an internationally renowned centre of excellence in textile conservation, whose work included postgraduate teaching, research and consultancy. Then based in Hampton Court, it had sought to develop its academic role and services but had been frustrated by the limitations of its location. A new building was constructed for the Centre, at the same time as further building work on the campus, with HRH The Princess Royal formally opening the Textile Conservation Centre in 1999.

In 1997 La Sainte Union was absorbed even more rapidly, but for different reasons. La Sainte Union College (LSU) had had its qualifications validated by the University for many years. Located on The Avenue, close to the centre of the City, it had been founded by an order of French nuns in 1905 and for most of its existence was a small residential Catholic women's teacher training college. Like other colleges of education it grew and diversified its academic activities and by the mid-1990s had some 2,000 students. In the summer of 1996 the College's teaching-training programmes were subject to inspection by the Office for Standards in Education (OFSTED) and were not found to be satisfactory by their criteria. A re-inspection was scheduled for March 1997 and it became known that unless the programmes were then found satisfactory the Teacher Training Agency (TTA) would withdraw funding for all teacher-training programmes, involving some 800 students in the College in the summer of 1997. This in turn was likely to lead to the financial collapse of the College and the need to close all its remaining programmes.

Early in 1997 the Higher Education Funding Council approached the University with a request that it prepare a contingency plan to take over the College if the OFSTED re-inspection again led to an unsatisfactory rating. This turned out to be the case and over a frenetic few months the senior officers of the University had to work very hard and very quickly to rescue the situation. The first concern was that the students in mid-course should not be left abandoned and with a General Election taking place in May 1997, the TTA and HEFCE were more than anxious to avoid the political embarrassment that could have occurred had an effective rescue plan not been devised.

Through the co-operation of Chichester Institute of Higher Education the teacher-training students in mid-course were taught through to completion by the staff of that institution who took over and delivered the programmes at the LSU site. The University moved the Department of Adult Continuing Education to join with the non-teacher-training programmes of the former LSU College and created a new entity, New College. The University, via some very complex negotiations, purchased the site and assets from the LSU Trustees, including the new student residences in Archers Road, and by October 1997, New College became a new part of the University, adding another campus and activity.

The year of the amalgamation, 1997, was also the year of the Dearing Report on higher education and New College fitted well with some of Dearing's proposals: that institutions of higher education should provide more opportu-

A University preview day: prospective students pore over a campus map.

nities for lifelong education, both part-time and full-time. The idea was not new at Southampton. Since the war Adult Education's 'Return to Study' had been only one of a number of the Department's courses launched with the same purpose. 'Higher education is no longer something which people undertake only in the early years of their lives,' Newby told *Hartley News* soon after he arrived. 'We are in an era of lifelong learning.' Since many of New College's students were likely to be local, it would also contribute to fulfilling another of Dearing's recommendations: that universities should co-operate more closely with their communities. Commenting on New College, the Executive Director of Education for Southampton said, 'it will assist us in our ambition for Southampton to become *the* "city of learning".' Dearing also recommended that more of the country's 'lower socio-economic groups' should receive higher education. In 1995 Southampton had been awarded a grant by the Higher Education Funding Council to enable it to establish a 'Widening Provision' project with this as its aim.

A significant further expansion began in 1995 when the University greatly increased the number of nurses it was training, from the 20 or so it had been taking since its nursing degree course was launched in 1982 towards an eventual figure of 1,500. This was a result of the Government's recognition that most nurses should have degrees, and its decision to hand over the training of nurses from the NHS to universities. Southampton's Medical Faculty had recognised early that activities in hospitals were increasingly carried out by teams in which nurses were as important as doctors, and welcomed the opportunity to take more nurses. A new school of Nursing and Midwifery was formed in 1995 by the amalgamation of the NHS College of Nursing and Midwifery with the existing nursing group in the Faculty of Medicine. The community nursing

University sporting activities, anticlockwise from top:

Cowes Week, 1999; Three Peaks Cyclo-Cross 2000 (Alex Forrester); the women's VIII on the River Itchen; netball; football; Hockey (Jon Potter, member of the England 1st XI); ladies' rugby.

Freshers' Fair, 1997.

group transferred into the new school from the Faculty of Social Sciences in 1996.

The following year Southampton was one of two universities selected following a competitive tendering exercise by the NHS to provide education and training for nurses, midwives and health visitors in central-southern England. This involved a huge increase in student numbers and the establishment of sub-campuses in Basingstoke, Winchester, Portsmouth and Newport, Isle of Wight. The contribution of library and IT equipment study centres at the sites meant that students based there needed to commute to Southampton for only a few days each month. Those to train in Southampton would have a new building on the west side of University Road. In 1997–8 the University had 436 pre-registered nursing and midwifery students. By 2001–02 this had increased to around 1,275, many of these based away from Southampton. Numbers of post-registered students and of staff in the school also increased and a feature of the expansion of nursing was the development of a new research strategy in the school.

The University had already bid successfully for a new school of Occupational Therapy and of Physiotherapy, to be accommodated in a Norman Foster-designed building next to the old Unigate dairy on Burgess Road, which would similarly provide degree courses. Space for another expansion remained close by at the old Hampton Park School.

The University's commitment to research was soon rewarded by results exceeding the targets set in the first Strategic Plan. In the 1996 Research Assessment Exercise three of its groups which submitted themselves for assessment scored the very top rating of 5*: Electronic Engineering, Electrical Engineering and Nutrition, while another 15 scored 5. These included Law, Geography, Economics, Archaeology and Music, demonstrating the breadth of the University's research. Nevertheless, groups more firmly science-based predominated, and included Chemistry, Oceanography, Mechanical Engineering, Engineering Materials, Sound and Vibration, Computer Sciences, Aeronautics and Astronautics, Ship Science and Cryogenics. About these results Dr John Taylor, University Director of Planning, wrote that they placed Southampton ahead of 'comparable, broad-based institutions such as Leeds, Manchester, Sheffield, Liverpool, Newcastle and Nottingham'.

In 1995 student grants and tuition fees were still an issue. Soon after he arrived Newby told an interviewer that his preference was for 'a loan scheme that covers both fees and maintenance but which is repayable over the lifetime of a student's earnings, through the National Insurance Scheme – subject to their reaching a certain level of income.' Five years later this was more or less what happened, and students accepted what now seemed to have been inevitable.

It was more surprising that other issues were no longer raising the passions they once had. During the 15 years which followed the expansion of student accommodation in the 1970s virtually no more had been built – a period in which numbers had more than doubled. The Students' Union had not been totally silent about the resulting shortage, periodically resolving to 'look into the problem' of housing for students, and once resolving to 'put pressure on the University to build a new hall of residence', but with little effect. In 1992–3 just 250 new places had been built as a small extension to Glen Eyre.

Students outside the Students' Union shop.

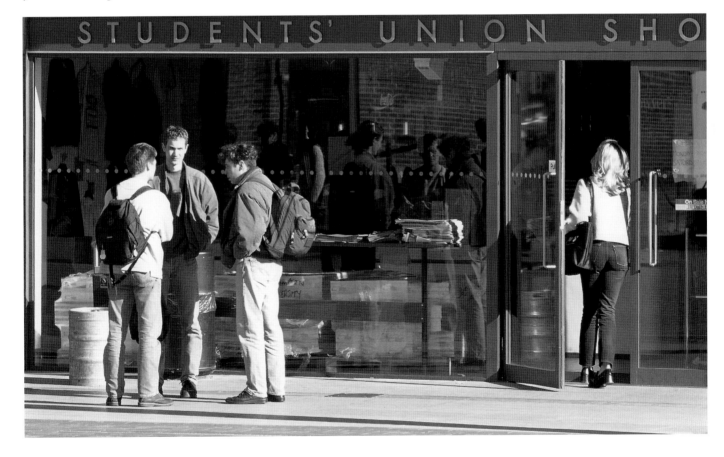

Two of the University services:

Above: *the campus play-group.*

Above right: *the Uni-Link bus service launched in 1998.*

Meningitis immunisation at the University, November 1997.

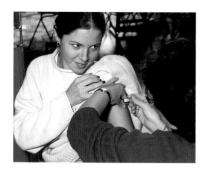

Now the University resolved at least partly to put things right and built further halls for 600 at Montefiore, and for 400 at Hartley Grove. Other residences, including Highfield Hall and the old courts at Glen Eyre, were extensively refurbished. But the University's total of 5,120 places for a student population of over 18,000 remained well below the 40 per cent once thought desirable. Furthermore most accommodation had been built with loans, and to service these rents had to rise sharply. The new halls of course provided greatly improved facilities, but George Clegg, Permanent Secretary to the Union, was nevertheless astonished at how willingly students paid. Increases which would have provoked strikes and protest marches 20 years earlier were accepted without protest, let alone sit-ins or boycotts. The Union and the University worked in close harmony to ensure that students were properly informed about what had happened. New services, including an inter-campus bus service, Uni-link, were also introduced.

The autumn of 1997 was distressing for the whole University, and above all for students. On Saturday 11 October, just two weeks into term, a first-year student died of meningitis in Montefiore. Two weeks later, a second first-year student also died of meningitis and three further cases were confirmed; all were students resident in the Wessex Lane halls. The University worked closely with the health authority and all first-year students in the Wessex Lane residences were offered immunisation against type C meningitis. Remarkably over 95 per cent of students came forward for immunisation.

The crisis deepened and raised huge additional concerns when a third student died over the first weekend of November. Unlike the previous cases, this student had no apparent connection with the Wessex Lane residences. It was recognised that a real sense of panic could ensue and a five-hour crisis meeting was held on the Sunday evening to consider what action should be taken involving University and Health Authority representatives. The University pressed for vaccination against type C meningitis to be made available more widely, so that all students, and indeed staff, who felt concerned and wished to be vaccinated, could be. The Health Authority did not believe it was necessary and justifiable to extend this option to all staff and students, although it extended its programme to all remaining first-year students, all other students living in halls and staff working there.

The climate of concern in the University was at a very high level by this stage, and on the next morning, the Vice-Chancellor and Secretary and Registrar took the decision to offer vaccination to all other members of the University starting on the following Wednesday afternoon. In theory this applied to some 15,000 staff and students and the logistics of making good this undertaking proved formidable. The vaccine had to be purchased very quickly (5,000 were ordered from the total national stock of only just over 40,000 vaccines) and staff from the Medical School, School of Nursing, University Health Service and the Administration were drafted in to organise the mass vaccination programme, which in the following days enabled over 4,000 staff and students to be vaccinated. At one stage, some 500 staff were dealing with one aspect of the crisis or another.

By now a media storm had broken; over the three weeks of the crisis, several thousands of phone calls were received from students, staff, parents and the general public. Thankfully, there were no further cases, but nevertheless, it was the worst outbreak of meningitis ever suffered in a British university.

The Public Health Service in Southampton subsequently took the ground-breaking decision to advise all new students starting courses in the Autumn of 1998 to seek vaccination against type C meningitis. By the following year the Department of Health extended this advice across the UK and the subsequent incidence of meningitis cases declined markedly. The tragic Southampton outbreak of 1997 had therefore a major influence in changing national policy towards the prevention of meningitis.

That Southampton should have suffered in this way was ironic since the Medical Faculty had for many years been researching meningitis, and had made a particular study of the outbreak at Stroud. One University reaction was to grant £204,000 to the team at Southampton General Hospital led by John Heckels, Professor of Molecular Microbiology, which was attempting to develop an improved vaccine against strain B. At the same time (June 1998) the University organised a London conference entitled 'Meningitis: Protecting our Students'. It had already passed to other universities an account of the outbreak and of lessons it had learned in dealing with such an event.

During the 1990s the Union continued to support traditional political causes, or new ones as old ones disappeared: anti-apartheid, anti-racism, pro-abortion – though on another occasion it resolved 'to have no policy stance on abortion'. An event of 1996, however, suggests that there had been a change in students' attitude to the Union. That year it resolved to hold Union meetings every three weeks instead of

'Carols on Campus' in the Turner Sims Concert Hall, December 1997.

The Grad Ball, 2000.

fortnightly because of low attendance.

Meanwhile student athletes and University teams continued to win medals and score successes – oarsmen and sailors now particularly distinguishing themselves. John Cooney and Nick Phillips won Gold and Silver medals respectively for rowing at the Commonwealth Games of 1994. At the 1996 Olympics Guin Batten came fifth in sculling and her sister Miriam seventh in the eights. Miriam went on to win Silver then Gold medals at the 1997 and 1998 World Rowing Championships, and Miriam and Guin won silver medals in the Ladies' Fours at the 2000 Sydney Olympics. In the year 2000 the men's sailing club came first in the Cowes International Youth Week and British Universities Match Racing championships. The same year the Ladies' Sailing Club won the National Student Championships. Andy Beadsworth was chosen to sail for Britain in both the 1996 and 2000 Olympics.

Other sporting teams to flourish were hockey, with its 1999 synthetic-turf (water-based) pitch; and other individuals Rebecca Humphreys (Ultimate Frisbee) and Pauline Boxall (Ladies' Rugby).

A New Millennium

As the year 2000 approached Newby (by this time the first-ever President of the Committee of Vice-Chancellors and Principals) encouraged the University to ask itself where it would be in ten or fifteen years' time. To do this with any hope of a probable answer it should ask the same question about higher education as a whole, not merely in the UK but in the world. It was certain, Newby believed, to have become globalised.

There were two main reasons for this. First, because it would have become possible, as a result of information technology and of the use of English as a world language. Second, because, for any university which wanted to remain in the top league, it would have become essential since the cost of achieving this alone was beyond any but a very few of the largest.

Among the consequences of IT and a world language would be the creation of new so-called virtual universities which did not exist in that they had no campuses. Students would pick from the offerings of such universities what they wanted, behaving as clients rather than pupils. The Dearing report had not foreseen such a change, but had supposed that the reforms of UK higher education which it recommended, most of them desirable, would take place on traditional campuses.

One possible future for Southampton was to continue to qualify for member-ship of a global superleague, both with its research and teaching, but at the same time (of necessity because it was small) join a group of similar institu-tions to form a global alliance. Only such an alliance could attract the investment it would need and have the ability to market itself worldwide. Such an idea was soon no mere theorising. The Worldwide Universities Network (WUN) was formed in 1998 as a global strategic alliance bringing together a group of research-led institutions committed to innovation in research and education. In the UK, the initial members were the universities of Leeds, Sheffield, Southampton and York, with Manchester and Bristol joining later. Four US partners also joined at the outset, with a fifth to join later, and with discussions initiated with other possible members outside both the UK and the US. WUN was set up to take advantage of the opportunities that globalisation presents and the pervasiveness of IT.

As Newby saw the scheme developing, it would move from, for example, the setting of similar standards of teaching and research, collaboration between research groups, student and staff exchanges and the joint development of courses, to a system which would enable students to accumulate credit towards a degree from associated universities all over the world.

Newby, who was knighted in the 2000 Birthday Honours list, left Southampton at the end of the 2000–01 session, following his appointment as Chief Executive of the Higher Education Funding Council for England. In his term of office, Newby had been well supported by the principal officers of the University. Earl Jellicoe, who had been Chancellor of the University since 1984, was succeeded by Earl Selborne, an active member of the House of Lords who was a Fellow of the Royal Society, Royal Geographical Society and also a former Chair of the Agriculture and Food Research Council. Dame Rennie Fritchie, the former Chair of the South and West Regional Health Authority, had succeeded Kingsley Williams as Chair of Council in 1998; two years later, Dame Yvonne Moores, a former Chief Nursing Officer, succeeded Dame Rennie, who had been appointed to the demanding office of Commissioner of Public Appointments.

Newby was succeeded in October 2001 by Professor Bill Wakeham, previously Deputy Rector of Imperial College London (see p.282). By the time he left, Newby had completed seven years as Vice-Chancellor and had seen the University almost double in size, from 9,000 full-time students in 1994 to 15,500 in 2001. Together with 4,500 part-time students, the University's student population reached 20,000 for the first time in 2001.

Each year the University consistently hit its targets for undergraduate numbers, as applications remained buoyant. But despite the dramatic growth in student numbers the University failed to meet the targets it set for itself in increasing postgraduate and overseas student numbers. The latter remained a cause for concern, stubbornly remaining below expectations despite increased and most determined efforts to internationalise the student body at the University.

During the same seven years the University turnover almost doubled from £127 million in the 1993–4 financial year to £214 million in 2001–02. The University maintained a financially prudent course throughout the period, returning a surplus each year, although in the mid-1990s it was sometimes a close call.

The University's research income continued to increase as a proportion of the University's total income and by 2001 over half of the University's income was attributable to research. Southampton was consistently in the top ten on a number of indices of University research income including that for income for collaborative research received from industry and commerce, and the

Graduation 2000. Photographs taken on Highfield Campus and in the Nuffield Theatre, where the ceremony took place.

amount of research income received for each member of academic staff.

When his departure was announced, Newby commented: 'As Vice-Chancellor my aim has been to see the University of Southampton consolidated in the leading group of UK universities and recognised as one of the global élite. The University has developed greatly in the past seven years, and has further strengthened its international reputation for excellence in both teaching and research . . . I've enjoyed enormously my time at Southampton and will greatly miss the University and the people here. I couldn't have imagined leaving Southampton for any other university.'

III

THE FACULTIES AND PROFESSIONAL SUPPORT SERVICES

1. Arts

Arts has undergone a radical transformation over the past two decades, which has seen it emerge as one of the largest Faculties in the University (approximately 3,500 students) with an innovative, cross-disciplinary approach that is now recognised worldwide. During that period the Faculty has built up a sound reputation for moving into specialist areas of research, study and practice: examples include the Textile Conservation Centre, the AHRB (Arts and Humanities Research Board) Parkes Centre for the Study of Jewish and Non-Jewish Relations, and the Centre for the Archaeology of Human Origins. Successes such as these demonstrate that a concerted attempt to reposition the Faculty as a leader in international research in the arts and humanities in the recent past has been successful. But perhaps the greatest change has been in image: the Faculty has created the cross-disciplinary ethos generally associated with the post-1992 universities, while retaining the scholarly standards associated with the older ones. Masters and research students are arriving in increasing numbers, partly as a result of the diverse range of subjects on offer, some of which are unique, such as Textile Conservation.

In the pre-war era Arts had been a small part of what was primarily a science, engineering and teacher-training college. With the influx of ex-servicemen in the post-war years, the Faculty was able to expand and, even when they had gone, student numbers continued to rise, with a record 142 in October 1955. In the 1960s the first signs of the Faculty's now established multi-disciplinary approach appeared when the General Degree was replaced with a new Combined

Honours Degree; this was followed by the launching of a one-year MA programme in 1966, the degree being awarded mainly on examination results.

By this time the Faculty encompassed distinct Departments of Classics, English, French, Geography (which became part of the Faculty of Science in the early 1970s), German, History, Music and Philosophy. In the mid to late 1960s there was a serious attempt to widen the range of disciplines on offer, with four additional areas starting up: Russian, Italian, Theology and Archaeology. However, it was not the best timing for the introduction of new subjects because university expansion was drawing to a close, and existing Faculty members now concede that these initiatives were 'maybe too small and too late'. Three of those subjects no longer exist: Russian, Italian and Theology all closed by 1988, and were followed by Classics. Of the new subjects, only Archaeology continues to thrive.

Until the early 1970s, Southampton's Arts Faculty was organised within the same structure as that in most of the older universities, with strong individual departments. The funding crisis in the early 1980s led to the consolidation of the departments – apart from Archaeology and Music – into three schools; in the long term, the only School to survive and flourish was the School of Modern Languages, with the rest of the Faculty reverting to a departmental organisation. At this time there tended to be one Professor in each department and that person was generally appointed Head of Department for life, a state of affairs which endured until the 1990s. (In Music the foundation Professor, Peter Evans, who retired in 1990, had been there for 28 years and his secretary for 20.) As a consequence these senior staff tended to loom large within the Faculty and one thought of the department as being almost synonymous with its Professor. That has now changed: the size of many departments, and the administrative load of running them, has grown considerably. In order that senior departmental members can remain research-active it has become the norm for the headship to rotate between them, usually every three years. This also helps to create the consensual and non-hierarchical style of management that generally characterises the Faculty.

In the late 1990s the Faculty underwent a number of transformations, two of which took place in quick succession in 1996: Winchester School of Art (until then an autonomous institution) became part of the Faculty, and a few weeks later all the rest of the new Faculty (with the exception of Music) moved to a new campus a few minutes away from Highfield. Named the Avenue Campus, this is an architecturally distinguished conversion of a former school (Richard Taunton's College), a particular feature of which is the central courtyard, flanked by glazed aisles and occupied, in summer, by café tables and umbrellas.

In the new millennium, Arts has emerged as one of the most dynamic Faculties in the University with a growing reputation for research in a wide number of subjects, some of which can be studied only at Southampton. The sheer scale and ambition of many of the innovative projects and conferences taken on by Arts underline the manner in which the Faculty has succeeded in reinventing itself.

Research

The major part of the Faculty's research output consists of books, articles, musical performances, sculptures and other forms of individual production. Its success in these areas is measured by all the standard indicators – publication, prizes, keynote addresses, FBAs, and of course the national Research Assessment Exercises. In the 1996 RAE, almost half of those departments improving their grades were in Arts, with Archaeology and Music both rated at the fully international grade of 5.

Alongside such work, however, the Faculty has in recent years made large strides in developing collaborative research projects. Most of these involve external funding – the Southampton Arts Faculty is the sixth best-funded in the country in terms of research support from sources other than the Higher Education Funding Council for England (HEFCE), with only well-known names such as Oxford, Cambridge, University College London and King's College London receiving more. Among the sources of such funding are the AHRB (as in the AHRB Parkes Centre for the Study of Jewish and Non-Jewish Relations), and the EU (as in the case of the Fifth Framework project CULTOS, centred on the Department of English in collaboration with the School of Modern Languages and academics in Britain, Europe and Israel). This is designed to produce a multimedia intertextual database of key works in the European cultural heritage. Another huge undertaking, again in English, has been the development of Chawton House – the 'Great House' owned by Jane Austen's brother in the Hampshire village where she lived and wrote. This is set to become the future home of the Centre for the Study of Early English Women's Writing (1600–1830).

Like the other examples listed here, Chawton – which will open in 2003–04 – is an excellent example of a project which plays to the Faculty's cross-disciplinary strengths: although firmly located in the English Department, it also encompasses researchers working in film (School of Modern Languages), and in costume and dress history (History of Art and Design). A number of Faculty Centres have been set up specifically to promote cross-disciplinary work: these include the Wessex Medieval Centre (which brings together colleagues from English, History and Archaeology) and the Centre for Post-Analytic Philosophy (set up jointly by the Departments of Philosophy and Politics), while the position of Archaeology as an international leader in Palaeolithic Studies has been recognised with the establishment in 2001 of the Centre for the Archaeology of Human Origins.

There are many other Centres and collaborative projects within the Faculty: in the Winchester School of Art, there is a Centre for the History of Textiles and Dress, and a Centre for Contemporary Art Research set up in collaboration with the John Hansard Gallery; there are also a newly established Centre for Architecture, Urbanism and Design (which links with other Departments in the Faculty and with the Department of Civil and Environmental Engineering) and a Centre for Contemporary Sculpture.

The Textile Conservation Centre, an internationally recognised centre of excellence established in 1975, moved to the Faculty's Winchester campus in 1999, and has already established collaborations with the Department of Chemistry and the Faculty of Engineering. The Centre commands a leading role in the teaching of textile conservation and for research into the field. Unusually, it combines conservation with consultancy, professional training and research and development.

The AHRB Parkes Centre for the Study of Jewish and Non-Jewish Relations builds on the internationally renowned work of the Parkes Centre at Southampton, in collaboration with the Classics Department of the University of Reading and the Institute of Jewish Policy Research, London. Research projects carried out in 2001 included an examination of Jewish and non-Jewish peoples in cosmopolitan maritime trading centres, a translation of the Greek bible, literary representation of Jews in Britain, along with race, ethnicity and memory in twentieth-century Britain.

In the School of Modern Languages an important research project focuses on the discursive construction of identities in European border communities. An international research consortium, co-ordinated and directed by the Professor of German, forms part of an EU Fifth Framework key action project, 'Improving the socio-economic knowledge base'.

In Music a number of projects involve collaboration between academics and professional performers. One example, funded by the AHRB and entitled 'Female Musicians and Performance Practice in Parma and Ferrara', is being pursued in conjunction with the vocal and instrumental group 'Musica Secreta', while another joint project with the University of Texas at Austin focuses on improvisatory practices in historical repertories.

Conferences

One of the ways in which the Faculty has disseminated its new image is through staging conferences; these have helped put it more firmly on the national and international map. An early and notorious example was the negative press coverage attracted by the Faculty for its refusal to accept South African delegates to the World Archaeological Congress in Southampton in 1986; this was part of the widespread academic pressure brought to bear against apartheid at that time, but also reflected the Congress aim of reorientating archaeology towards a more socially aware attitude as regards its responsibilities in the community, such as acknowledging the rights of local people.

Many departments have held national or international conferences in their particular specialist areas (for instance the 'Performance 2000' conference put on by the Music Department in the Turner Sims Hall, interdisciplinary conferences on musicals and the influence of Darwin's thought on the arts and humanities). The largest of recent conferences was the annual meeting of the Association of Art Historians in 1999, which showcased the facilities of the Avenue Campus and placed Southampton at the centre of contemporary artistic thought and practice. A major international conference called 'Adaptation, Costume, Heritage', planned for 2003, concentrates on the

The Department of Archaeology.

Top, and middle right: *The Beaulieu River Project, 1997.*

Middle row, left: *a student in Namibia.*

Bottom, left to right: *a student on a dig; the Centre for Applied Archaeological Analyses.; in the laboratory at the Centre.*

'afterlife' of the classic novel in its adaptation for film and television; it will provide a forum for discussing individual film and television adaptations, their film-makers and their audiences, and for addressing the connection between source, text, and screen image. The conference will include screenings of significant and rare productions, and a trip to Chawton House.

Philosophy

Philosophy was a small department in 1948 when Arthur MacIver arrived from Leeds University to establish it as a degree subject. MacIver was joined a year later by Guy Robinson who brought the study of formal logic and of the philosophy of science to what had started as a very historical course. Around this time they were joined by Tony Manser, already a widely read and original young philosopher. With the Robbins expansion in the 1960s, three more staff were added to this still very small Department. From this point onwards, right up to the 1980s, the philosophers had close personal and working relationships with people in other subjects in the arts, social sciences and occasionally even in the natural sciences.

British philosophy from the 1950s through to the 1980s was relentlessly dominated by the analytic tradition that had developed in this country in the twentieth century. The two major streams were Oxford linguistic philosophy, deriving from figures such as John Austin and Gilbert Ryle and the rather bolder conceptions of language, thought and world recently inherited from Ludwig Wittgenstein. Manser developed a lively interest in Wittgenstein and cultivated an interest in Continental philosophers, especially Sartre. In the 1980s, Philosophy generally became much less sectarian. Sophisticated relationships with the Continental traditions began to develop more widely, and fertile confluence developed between the philosophy of language and the emerging fields of cognitive science, artificial intelligence and brain science. It also developed powerful relationships to political thought and to public thinking about ethics in many areas (collectively known as 'applied philosophy'). Today, the philosophy of Wittgenstein remains strongly represented but the treatment is now more reflective than evangelical and the study of Continental philosophy has expanded. Indeed, the earlier approach of the Department to philosophy could be seen to prefigure the founding (with Politics) of the Centre for Post-Analytic Philosophy. Since its inception, the Centre has held several conferences and there is an annual lecture by a distinguished figure.

Archaeology

Over the years Archaeology has developed a number of core areas of activity. Some of the main ones include the analysis of pottery and ceramics, and the applications of computing techniques to archaeology and maritime archaeology where Southampton is probably the world leader in postgraduate instruction.

As a Department, growth was slow from the late 1970s, when there were about eight staff, until the early 1990s. Student numbers also rose significantly over a period of about eight years – from few postgraduate students to 64 in 2000–01.

Southampton has always been at the forefront of developing innovative analytical approaches to archaeology, and has excellent facilities to underpin this. The Department believes in the importance of archaeological computing and rapidly embraced Geographical Information Systems as a fundamental tool for managing and analysing spatial archaeological data. The main emphasis of research into archaeological computing has been in its application to the role of spatial technologies in the understanding of prehistoric and classical landscapes, interpretative archaeology using 3D, and virtual-reality technologies.

The Department's traditional expertise in the analytical study of artefacts continues, with studies of ceramics which contribute to the study of ancient trade. The analysis of ancient stone has been reinforced by recently enlarged laboratory facilities, and an extensive rock collection in a new Resource Centre. The Department also continues to provide major research support in the analysis of animal and, more recently, human bone. Links with the Southampton Oceanography Centre have enabled the Faculty's Centre for Maritime Archaeology to be at the forefront of the development of new remote-sensing techniques. A new paradigm for the study of submerged archaeological sites is being developed. At the same time, the Department has also expanded into the field of Archaeo-botany and Geo-archaeology, undertaking valuable work on Roman and Saxon soils. In 2001 the Department was involved in excavations in a Roman town on the Red Sea coast of Egypt. The excavational culture centred on an ongoing discourse with the people who live there, so that they can contribute to the understanding of what has been found. The aim is to develop 'community archaeology' where staff members at the site liaise with schools and use local guides. Some of the real achievements have been the creation of a local museum and the development of tourist goods for the heritage industry.

Modern Languages

Modern Languages at Southampton dates back to the University's beginnings in the early 1860s. With the establishment of the University College in 1902, Modern Languages became one of the eight founding Chairs, and in the early 1950s separate Departments of French and German were created, followed by Spanish in the early 1960s. The Language Centre developed from the late 1960s in response to the need for language laboratory facilities and the growing demand for language-teaching for non-specialists, such as English as a Foreign Language and languages not offered by the three academic departments. At the same time, degree-level provision was also introduced for Italian, Russian, Portuguese, Latin American Studies and Linguistics. During the 1970s the French, German and Spanish Departments developed a close working relationship with the Language Centre. Together they created a range of new

Students in a Language Lab.

combined-honours degrees within the Arts Faculty, as well as introducing a growing number of inter-Faculty degree programmes.

In the early 1980s the three language Departments combined with the Language Centre to form the School of Modern Languages. Since then, the School has grown considerably and is now organised as a unitary Department. The demand for languages in a range of careers has resulted in the introduction of many combined-honours programmes with other Faculties, such as Social Sciences, Science and Engineering. Growth of international links, particularly through the ERASMUS/SOCRATES scheme, has also created the need for teaching in languages to support exchange programmes in many disciplines.

In the 1990s there was an enormous national downturn in the desire of students at all levels to study a second language. Despite the uncertainty and after endless debates about the future of modern languages, the University and Faculty came down firmly in favour of providing opportunities for study. However, one effect of the downturn is that the School is continually reinventing effective ways to study a modern language, whether through new subject combinations (such as Fashion and French) or through a new emphasis on the study of language in the context of the media. The School has also been awarded the prestigious status of hosting the national Subject Centre for Language, Linguistics and Area Studies funded by HEFCE, which promotes and disseminates good practice teaching and learning in the subject area.

The School of Modern Languages has a strong research culture and a lively research community of staff and postgraduate students. Over the past decade it has moved from its traditional emphasis on national languages and literatures since the Middle Ages towards an interdisciplinary focus on the languages, cultures and societies of contemporary Europe, with a strong awareness of the wider international context. This process has led to staff grouping themselves into four inter-disciplinary fields: Film and Television Studies; Linguistic Studies; Literary and Cultural Studies; Social and Political Studies. While each field has developed its own portfolio of activity, colleagues collaborate closely across fields and often belong to more than one, resulting in a broad and creative span of activity.

Although Spanish, German and French are the main languages studied, others include Portuguese and Catalan which reflect the School's interest in Latin American studies. A further development was the establishment of a Chair in European Film. This has proved a success and very high numbers of postgraduate students have been attracted to the film courses. Although Warwick and the University of East Anglia offer courses in film, Southampton's distinctiveness comes from its European dimension and the very successful development, in conjunction with the English Department, of undergraduate and postgraduate courses in European film.

Music

As in many post-war universities, Music began as a service unit, running orchestras and putting on concerts, but it had developed into an academic Department by the early 1960s, when Peter Evans was appointed the first Professor of Music since 1928; one of his first acts was to persuade Senate to offer Music as a single honours programme. At that time the Department, which grew by the 1970s to five staff members, had a reputation for quality in research and innovation in teaching (it was one of the first to integrate performance within its degree programme), which was consolidated by the opening of the Turner Sims Concert Hall in 1974. Student numbers remained virtually static until 1990, however, when a decision was made to revamp and expand the Department: a new curriculum was brought in which featured then

Below left: *Southampton University Symphony Orchestra, 1997.*

Below: *The Allegri String Quartet in the Turner Sims Foyer.*

unusual fields such as world music and pop, and in which the traditional core curriculum was replaced by a foundation year followed entirely by elective subjects. This made possible a rapid increase in student numbers from 40 to well over 200, including a substantial proportion of postgraduates; at the same time the staff complement more than doubled, supporting a progressive diversification of the subjects on offer. (The professoriate, still one in the early 1990s, had grown to four by 1999.) The Department's achievement was recognised through its grading as 'Excellent' in the 1995 Teaching Quality Assessment.

In terms of research the aim has been to build on the Department's tradition of high international quality while diversifying into new areas of work. For many years Southampton has been known as a centre for research in early music, and in theory and analysis; it now boasts equal distinction in nineteenth-century and contemporary repertories (including popular music), in multimedia and film music, and in a range of cultural approaches. High-level instrumental and vocal tuition (in classical, jazz, and rock styles) is fully integrated with academic studies, while the Department's complement of composers ranges from concert to commercial music. The most recent development in the Department's research portfolio is its work in research-based performance, building on existing editorial and consultancy work by Departmental staff through bringing professional performers into the Department to collaborate with music historians and theorists.

English

In the post-war years, the English Department has grown and the discipline it professes has changed – not quite out of recognition but very substantially. English did not take the opportunity to expand in the period from the 1950s to the early 1970s, and in the mid-1970s it still retained the values and the scale of its immediate post-war days. The education it provided reflected the conception of the discipline as taught by the University of London, which had previously validated its degrees, concentrating on the philological and historical study of literary works, and the techniques of traditional literary scholarship.

English, growing in popularity nationally, was about to be changed radically by the advent of new forms of critical theory, based largely on ideas which had been developed on the Continent in the previous 30 years. English as a discipline became more diverse in character, driven by a theoretical perspective which barely recognised disciplinary boundaries. The Southampton English Department appeared to leap from 'Practical' and 'New' criticism straight to post-structuralism without having had to go through the intervening periods. During this period, the strong demand for English meant that the Department found itself under pressure to expand its student numbers in order to sustain Faculty numbers as a whole.

Through the 1980s and 1990s the Department developed its prominence in women's studies from the medieval to the modern period and built on strengths in theory, adding Marxism and psychoanalysis to its portfolio, and extended its coverage of modern literature and culture, both American and British. It maintained a tradition from the pre-Charter days of making strong and innovative professorial appointments in the Renaissance. It was the first Department in the Faculty to develop a modular course structure, and to introduce a substantial element of continuous assessment.

English has been a fortunate Department in a University which has always been perceived as predominantly scientific and technological. It has moved from being a small Department to being a smaller middle-sized Department, but it has always maintained a quality of teaching and research disproportionate to its size (in the 1990s: 'excellent' in Teaching Quality Assessment, and one of the smallest Departments in the country to gain 4A in the Research Assessment Exercise). The English Department of the current millennium looks very different in disciplinary terms from that of the post-war years, but a creative use of change has been for the past two decades an essential characteristic of the Department.

History

Like other parts of the Faculty of Arts, the Department of History has changed dramatically over the past 30 years. For one thing, student numbers have increased at a steady rate. The Department now regularly recruits as many as 100 students each year. Most of these are still single honours students, but many follow combined programmes – for example, Modern History and Politics, History and Sociology, History and Spanish/French/German. Most recently, the Department has launched a new programme in History and Jewish History and Culture. The Department also receives more students from abroad, largely through its links with European universities participating in the SOCRATES programme. Another significant change has been a shift in approach and subject focus. Broadly speaking, the Department offers a good deal more social history than it once did. Staff appointed in the past ten years or so tend to specialise in areas such as race, ethnicity, gender, and history and memory. Perhaps the most striking and successful example of this trend has been the growth of Jewish History and Culture, as reflected in the success of the Parkes Institute and the Parkes AHRB Centre for the Study of Jewish History and Culture.

Whereas in the past the Department spread itself quite widely (taking in Latin America, the Netherlands and Eastern Europe) it now concentrates its research and teaching interests around a number of distinct clusters: for example, US History, Jewish History and Culture, Medieval History. This emphasis has led to a distinctive undergraduate curriculum, as well as a successful Master's programme in History (another important innovation). Like other parts of the Faculty, the Department has many more postgraduate students than it did, say, ten or fifteen years ago, and is keen to expand its postgraduate numbers even further.

Winchester School of Art

The Winchester School of Art was integrated with the University of Southampton in 1996. This marked an important milestone in the Faculty's history as it opened up an unusual range of disciplines, giving the Faculty an opportunity to develop a quite distinctive identity.

With the merger the Faculty took on an exciting new mix of subjects: Fine Art which includes painting, sculpture and printmaking; and Design which includes textile design, textile art and fashion design, and the History of Art and Design (HAD). This gave the Arts Faculty a more distinctive range of disciplinary expertise and offered teaching and research in art and design practice. The Arts Faculty was immediately catapulted into a different league in terms of size. Before the merger the Arts Faculty was small compared with similar faculties in other universities. Winchester School of Art was about 60 per cent of the size of the old Faculty and as such was bigger than any of the existing departments. It still accounts for 40 per cent of the Faculty size in terms of student numbers and has raised the profile of the Arts Faculty within the University and within the region. Much of the research and teaching in HAD was empathetic with the work that existed in the original Faculty of Arts.

The number of students increased from approximately 350 to 1,000 over the decade to 2002. The School premises were purpose-built in the 1960s. After the merger, investment was made by the University in the development of two new buildings designed to house the expansion of its student numbers, and new facilities for fashion design, a digital media campus and also to include the internationally respected Textile Conservation Centre which moved its premises from Hampton Court Palace to the University in 1999. The Textile Conservation Centre has gained its reputation for the conservation of historical and contemporary textiles. Having the Centre on campus enables the School to link textile art and design, the history of textiles, and dress and textile conservation in new and exciting areas of research and the development of new curricula. The School also has one of the best specialist libraries in the sector and a gallery that works closely with Southern Arts in the curation and development of major exhibitions of art and craft in the region.

The School of Art has reinforced the Faculty's European focus and approach to teaching and research. Some students, particularly those studying design, have had work experience throughout Europe, particularly in Italy and France. A large number of students have benefited from exchange schemes with other universities across Europe. More recently, work placements and exchanges have extended beyond Europe to such countries as the USA and Australia. Some students have used video conferencing to link Winchester with its Studio and partner institutions in Barcelona, and the School has spearheaded the development of an MA programme within its own premises in Barcelona. The extension of research activity, both at postgraduate level and among the academic staff, is already planned with the expansion of its activities in Barcelona.

The School has always been interested in the development of inter-disciplinary work and to this end many of its single honours and postgraduate taught

Work at the Textile Conservation Centre.

The Winchester School of Art.

courses have offered students the opportunity to work across a broad spectrum of media and techniques. More recently, developments have included an increased use of video and computer technology in the production of art and design work. The School has also developed combined honours courses with the School of Modern Languages, with the result that it is one of the few places in the country where it is possible to study Fashion and French or Spanish.

In the development of the School's research and teaching, links are being forged with other Faculties within the University. Staff are teaching on the MEng course in Engineering and are also linking with the Engineering Faculty in the development of SMART fabrics. Academic staff at the School are respected international artists, designers, historians and conservators. This community of staff active in research continues to contribute to and enhance the reputation and excellent work that emerges from the School.

Top left and bottom: *pieces in a students' degree show at the Winchester School of Art.*

Top right: *the John Hansard Gallery.*

2. Engineering and Applied Science

In 1952 the Faculty of Engineering already had a national reputation. John Eustice, the first Professor of Engineering, had retired in 1931, to be succeeded by Thomas Cave-Browne-Cave, who had been a member of the engine design team of the airship R101. When Professor Cave-Browne-Cave retired in 1950, the Faculty of Engineering was awarded a second Chair. Archie Black came from Oxford to be Professor of Mechanical Engineering and Elfyn Richards, who had been chief aerodynamicist and assistant chief designer at Vickers Armstrong, became Professor of Aeronautical Engineering. At that time, the Faculty had four Departments: Aeronautical, Civil, Electrical and Mechanical Engineering. In 1953, Professor Eric Zepler brought Electronics into the Faculty, although it also maintained its presence in the Science Faculty. At that time, including Electronics, there were 20 academic staff members, with support from others in the Mathematics Department (which 'belonged' to three Faculties – Engineering, Science and Arts).

Engineering was seriously short of space, so it took advantage of the Government's 1952 invitation for institutions to submit plans for 'urgent extensions' of their facilities for technology, research and teaching. Black and Richards worked on a plan to provide the Engineering Departments and the

Left: *two students with Professor Eustice (top left) and the Crossley Engine, owned by the Engineering Faculty since 1897. Originally bought to provide engineering students with practical experience in the operation and performance of contemporary engines, it is still used regularly for undergraduate teaching.*

Below: *the Crossley Engine today.*

Department of Electronics with adequate accommodation. Although this was accepted in 1954, none of the new buildings was occupied until October 1959.

In the mid-1950s, the Faculty undertook the building of a hydraulic tidal model of Southampton Water and the Solent, providing a popular demonstration for visitors. It did this at the request of the Harbour Board which was anxious about the consequences of a proposed oil refinery on the east side of the Solent. The purpose of the model was to show whether the dredging of a deep channel to enable tankers to reach the planned refinery terminal near Hill Head would affect existing tidal streams and sedimentation. The model was so large that it required its own building and Edwin Gifford, a local consulting civil engineer, designed one. The model showed that the dredging would have no serious consequences but, for other reasons, the company involved – Caltex – abandoned its refinery plan. Caltex, which had paid for the model, then gave it to the University which used it for other studies concerning power stations and sewage discharges. It was also used by the University Sailing Club to study tides which might help in Solent racing. The model was demolished in 1978 and its building turned into the University's John Hansard Gallery (see pp.72–3).

During the second half of the University's first decade, the Faculty expanded rapidly. By the beginning of the 1962–3 session, the total teaching staff had increased to 46, with Peter Morice appointed to a new Chair in Civil Engineering in 1957, and Geoff L. G. A. Sims promoted to a new Chair in Electrical Engineering in 1959. Professor Zepler had just retired and had been replaced by Geoffrey G. D. Sims who, during the following 11 years, greatly influenced developments both within the Faculty and throughout the University.

On 6 May 1960 Sir George Edwards formally opened the Lanchester Building, named after Frederick W. Lanchester, the college's best-known engineering student of the nineteenth century, and the Tizard building, named after Sir Henry Tizard, Pro-Chancellor of the University from 1952 to 1959. The Lanchester Building contained the Faculty's administrative offices and many lecture rooms and laboratories. The Electronics Department moved into the top floor. The Tizard Building contained more laboratories and the Department of Aeronautics and Astronautics' 7' × 5' (2.1 × 1.5 m) wind tunnel. This wind tunnel, which had been a gift from Vickers Supermarine at Swindon (originally located in Southampton), was refurbished and a second large working section was added for helicopter rotor, industrial aerodynamics and yacht sail research. The third new building was occupied for the 1963–4 session. Called the Faraday Building, it consisted of a ten-storey tower for Electrical Engineering and a large laboratory block for Civil Engineering. The move of Electrical Engineering was the final stage in the career of Professor Sims, who had built up that Department as a senior lecturer. He was succeeded in 1964 by Percy Hammond, who became Professor of Electrical Power Engineering.

Meanwhile, Richards was continuing to lead research on the environmental and industrial effects of noise and by 1963 acoustics and vibration had become such an important part of the Faculty's activities that an Institute of Sound and Vibration Research (ISVR) was formed. As its head, Richards was retitled

Professor of Industrial Acoustics in 1964. He was succeeded as Professor of Aeronautics and Astronautics by Geoffrey Lilley, who joined the University in January 1965 from the College of Aeronautics, Cranfield. More professorships followed rapidly. In 1964–5 a new Chair of Engineering Materials was created in the Department of Mechanical Engineering and Ron Bell from Imperial College joined the Faculty, while Alec Gambling was appointed to a second Chair of Electronics. In the following year, Jim Nightingale from Leicester University became Professor of Control Engineering in the Departments of Electrical Engineering and Electronics. In 1968, Professor Black was exempted from teaching duties in order to help the Vice-Chancellor and, in the following year, Stan Hutton took over as Professor of Mechanical Engineering, having come from a similar Chair at University College, Cardiff.

Already by 1964–5 the Faculty had 344 undergraduates and 118 postgraduates, resulting in a new 'acute shortage' of laboratory and office space. This was eased by adding three further floors to the Tizard Building, shared between the ISVR and Aeronautics and Astronautics, and occupied from early 1969. This was preceded by the Rayleigh Building, opened late in 1968, to provide special acoustics, vibration and other test cell facilities.

Another post-Robbins development was the launch of two new degree courses. One was in Nautical Studies, for deck officers in the Merchant Navy. The second arose from the yacht research introduced into the Department of Aeronautics and Astronautics by Thomas Tanner, and the need to overcome the lack of a degree course in Naval Architecture in the South of England. Thus Ship Science was introduced as a sub-Department in Aeronautics and

The 1929 Dennis 'Toastrack' – the Engineering Faculty's long-serving minibus – being readied by Geoff Thomas for an outing, with encouragment from Lord Montagu of Beaulieu.

Astronautics. The first holder of the Chair in Ship Science was Geoffrey Goodrich, who joined the University in 1968 from the Ship Division of the National Physical Laboratory.

The close ties between the ISVR/Department of Aeronautics and Astronautics and industry, as pioneered originally by Professor Richards, were continued under Professor Lilley. In 1967 the Department established a new Industrial Advisory Unit for Yacht Research, Design and Development. This later became the Wolfson Advisory Unit for Marine Technology and Industrial Aerodynamics. Other Departments in the Faculty expanded their ties with industry through a generous grant from the Wolfson Foundation. In 1968–9, this awarded £30,000 to the Industrial Noise Unit, and in 1970–1 £90,000 for the Industrial Advisory Units in Engineering Materials, Applied Electronics and Marine Craft Design. All these units eventually became self-supporting.

For some years a number of Faculty members, including Geoffrey Sims, Henri Kemhadjian and Bill Bright, had felt strongly that Britain's growing association with the wider Europe made it a good idea to offer students modern language courses. In the early 1970s, first French, then German, were included as options in the third year of the BSc courses, to make it easier for graduates to liaise more effectively with continental European engineering companies.

In 1974 Lord Zuckerman visited the Faculty. As a trustee of the Wolfson Foundation, he had initiated its policy of founding advisory units at universities. That year Southampton's units had a total of 45 staff and an income of £223,000. Next year Leonard Wolfson visited the University and soon afterwards the Wolfson Trust made a grant of £250,000 for an extension of the Rayleigh Building. On 26 September 1978, Zuckerman returned to open what now became the Wolfson Building and provided accommodation for the ISVR's advisory units.

The teaching event of the decade was the introduction of a four-year engineering degree under the leadership of Professor Bob Smith. The idea behind this was the need of students for a course which included a larger amount of industrially-based professional work than they could be given in three years. Those participating would take the first two years of the existing BSc course, before changing to the 'design-enriched' four-year course for the next two years, as opposed to the 'management-enriched' degrees proposed elsewhere. During these they would take part in real-life, multi-disciplinary and design group projects. They would also spend 20 weeks in industry. In 1979 the Senate approved the course and in October that year the 22 students selected for the pilot scheme began their third year, graduating in July 1981. Prior to the establishment of the four-year course, Professor Hutton had collaborated with Professor John Smith of the Sociology Department on a survey of mechanical engineering education in Germany. Financed by the Department of Industry, the survey's findings helped to encourage the initiation of the four-year course.

At that time, the Faculty, in common with the rest of the University, was still wrestling with severe budgetary constraints. In 1982 it was pressed by the

University to reduce its intake because of its four-year course, in spite of this being recommended as the future national model for such courses. The Faculty was frustrated by not being allowed to educate as many engineers as it might have done, at a time when the Government repeatedly said that the country needed more.

Despite such troubles, there were successes and expansion. By 1982, the advisory units had grown to 12, with an annual turnover of £1 million. The recently formed Institute of Irrigation Studies under Dr Janusz Rydzewski's leadership was proving an outstanding success, while Professors Gambling and Payne had had new recognition for their work on optical fibres. By 1984 there was hope of a new building for Electronics. Only in 1986, however, could the Faculty report that it had weathered the financial crisis and balanced its budget, with a fully devolved and accountable budgetary system introduced by Professors Geoffrey Goodrich and Roy Farrar.

During the final 15 years of the century, the four-year course continued to flourish, leading now to a four-year MEng as well as a three-year BEng, and the quality of new students remained high. An important enlargement of the Faculty occurred in 1986, when Computer Studies was transferred from the Faculty of Mathematical Studies (see page 182) to the Electronics Department, as a result of the University's successful bid for extra student places in both subjects. In terms of staff and students, the Department then became one-third of the Faculty. In 1986, David Barron, who had been appointed Professor of Computation in 1967, wrote that it was probably the only Department in the country which encompassed the whole extent of the subject 'from theoretical computer science to the fabrication of silicon chips.'

At the beginning of the 1990s, research assessment ratings had been excellent for Electrical and Electronic Engineering and the ISVR, good for Civil Engineering, but disappointing for Mechanical/Aeronautical Engineering and Computer Science. To improve on these results the Faculty set up a Forward Look Working Party to make proposals for the years up to 2000. It recommended concentrating on inter-Departmental and cross-Faculty work in Marine Technology, Space and Transport, and in Innovative Manufacture. Two cross-Faculty results were the creation of an Engineering Business Centre (with Social Sciences), and a Human Sciences and Biomedical Engineering Research Group (with Medicine). The Faculty was already directing much effort towards European Community support, which in 1992–3 amounted to 17 per cent of total Faculty funding.

In 1992 the Faculty introduced a foundation year for students with inappropriate entry qualifications. Around 500 students who would otherwise have been excluded from studying engineering at Southampton have since benefited from this route. The proportion of first-class honours degrees awarded to these entrants has been comparable with that of other entry routes. The course is taught at Southampton City College and Weymouth College. Two years later, the Royal Navy Engineering sponsorship scheme was formally inaugurated. This followed an open-tender bid by the then Dean, Professor Chris Rice, to the Navy to transfer training from the Royal Naval Engineering

College at Plymouth to a civilian university. Now, about 100 Navy students are studying for engineering degrees.

The Faculty had reason to be pleased with the results of the 1996 Research Assessment Exercise. Electronics and Computer Science and Electrical Engineering both received 5* ratings and academic staff engaged in research in Departments which received 5 or 5* ratings formed 85 per cent of total research staff. The following year the Higher Education Funding Council for England gave teaching in the Faculty equally good results. Electronics and Computer Science and Electrical Engineering scored 24 out of 24, ISVR and Ship Science 23; Aeronautics and Astronautics, and Civil and Environmental Engineering 21. Nevertheless, the Faculty now began in a systematic way to plan for even better results. One form this took was to concentrate Faculty research into four groupings working in common or overlapping fields: Electronics (with Optoelectronics), Computer Science and Electrical Engineering; Civil and Environmental Engineering; Engineering Sciences (Aeronautics and Astronautics, Engineering Materials, Mechanical Engineering and Ship Science); and ISVR. The groupings recognised that research projects increasingly involve staff from more than one Department. The Faculty also demonstrated even more firmly its commitment to research by increasing to 95 per cent the members of its academic staff who were research-active. The results of the 2001 Research Assessment Exercise were published on 14 December 2001. The University made a dramatic leap up the national league tables for research quality, with the Engineering Faculty achieving a spectacular outcome. The Departments of Electronics and Computer Science, Civil and Environmental Engineering, the ISVR and the School of Engineering Sciences each gained the top grade of 5* making Engineering at Southampton the UK's leading Faculty for research. The remainder of this chapter looks at the growth of this research over the past 50 years on a Departmental basis.

Aeronautics and Astronautics

In its early years, research in the Department of Aeronautics (or, as it became in 1959, Aeronautics and Astronautics) was dominated by Richards's work on noise. He and his team published papers on helicopter noise, jet noise and ground silencing installations. By the late 1950s, they had begun work on underwater noise and had investigated noise nuisance around several German airports. By 1963, acoustics had become such a large part of the Department's activities that the Institute of Sound and Vibration Research was formed (see pages 153–6).

When Ken Bray arrived in 1957 as a lecturer, his research was initially into hypersonic aerodynamics and the associated aerothermochemistry problems. However, after some years his interests developed in the direction of turbulent combustion, for which he became internationally recognised. He later became Professor of Gas Dynamics and Head of Department, before moving to Cambridge in 1985.

Following Richards's move to the ISVR, Geoffrey Lilley, who had assisted Professor Cave-Browne-Cave in conducting the first experiment on supersonic flow at the University, was appointed Professor of Aeronautics and Astronautics. Under Professor Lilley, the teaching of the undergraduate course was reorganised and research initiated in many of the major disciplines of aeronautics and astronautics. After lengthy negotiations, the Westland Helicopter Co. agreed to the endowment of the Westland Chair in Helicopter Engineering, and Jeffrey Jones, who had pioneered helicopter research in the Department, became its first holder. After Professor Jones left to become Technical Director of Westland, Ian Cheeseman, from NGTE, Pyestock, became second holder of the Chair. He continued his researches on helicopter noise and aircraft for short take-off and landing.

In 1965, Lilley negotiated a formal link with the Royal Aircraft Establishment (RAE), Farnborough, which put many of the research scientists at Farnborough in touch with their colleagues in similar disciplines in the University. Both theoretical and experimental research conducted at Farnborough by RAE staff under University guidance could now lead to the University's higher degrees. The link remained an important bridge between University teaching and research and government research in aeronautics and related fields for the next 25 years.

By the mid-1970s, the Department had established the widest range of experimental aerodynamics facilities among UK universities. This covered the range from low speed through to hypersonic, reaching Mach numbers in excess of 10 (by comparison, Concorde cruises at Mach 2). This range of facilities and accompanying expertise attracted wide support from the Ministries of Defence and Industry. In the same period, Mike Goodyer demonstrated the principle of the cryogenic wind tunnel. The world's first wind tunnel operating at liquid nitrogen temperature (-196 °C) was designed and demonstrated in the Department. The principle was subsequently used in major national and international wind tunnels in the USA and Europe.

In 1981, the RAE No. 2 11' × 8' (3.2 m × 2.6 m) wind tunnel was presented to the Department by RAE, Farnborough. This was installed next to the Wolfson Building in a new building, later to be named 'The R. J. Mitchell Wind Tunnel' after the famous Southampton aeroplane designer of the Second World War *Spitfire*. A moving ground section was added to the tunnel, its working section was lengthened and a new anechoic section was added for aerodynamic noise studies. This assumed national importance in studying road-vehicle aerodynamics, such as spray from lorries, and was a major influence in stimulating advances in racing-car design. It also made possible a new research programme on aerodynamic performance and noise from propellers. In the wake of the oil crisis of the 1970s, there was renewed interest in the development of more efficient propeller-powered commercial aircraft. This research was initiated by Professor John Williams, who had joined the Department under the University/RAE link agreement, and grew out of the Department's long-standing interest in the performance of helicopter rotors. In 1992, extensive improvements were made to the 11' × 8' and 7' × 5' tunnels to

The Southampton University Manpowered Aircraft (SUMPAC), constructed by the Aeronautics Department, making the first ever manpowered flight at Lasham airfield, Hampshire, 1961.

meet the increasing technical demands of commercial users. These modifications resulted in an extension of the operational performance of the wind tunnels to match the increased speeds required by Formula 1 and Indy racing cars.

In the early 1980s, a sub-Department of Engineering Materials had been created under Professor Geoff Chadwick. During its first year, the title of Professor of Electronics Materials was conferred on Dr Arthur Willoughby, and studies on materials for use in the electronics industry were an important research strand. Other research programmes included application of advanced casting techniques to various alloys and steels and research into fracture mechanics for aircraft applications. Within a couple of years, the sub-Department had begun to turn its attention additionally to materials for surgical implants.

By the early 1990s, engineering materials research had been grouped into three main areas: Aerospace structural materials and shape memory alloys; Electronics materials, including solar cell materials; Biomaterials. Electronics materials had a very high profile and, together with other Departments and Faculties, it was proposed to establish a Centre for Solar Energy Conversion and Applications. By the mid-1990s, the Southampton Test and Reference Facility (as it was called), one of three in the UK, was studying ways in which solar energy could be produced and integrated with the national grid. Biomedical materials research had broadened to cover dental materials and failure mechanisms, while research on composite materials and light alloys – fibre-reinforced alloys based on magnesium and aluminium – had also increased.

By the mid-1990s research within the Department had been reorganised into three main areas: Structures, Dynamics, Control and Rotorcraft (SDCR); Aerothermofluids and Computational Fluid Dynamics (CFD); Astronautics. The work in SDCR encompassed the study of noise and vibration in engineering structures, the application of active control technology to fixed- and rotary-wing aircraft, and the aero-elastic behaviour of helicopter rotor blades. In

Aerothermofluids and CFD, experimental research was undertaken in both low- and high-speed aerodynamics; the Department had a strong reputation in CFD and ongoing work encompassed steady, unsteady, and reacting flows, and there was particular emphasis on parallel and vector processing. Astronautics had well-established research activities, including orbital mechanics and the ground simulation and in-orbit measurement of atomic oxygen effects on spacecraft materials.

Institute of Sound and Vibration Research (ISVR)

The foundation of the Institute of Sound and Vibration Research in 1963 depended on a number of factors, but primarily it was due to the foresight and inspiration of Elfyn Richards. In the decade before 1962, he had encouraged and directed the development of a major research effort into noise and vibration in the Department of Aeronautics and Astronautics. In the same period there had been growing public concern about the increasing environmental and social impact of noise.

On his appointment to the University, Professor Richards began to seek funding for research into noise and noise-induced fatigue in aircraft structures both from industry and government agencies. By the time that the University Council approved the formation of the ISVR from October 1963, Richards had again approached a number of industrial acquaintances for financial support. From Hawker-Siddeley, he had obtained agreement to support both a readership and lectureship in acoustics and vibration, and from Westland support for a readership in helicopter-blade vibration. Richards also negotiated with Academic Press to establish a new international *Journal of Sound and Vibration*. Philip Doak, who joined the University in 1962 as the Hawker-Siddeley lecturer, became the editor, a post which he has retained to the present day, although now as an Emeritus Professor.

During 1962 proposals were put successfully to the Department of Scientific and Industrial Research (DSIR) for a major grant to develop the Institute and its work on applied acoustics and noise control. Architects for the new acoustics laboratories were appointed in July 1963. The building grant was supplemented early in 1965 by the Science Research Council (which had by then replaced the DSIR). The new acoustic and vibration facilities were completed in March 1968 and opened as the Rayleigh Building in that November. By that time three more floors had been added to the Tizard Building to house the expanding activities of the Institute and the Department of Aeronautics and Astronautics.

As well as continuing established research in aeronautical acoustics and vibration, new research was begun in industrial acoustics and vibration, supported by industrially sponsored research fellowships, contracts and payments for consultation. This included road-transport vehicles, hovercraft, structural fatigue in nuclear reactors, commercial-fan silencing, other machinery and manufacturing processes, building vibration, traffic- and

Clinical assessment in the ISVR Hearing and Balance Centre.

airport-noise studies, subjective acoustics, subjective and physiological aspects of noise and, in particular, of impulsive noise and community reaction to noise. According to Professor Brian Clarkson, senior lecturer in structural vibration when the Institute started and later (1967–78) its Director, 'From the early days, the research was aimed at longer-term industrial problems. The team approach allowed a comprehensive attack which usually ranged from purely theoretical studies through physical models in the laboratory to full-scale tests in industry or government research labs. Now, of course, computer modelling is inserted as an essential component of the chain. Even today few research organisations in the world can claim such a comprehensive cover of their subject.'

In parallel with the research programme, there had been a growing demand in industry for help and advice on everyday noise-control problems. The demand for such short-timescale projects far exceeded the time that the academic and senior research staff had available to respond effectively. With the help of a pump-priming grant from the Wolfson Foundation, the University

Professor Philip Nelson, Yuvi Kahana and Takashi Takeuchi experimenting with virtual acoustic imaging in the ISVR anechoic chamber.

approved the formation of the Wolfson Industrial Noise Consulting Unit within the Institute in 1968. Its specific tasks were to provide the main interface with industry and the community, to make available the expertise within the Institute, and feed back ideas and specific requirements into the research and teaching programme. The Wolfson unit continues as the ISVR Consultancy Services. The Automotive Design Advisory Unit was formed in 1972 to provide specialist services to the automotive industry and was equipped with laboratories at Chilworth Manor.

Another development was audiology research, with the establishment of working links with the staff of the Southampton and Wessex Regional hospitals and with the co-operation of the University's Department of Physiology. Among other factors, appropriate noise-control specifications depend on a knowledge of auditory physiological and psychological function and auditory damage risk criteria. Such studies had been a subject of research in the Institute since its foundation. Clinical studies and audiology research were encouraged by the provision of a suite of special rooms and facilities in a substantial extension to the Tizard Building to which they moved in 1970, forming the Wessex Regional Audiology Centre. In 1993, the Centre was restructured as the ISVR Hearing and Balance Centre. This was intended to strengthen the research base in audiology, particularly in relation to cochlear implants and the assessment of hearing and balance functions. This is part of the Human Sciences Research Group which also includes the Human Factors Unit developed by Professor Mike Griffin to study the response of humans to motion and vibration.

The first six directors of the ISVR on the occasion of the Scientific Advisory Committee Meeting, October 1992. Left to right: Bob White, Joe Hammond, Brian Clarkson, Chris Rice, John Large, Elfyn Richards.

In the late 1960s, the ISVR recognised the need to have distributed computational facilities for the capture and analysis of experimental acoustic and vibration data. This Data Analysis Centre later became the Data Analysis Research Group with the appointment of Joe Hammond, later Dean of the Faculty – the first former undergraduate of the Faculty to become its Dean.

In the early and mid-1970s, there was considerable national interest in fuel economy. This led to an increase in the activity of the Automotive Engineering Group, under the leadership of Professor Theo Priede. High-speed diesel engines for passenger cars were one subject of study. Over a period of years automotive work and, more recently, rail system research have come together with structural dynamics in the relatively new Dynamics Research Group.

During the 1980s, research expanded further and, reflecting this, the Signal Processing and Control Group was formed, bringing together the work of Joe Hammond with the work on active control led by Philip Nelson and Steve Elliott. There was considerable interest in active noise-control ('anti-sound') for both automobiles and aeroplanes. By 1988 this research had progressed enough for flight trials of the first propeller aircraft to incorporate an active noise-control system (a BAe748 48-seater). Today, more than 500 aircraft in service have such systems fitted. Another area to expand during the 1980s was research in underwater acoustics. This represented a development of work in the Fluid Dynamics and Acoustics Group of the Institute which included long-serving ISVR staff such as Dr Mike Fisher, Professor Frank Fahy, Professor Chris Morfey and Professor Peter Davies. This led to the building of the A. B. Wood Laboratory dedicated to research in this area and to the appointment of Professor Tim Leighton to work in this field.

During the 1990s, Professor Philip Nelson, currently Director of the ISVR, worked with a consortium of Japanese companies on fundamental studies of stereophonic sound-reproduction. This led to a revolutionary new sound-reproduction system which can control the direction from which a sound appears to come. This Stereo Dipole offers a wide number of applications, particularly in entertainment and multimedia.

Over its lifespan of nearly 40 years, the ISVR has established an international reputation as a world centre for the study of acoustics and vibration. From relatively small beginnings – in 1965 its total income was barely £200,000 – it has grown to an organisation with an annual turnover of £7m. It plays a key role in European Union initiatives in sound and vibration and has strong links with many academic institutions and industrial companies around the world.

Ship Science

In his 1979 report as Dean of the Faculty, Brian Clarkson wrote that 'The distinctive discipline of Ship Science was born and nurtured in the Department of Aeronautics and Astronautics but the growth of the undergraduate course and the postgraduate activities has now reached the stage where a separate identity is required.' In the period during which it had been in Aeronautics and Astronautics, Ship Science had built up research interests under the leadership of Professor Goodrich. Now there was a gradual expansion of these activities, covering subjects such as the capsizing of ships, measurement of forces and moments on ship rudders, and the prediction of ship response in waves. Most of the research at this time was supported by the Ministry of Defence, although the Wolfson Unit for Marine Technology was receiving money from industry, notably for development of the use of microcomputers in ship design.

By the late 1980s, work was continuing on low-speed aerodynamics of thick aerofoil sections. The problems associated with stall regulation of wind turbines had been studied extensively in the large wind tunnel using liquid-crystal flow-visualisation techniques. A large contract had been started on the study of ship propeller–rudder interactions, sponsored jointly by SERC and the MOD. This followed from work on the fundamental design of ships' rudders. The MOD had also awarded a contract for the development of a new system for the control of roll stabilisers, with the aim of minimising the lateral motion of ships at specific points along their length, using the fin stabilisers rather than minimising the roll angle.

In 1990 Goodrich retired and Professor Geraint Price was appointed his successor. This meant that the Department gained an active and enthusiastic research group studying hydroelasticity theory of marine structures. Software tools for the solution of general computational fluid-dynamics problems using parallel computing had been developed on the Department's array of transputers. The prediction of ship motion was reaching a successful conclusion. An area of expanding interest was the use of composite materials in ship and boat construction. The Department's towing tank facility proved immensely valuable in an investigation into the resistance of components of catamarans.

In the early 1990s, the Department completed a unique new facility, affectionately dubbed the 'Fortress' (Flexible Orthogonal Rig for Testing Real Ship and Boat Structures) which allowed basic research into ship structures to be undertaken. The rig underpinned a growing basic and applied research programme and was also used for Wolfson work, so establishing a clearly defined mechanism for technology transfer within the Department. In 1994, the Department signed a collaborative research agreement with the Solid Mechanics Research Centre at the Beijing University of Aeronautics and Astronautics and the Chinese Ship Scientific Research Centre, Wuxi, to study damage and failure criteria in metals and composite materials.

The Ship Science Department's towing tank.

The Department of Ship Science.

Above: *the 'Fortress' rig (Flexible Orthogonal Rig for Testing Real Ship and Boat Structures), specially developed for a three-year research programme in conjunction with Britain's Royal National Lifeboat Institution (RNLI), the Department of Trade and Industry, and the Engineering and Physical Sciences Research Council to develop faster and lighter lifeboats.*

Left: *Mr Peter Nicholson, Chairman of the RNLI, and Professor Sir Howard Newby, Vice-Chancellor, at the RNLI partnership launch, February 2001.*

Civil and Environmental Engineering

Civil Engineering was something of a Cinderella subject in the Engineering Faculty until the appointment of its first full Professor, Peter Morice, in 1957. Some civil engineering research had been carried out earlier, but the Department had been administratively under Archie Black. For the newly independent Department, 'some of the first battles which had to be fought,' Professor Morice recalls, 'were to gain control of certain laboratories. The Tidal Model was an obvious Civil Engineering facility but others had to be prised from Mechanical Engineering.'

Early in 1959, the Department was visited by a representative of Ove Arup and Partners, consulting engineers for building the Sydney Opera House based on a design by the Danish architect Bjorn Utzon. The structure was to be a novel multi-thin shell form and Arup required analytical studies as well as structural and wind-tunnel model tests. One of the first jobs was an aerodynamic study using a small-scale wooden model of the main hall. This was carried out in the Aeronautics and Astronautics Department's wind tunnel and, although it was satisfactory as a preliminary test, it demonstrated the need for a large, low-speed facility. At this time the new wind tunnel was being designed for the second of the Faculty's new laboratories, the Tizard Building. This new wind tunnel incorporated a large 12-ft. square low-speed section, a facility which was often used by the Department during the next few years for building studies.

There was by this time a wide range of research activity in the Department, especially structural engineering under the guidance of Hugh Tottenham, who later became Professor of Structural Engineering. The number of research students was increasing and studies were in hand in the field of thin shells generally, in computer studies and finite elements, in thick shells for nuclear reactors, in concrete and timber, in industrial aerodynamics and in plastics structures. Research was also continuing in various aspects of hydraulics, such as channel flow and coastal and maritime hydraulics.

The arrival at the beginning of the 1962–3 session of Roy Butterfield was the start of a very productive research development within the Department, especially in the field of foundations and piling. One study in which Butterfield, who was appointed to a personal Chair in 1978, was deeply involved, was concerned with relieving the problems of the sinking of Venice. Another field of research was developed by Howard Allen on the structural use of plastics, particularly fibre-reinforced plastics. In the late 1960s, the Faculty acquired additional laboratory facilities at Chilworth Manor and a structural plastics laboratory was established. It was here that Professor Allen's team developed work begun in Russia on glass-fibre reinforced cements. It did some of the

The Sunsurfer came third in the 1999 Alice Springs to Adelaide World Solar Challenge for solar-assisted racing cycles.

first research using Zirconia glass which was essential to resist alkaline attack by cement.

In 1963, following discussions with a number of senior consulting engineers, Dr Rydzewski had concluded that there was a shortage of young irrigation engineers throughout the world. He therefore started discussions with the government's Department of Technical Co-operation with a view to the Civil Engineering Department establishing a postgraduate course in the field. The Southampton course was the first in this subject to be run in Western Europe. During 1978 discussions took place concerning the future of irrigation studies. There seemed to be a need to expand the work and build up a stronger lecturing team as well as to strengthen research. Following discussions with the government department then concerned (the Overseas Development Administration), further funding was offered and the establishment of an Institute within the Department, having some degree of separate financial status, was suggested. The Institute of Irrigation Studies was set up and Rydzewski became its first Director, which he remained until his retirement as a Professor in 1990.

Professor Tom Williams was appointed in 1967 to a Chair which was originally described as construction engineering. However, after his arrival Williams felt that a more important field of work was presenting itself with the increased national concern with transportation problems, especially in respect of highways. He therefore set about building a team which could teach and research in this field. Research in transportation was underpinned by the establishment of the Transportation Research Group when the Department was awarded a Ministry of Technology research contract to study the business traffic potential of vertical take-off and landing facilities in the UK. Other contracts soon followed concerned with various aspects of surface transport by road, rail and sea. It was not long, however, before highway studies dominated the work of the group, drawing funds from many sources including the Transport and Road Research Laboratory, the Departments of Trade and Industry, Environment and Transport as well as the Science Research Council. This research formed a basis for Tom Williams's leading role as a UK government adviser in the 1970s and 1980s.

Mike McDonald took over the group in 1982 and it has grown to be one of the leading units of its kind in the UK, with a particular emphasis on the application of Intelligent Transport Systems (ITS) to a wide range of traffic and transport problems. The group has contributed substantially to the development of road traffic accident prediction models, on-line priority for public transport and the development of integrated traffic management, significantly through extensive research links with Hampshire County Council and Southampton City Council. The group has recently been at the forefront of setting the ITS research agenda for the European Union. While many of the group's activities have been concerned with UK transport problems, it has also been active in both research and advisory work in Africa, North and South America, Europe, the Middle East and the Far East.

In 1993, the name of the Department was changed to Civil and

Environmental Engineering, reflecting the growing importance of teaching and research in the latter area. In 1994, Trevor Tanton was appointed British Gas Professor of Environmental Technology, a post linked to the development of a substantial research effort targeting environmental problems in Kazakhstan. William Powrie was appointed Professor of Geotechnical Engineering in succession to Roy Butterfield and subsequent work in this area has included field-based research in landfill engineering and transport infrastructure. Projects of particular interest included studies of temporary prop loads on the London Underground Jubilee Line extension, and the behaviour of embankments and retaining walls on the Channel Tunnel rail link. In structures, the Department collaborated with Ship Science in the design of the 'Fortress' rig and on studies of foam-cored structural panels for RNLI lifeboats, as well as structural strengthening using carbon-fibre composites.

In recent years, the Department has seen significant changes. Twelve of the current members of academic staff have joined since 1995, with the most recent professorial appointments being in Infrastructure Engineering (Chris Clayton, formerly of Surrey University), Hydraulics (John Chaplin, formerly of City University) and Structures (Marcus Lee, Swansea). The Department collaborates widely with industry and other academic groups. Its activities are now focused firmly on the key problems facing society at the start of the twenty-first century: transport, the environment (including energy and waste management) and infrastructure.

Electrical Engineering

Electrical Engineering got its first Professor in 1959, when Geoff Sims, who had been senior lecturer in the subject since 1952, was awarded a Chair. Initially, little research was undertaken, but this changed with the appointment in 1964 of Percy Hammond as Professor of Electrical Power Engineering and Head of Electrical Engineering, a double post which he occupied for the next 25 years. Financial support for research came in the form of a large rolling grant from the Science Research Council, which was concerned by the national shortage of electrical power engineers. The Council invited the Department to submit an application for a grant to enable it to become a centre of research for electrical machines. The first instalment of this grant, in 1966, enabled the University to appoint additional academic and technical staff and to equip a state-of-the-art laboratory.

By the mid-1970s, the Department was investigating new types of motors and generators, in particular permanent magnet and superconducting machines. By 1981, the University was able to report that the permanent magnet machine 'has a secure future and will replace some of the traditional forms of motor and generator . . . the University now holds most of the significant patents in this area.' Work in the superconduction field not only covered motors, but also aspects of electrical transmission, such as the ageing of insulating materials at the low temperatures required for superconductivity. In

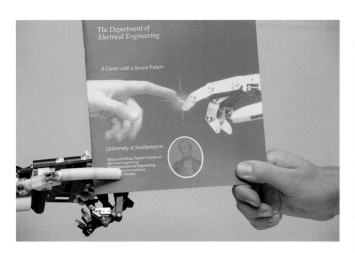

Dr Paul Chappell's Southampton-Remedi Artificial Hand and a natural hand holding an undergraduate booklet.

1965 Jim Nightingale was appointed Professor of Control Engineering, jointly with the Department of Electronics. Nightingale initiated research into the development of medical prostheses, notably an artificial hand. Work on this, which was supported by J. E. Hanger Ltd, manufacturers of artificial limbs, had progressed to clinical trials by the early 1980s. It had also led to the Department developing an interest in robotics, particularly in the control of tactile manipulators, where applications in automatic assembly, inspection and sensing were studied. By 1987, this applied research and development programme had resulted in the delivery to the Ministry of Defence of a whole arm manipulator, an instrument similar in size to the human arm and designed to operate where there was a radiation hazard.

As a result of the increased emphasis on electromechanical subjects, coupled with indications from industry – especially the automotive sector – that graduates in this specialism would be eminently employable, an Electromechanical Engineering degree course was introduced in 1988 by Professors Hammond and Farrar as a joint venture between the Departments of Electrical and Mechanical Engineering. The course was designed to gain a broad-based understanding of a blend of electrical and mechanical technologies with some specialisation in the senior years. It still operates today.

Electrostatics research at Southampton was launched in 1965 when Bill Bright was appointed as Reader. He was promoted to a personal Chair in Applied Electrostatics four years later. Under his leadership, the Electrostatics Group established an international reputation and several industrial partnership research programmes were set up in powder-handling hazards, explosions in oil tankers, electrostatic painting and spraying techniques and electrostatic powder coating. After Bright died in 1978, the value placed by British industry on the pioneering work in electrostatics done by the Department was demonstrated by the establishment of the Bill Bright Chair in Applied Electrostatics, supported by ten companies.

Adrian Bailey became the first holder of this Chair in 1981. He increased the existing co-operation with industry, especially on powder-handling hazards in collaboration with the Wolfson Electrostatics Unit (which Bright had pioneered) and on electrostatic precipitation projects. The powder-coating work continued and was extended into liquids spraying/atomisation programmes with an early emphasis on crop-spraying applications. This latter research became more and more refined and developed applications in the medical field. Drug and other therapeutic aerosols were electrically charged so they could be administered to the lungs or nasal regions of human beings in a controlled and precise manner.

As a result of substantial industrial funding, a Bioelectrostatics Research Centre was established in 1995 to promote the collaborative research activities initiated by Professor John Hughes of Electrical Engineering and colleagues in the School of Biological Sciences. Funding in excess of £2.5 million has supported a unique multi-disciplinary research team, bringing together expertise in electrostatics, health care and biological science. Evaluation of electrostatic techniques for the control of asthma and for killing bacteria is a novel research activity established within the Centre.

The benefaction in 1991 of £256,000 by Alcatel Submarine Networks (formerly STC Submarine Systems) enabled a modern dedicated high-voltage laboratory to be built. It was designed to accommodate research and testing of high-voltage insulation systems, an essential area of electrical power engineering, headed by Professor Tony Davies. Further industrial funding and University support provided a substantial base of equipment resulting in a research facility which is unique in the UK. It contains the most up-to-date equipment for the generation of DC (600,000 volts), AC (300,000 volts) and impulse voltages (1,000,000 volts) providing a facility for the research into the electrical properties of polymeric insulating materials with particular emphasis on power cables.

In order to maintain the stability and ensure the future growth of electrical engineering in the University, the Department amalgamated in 2000 with the larger Department of Electronics and Computer Science. Both the undergraduate degree courses in Electrical and Electromechanical Engineering continued, as there is still a strong and growing need for electrical engineers in industry. The research group became an Electrical Power Engineering Research Group in Electronics and Computer Science and, because of its relatively small size, its research activities became narrower in breadth but with increased depth. It maintains its high profile in the fields of high voltage, electrostatics and electromagnetics.

Electronics and Computer Science

In 1949 Eric Zepler became Professor of Electronics. Between the Wars he had been chief of radio design at Telefunken in Germany, before escaping to Britain in 1935 and joining Marconi at Chelmsford. Zepler was interned as an enemy alien in 1939, released and appointed lecturer in physics at Southampton in 1941, but then seconded to the Cavendish Laboratory, Cambridge, returning to Southampton to be made Head of the new Department of Electronics, Telecommunications and Radio Engineering in 1946.

In the first few years after Southampton gained University status, research in electronics was concerned mainly with paramagnetic and electron spin resonance spectroscopies. It is worth remembering that, at this time, the modern world of electronics had barely begun: the transistor, ancestor of today's micro-electronic circuits, was not invented until 1948, and the first demonstration of a laser took place only in 1960 – coincidentally, the same year as the Department shortened its name to just Electronics.

Alec Gambling joined the Department in late 1957 and initially carried out research on microwaves, but soon after developed an interest in lasers as an optical source for communications. Research was then aimed at overcoming two basic disadvantages of lasers: they were crude and they were short-lived. To turn them into coherent, stable, optical sources took many years. Even so, the problem remained of how to transmit modulated laser light over very long distances. Gambling took the first, revolutionary step in 1964 when he suggested that glass fibres might be the least unlikely way of doing so. This prediction proved to be spectacularly realised.

In 1962, research in the Department took another step towards its present eminence, when a new research group was formed by Ken Nichols and Greville Bloodworth to study the philosophy, design and construction of microcircuits. This activity grew rapidly and soon had an experimental electron beam welding machine for making microcircuits and was looking at the properties and applications of thin films and integrated circuits.

Zepler retired in the following year and was succeeded by Geoffrey Sims, who remained Professor and Head of Department for the next 11 years before leaving to become Vice-Chancellor of Sheffield University. Under his leadership, the Department's academic staff increased fourfold from 7 to 28 and research groups were created in pattern recognition, medical electronics and telecommunications.

By the mid-1970s, through the work of Nichols and Henri Kemhadjian, progress in computer-aided design of micro-electronic circuits had been such that Gambling (then the Dean) could report that 'New circuits can now be conceived, designed and made in the Department, all in the space of a few weeks – something which cannot be done in any other university laboratory and in few industrial ones.' In 1977–8, the Department received a special SRC grant of £200,000 to extend these facilities so that devices and circuits could be made for other universities. There was more to come. In 1980, the Department received a major SRC grant for the micro-electronics fabrication facility and two UGC grants for microprocessor applications engineering, one of which was specifically for the establishment of a Chair in the subject, to which John Brignell was appointed. Support for the fabrication facility continued over the years and when the Mountbatten Building was completed in 1991 it included a £5 million world-class facility for the fabrication of silicon microcircuits and optical fibres. By 1997, this had become the EPSRC National Silicon Fabrication Facility.

While micro-electronics and optical fibres continued to be major research activities, during the 1970s the Department also produced results in a rather different area. The Man-Machine Systems Research Group developed electronic aids for hearing-impaired people, which included both a transcription system and television subtitling system. The latter was developed in conjunction with the Independent Broadcasting Authority. By the early 1980s, both systems had been licensed commercially.

In 1983, Ray Steele joined the Department from Bell Laboratories as Professor of Communications to replace the late John Betts, and introduced an extensive research programme for improved worldwide communication based on cellular radio. This was supported by both SERC and British Telecommunications. One of the group's other developments was the DaRT system, a self-switching radio telephone which provided real possibilities for building telephone networks in rural areas where there was no infrastructure.

The Department's most significant work in electronics probably remains that in optical fibre communications. During the 1970s scientists and engineers throughout the world attempted to produce fibres that would carry light signals greater distances. At first, purifying the glass was thought to be the solution. Numerous innovations were made both at Southampton and elsewhere but, even by the early 1980s, signals needed to be reinforced with expensive electronic amplifiers every 50–100 kilometres. So far the fibres had been considered as purely inert carriers of the light. Now Southampton made the most important discovery of all by inventing amplifiers with cores doped with the rare earth element, erbium. 'For years we had been trying to purify the glass,' Professor David Payne explained. 'Now we put the dirt back into it.' During the next few years Payne and Dr Richard Laming turned this discovery into a practical device which would transform the world's communications systems: an amplifier consisting of a short length of doped fibre which could easily be inserted into existing fibre cables. Optical fibre cables were now set to replace virtually all other communication cables. The sort of economies which they made possible was shown in 1997 by a transatlantic fibre cable which provided 600,000 circuits, each circuit costing US$500. The previous transatlantic cable, laid ten years earlier, had a capacity of only 8,000 circuits, each costing US$30,000.

In 1989 the inter-Departmental Optoelectronics Research Centre was established under the Directorship of Alec Gambling. This was the first Inter-disciplinary Research Centre to be established at the University, with an initial six-year funding of £13m. (later supplemented with a further £5m.) from the EPSRC. It was organised into three divisions – Optical technology, Optical physics and Optical systems – and had a total staff of 100, many of them transferred from the Departments of Electronics and Physics.

In 1995, David Payne, who succeeded Gambling as the Centre's Director, pointed out that 'optoelectronics is poised to make a major impact in non-telecommunication areas, such as aerospace, oil and gas, and environmental monitoring.' An example was a trial of fibre sensors in California to increase the yield of oil wells. Despite this broadening of its activities – necessary, as it turned out, because the EPSRC funding was not renewed after the first six years – the Centre was still heavily involved in telecommunications. By 1997, Dr Laming and his team had found a new way to compensate for the way a light signal broadens out (or 'chirps') as it passes along a glass fibre. They developed a chirped grating which can be inserted at intervals along a cable to recompress broadened signals. This is being marketed worldwide by Pirelli Cables and Systems, which provided multi-million pound funding to the Centre for five years.

Professor Chris Harris, currently Head of Department, who graduated from the Faculty with a PhD in 1972, returned as the Lucas Professor in 1986 to the Aeronautics and Astronautics Department, before moving to Electronics and

The Department of Electrical Engineering's high-voltage laboratory, opened in 1991 for the testing of underwater telecommunications cables.

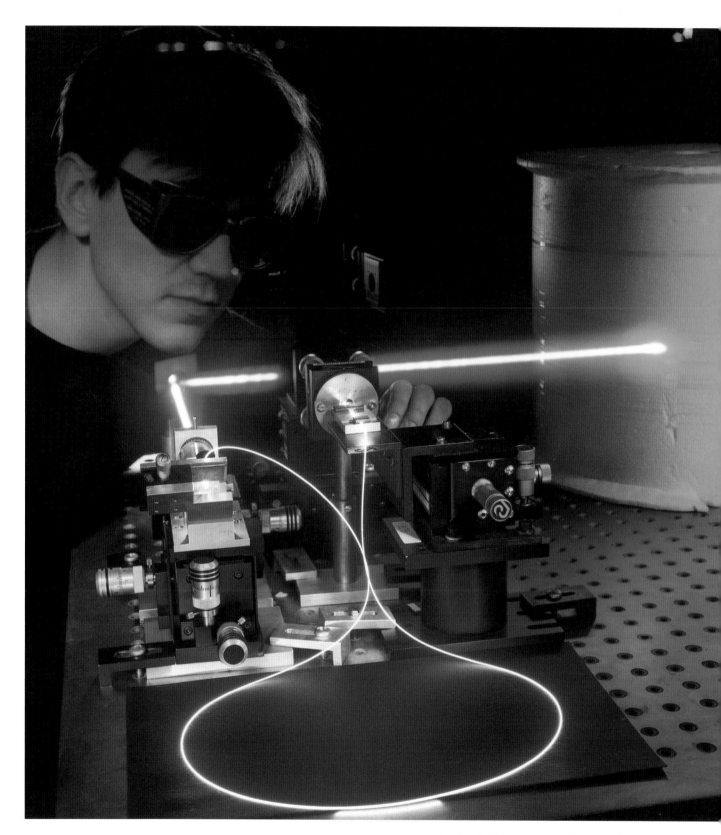

Study of fibre optics in the Optoelectronics
Research Centre.

Computer Science in 1994 to establish the world-renowned Image Speech and Intelligent Systems Research Group on neurofuzzy modelling and biometric research. Professors Harris and Gambling were uniquely awarded the highest recognition in electrical and electronic engineering for their research – the Faraday Medal in 2001 and 1982 respectively. Professor David Payne received the USA's equivalent award, the Benjamin Franklin Gold Medal in 1998, reflecting the esteem of Electronics and Computer Science research over the past two decades.

In the 1985–6 session, under the leadership of David Barron as the founding Professor of Computer Science at Southampton, Computer Studies was transferred from the Faculty of Mathematical Studies and integrated into the Department of Electronics, which now became the Department of Electronics and Computer Science. Two new courses were launched: an MEng in Integrated Information Engineering, and a BSc in Computer Science, which taught the subject as an engineering discipline.

In 1987, as part of the major expansion of Computer Science, two new Professors, Tony Hey and Peter Henderson, were appointed. Hey took charge of the Regional Transputer Support Centre, which was initially funded by the SERC. This was established at Chilworth Research Centre, its purpose to introduce transputer technology to industry. Subsequently the Department's Concurrent Computer Group was to secure a £13 million grant from the DTI to establish one of the country's three Parallel Applications Centres at Chilworth. In 1994, the Parallel Applications Centre was the first UK customer to install an IBM SP2 parallel supercomputer, capable of 1,000 million calculations per second. This followed IBM's choice of Southampton as the (then) only UK university in its Shared University Research (SUR) scheme.

One of the projects in the SUR portfolio was networked multimedia, which was a key interest of Wendy Hall. An undergraduate and postgraduate student at Southampton, she had joined the Departmental staff in 1984 and subsequently founded the Multimedia Research Group (MMRG), which became one of the most advanced of its kind. In 1994, she became the Engineering Faculty's first female Professor. Her group's pioneering Microcosm hypermedia system was commercialised in 1994 and won a prestigious British Computer Society IT Award in 1996 as well as being a major influence on the WWW Consortium's XML/Xlink standard.

Computer Science at Southampton has continued to grow from strength to strength. Its excellent research track record is evidenced by the fact that in the recent round of EPSRC inter-disciplinary research collaboration (IRC) funding, Southampton was involved in two of the five successful bids, becoming the lead site in the Advanced Knowledge Technologies (AKT) IRC and a partner in the Equator IRC. Southampton is now one of the major international research centres in multi-agent systems and, in addition, strength in e-Science and GRID-based computing has led recently to significant funding being awarded to Southampton, making the University a leading centre for research in Computer Science.

Mechanical Engineering

In the late 1950s, two research initiatives were started in mechanical engineering which were to have a lasting impact on the Department. These were research into gas lubricated bearings and the separation of oil/water mixtures. The former, supported by the Atomic Energy Authority, had arisen from the Department's introduction of nuclear engineering into its courses in 1958. A further impetus to research was the appointment in 1964 of Ron Bell as the first Professor of Engineering Materials. He brought with him, from Imperial College, London, research into creep and semiconductor defects.

When Stan Hutton came in 1968, he brought with him several research rigs and a strong team to study cavitation in hydraulic turbines and pumps, and to develop precision-flow measurements in liquids and gases. Much of the research was financed by the Admiralty Materials Research Laboratory and ranged widely from non-toxic methods of antifouling for ship hulls, cavitation effects of corrosion and cavitation attack on ships' propellers.

In 1970, the Department decided to add an Automobile option to the final year of its undergraduate course. Ford Motor Co. supported a lectureship in the Department, and its interests in this area grew rapidly. During the 1970s, the Department carried out research into automotive cooling pumps and more efficient internal combustion engines. To these, during the 1980s, were added studies of plastics and composite materials as lightweight structural components for motor vehicles.

Under the direction of Dr Norman Grassam the gas-bearings research moved from the nuclear field into activities as diverse as long-life bearings for precision navigational gyros through high-speed machine-tool spindles to fluid-flow monitoring and dental drills. Dr John Powell, the son of a dental technician, recognised how unsatisfactory the conventional low-speed dental drill was and set about producing an ultra-high-speed version driven by an air turbine and using pressurised air bearings to enable it to be operated at up to 500,000 rpm. He took advantage of research within the Department into the damping properties of elastomers to produce a simple means of overcoming a particular vibration problem. The drill has been adopted worldwide for general dental use.

A Gas Bearings Advisory Service was offered between 1972 and 1982. This led to the creation of a number of companies in Hampshire and Dorset which design and manufacture a wide range of machine tool spindles and slides. These are now accepted globally as the most satisfactory solution in the manufacture of high-tech components requiring extremely high levels of precision linked to high volume of manufacture. In 1975, the Gas Bearings Advisory Service, and the Wolfson Industrial Noise Unit, together with staff from Mechanical and Electrical Engineering, designed for the British Gas Corporation a very quiet high-pressure toroidal blower having spiral groove grease bearings. This highly successful joint effort now provides the basis of many free-flue gas fires.

The research on separation technology also continued throughout the 1970s,

Prince Charles (seen here with Professor Martin Thew, right) examines the Vortoil hydrocyclone unit.

with studies of cyclonic separation coming to the forefront under the direction of Professor Martin Thew. By the end of the 1970s, the NRDC was applying for patents on Southampton-designed hydrocyclones for the separation of oil and water and, in 1984, the first commercial hydrocyclone unit was installed on Conoco's North Sea Murchison platform. As the Department moved into the 1990s, the hydrocyclone work reached its apex with the receipt of The Prince of Wales Award for Innovation in 1992. By this time, the 'Vortoil' hydrocyclone unit was operating in more than 150 installations throughout the world and was cleaning up eight million barrels of oil-contaminated water a day.

The Department's research also included topics which involved close collaboration with other Departments, such as the development of the robotic arm in conjunction with Electrical Engineering and studies of cryogenic pipe-freezing for repair and maintenance of offshore pipelines, with the Institute of Cryogenics.

Departmental interest in the problems of the automotive industry took a new turn at this time. Ford sponsored research on new recycling techniques to help identify vehicle plastics parts, the introduction of which had been an earlier research interest. The ultimate aim was to produce a more efficient dismantling process for stripping as many plastics as possible from vehicles and then separating them. In 1996, the world's first mobile spectroscopic plastics identification service, Portasort®, was introduced.

In 1998, the University became a partner in a new five-year University Technology Partnership agreement to carry out research into engineering design processes for the twenty-first century. Other partners in this venture, which involved the Department's Computational Engineering and Design Centre, were the Universities of Cambridge and Sheffield, together with British Aerospace and Rolls-Royce. This research seeks to identify ways in which complex engineering design processes can evolve to meet increasingly demanding customer requirements by producing better and more cost-effective products to tight timescales.

Cryogenic pipe-freezing.

Institute of Cryogenics

In 1979, the cryogenics group built up in the Department of Physics by Dr Ralph Scurlock was transferred to the Faculty of Engineering as the Institute of Cryogenics. It was already very active in postgraduate courses, short courses for industry, and research and consultancy, but as a result of its move it also began a greater involvement in undergraduate teaching. In 1981, its industrial activities received a boost when a £100,000 pump-priming grant from Wolfson allowed the establishment of a Cryogenics Industrial Advisory Unit.

In research the Institute collaborated with a number of the Faculty's Departments. One of its long-term interests has been superconductivity and, in the early 1980s, it carried out joint research with Electrical Engineering on superconducting rotors, the University having the only such rotor in the UK at that time. With the Department of Aeronautics and Astronautics it collaborated on cryogenic wind tunnels, with Mechanical Engineering on pipe freezing and with Civil Engineering on testing concrete at low temperatures. Other research interests at the time included energy conservation in large cryogenic plant (supported by the British Oxygen Co.), magnetic separation with superconducting magnets, and the application of laser doppler anemometry to study hazards of large-scale storage of cryogenic liquids.

Following the discovery of high-temperature (100 K) superconducting materials in the mid-1980s, the Institute became involved with their development. In 1987, it formed a High-Temperature Superconductivity Research Group in conjunction with the Departments of Physics, Chemistry, Electrical Engineering, Electronics and Engineering Materials. By this time, it had also begun to collaborate with Electronics on the development of integrated circuit devices capable of operating at very low temperatures, while the work on magnetic separation had been expanded from separation of mineral ores to include other areas, such as in-line filtration of lubricating oils.

By the early 1990s, the Institute had become increasingly involved with refrigerator design. A particular interest was the search for environmentally friendly replacements for the chlorofluorocarbon (CFC) refrigerants which had been shown to damage the atmosphere's protective ozone layer. By 1994, Calor was marketing a new refrigerant material, Care 30, based on a mixture of hydrocarbons suggested by the Institute.

The work on high-temperature superconducting materials was also bearing fruit by this time. By 1994, research on construction of long lengths of silver-sheathed wire and tape superconductors had developed enough to consider setting-up a UK production facility. Meanwhile, the magnetic separations work had expanded into medicine and biotechnology. This included research on the separation of blood components, a significant success in leukaemia treatment and the establishment of a company, Biopraxis Ltd, to market micro-organisms which could remove pollutants from contaminated water.

3. Law

Since the teaching of law first started in 1923, the Faculty has combined a reputation for excellence in research with a pioneering attitude that has spawned a variety of innovative courses such as Information Technology Law. Although the Faculty's early roots lie in the study of commercial law and maritime law – for which it is world-famous – a much wider array of disciplines is on offer today including European law, criminal policy and environmental law.

A Department of Legal Studies was formed in 1923 with just one full-time staff member. At that time students were mainly articled clerks working for the Law Society exams. It was not until the 1950s that they began to work for law degrees. With the Second World War student numbers fell and the Department closed in 1943 when the Law Society withdrew its financial support. It restarted only in 1950; a year later S. N. Grant-Bailey was appointed part-time Director of Legal Studies and then took up the role of full-time Director in 1954. Part-time lecturing was common at that time and during the 1950s there were a small number of part-time tutors including Norman St John-Stevas (now Lord St John of Fawsley). He became an assistant lecturer in the Faculty (1952–3), working alongside a number of junior barristers.

Southampton's School of Law became a Faculty in 1952, the very same year that the College became a University. Under Grant-Bailey, the Faculty was involved in two main areas of activity: continuing teaching of articled clerks and the teaching of students who were learning the principles of law. One of the landmark moments of the Faculty was the appointment of the first Chair of English Law which was awarded in 1956 to Arthur Phillips, formerly a law officer in East Africa. As founding Dean, Phillips immediately made his mark through restructuring the Faculty successfully and recruiting full-time staff.

Alec Samuels was the Faculty's first full-time lecturer while other influential figures included Gabriele Ganz – another lecturer who went on to a Chair – and John Wilson who became Professor of Law, Dean and later Deputy Vice-Chancellor. John Wilson was instrumental in implementing a number of changes to the degree structure which were new and radical for the time. One of those changes was the introduction of an undergraduate dissertation – unusual even today in LLB courses – and he also developed other options as a way of meeting the needs of students who did not intend to enter the legal profession but who wanted instead to join industry, commerce or the public services. Although in 1962–3 three-quarters of the student intake intended to be solicitors, the following year the Faculty noticed that more students were not planning on entering the legal profession in any capacity. The consequent shake-up to the degree structure included an expansion in the teaching of jurisprudence, the compulsory study of commercial law, and family law. This resulted in the renamed Bachelor of Laws degree (LLB).

In 1960 the Faculty also pledged to cultivate the area of Comparative Law; this has evolved over the years and in the new millennium students are studying Comparative European Law. In the early 1960s students from other Faculties began taking up Law in increasing numbers and an increasingly inter-disciplinary approach started to take root. Courses for articled clerks finally stopped after 1962. Other important changes in the late 1960s included the launch of LLM courses in maritime law and planning law. The undergraduate degree was made even more flexible in 1973 following suggestions made by the Ormrod Committee on which Professor Wilson sat. As a result, a larger range of course options was made available including Sales and Sales Financing, Common Market Law and Carriage of Goods.

In the 1970s, with the widespread restrictions on budgets, the Faculty's thoughts turned to finance. One of the consequences was an inevitable stagnation: the annual intake of undergraduates remained around the 100 mark for five consecutive years from 1972 to 1977. Despite the financial difficulties, the Faculty was keen to develop maritime law and so launched a three-week short course in 1975 which was so well received that it has remained a permanent fixture of the Faculty. Law wanted to concentrate its research efforts on both maritime law and intellectual property. This was followed by the setting up of the Centre for Energy Law and Policy which was the first of its kind in the country. In 1988, the Centre was rebranded to keep up with current concerns and became the Centre for Environmental Law. Connections with foreign centres of study were also being made at this time, in particular with the Universities of Utah and Oslo and with maritime institutes at Oslo and Gdansk.

In the 1980s some of the main influences on the Faculty included Peter Birks, who became Professor of Law and a Visiting Fellow in 1990, and Professor David Jackson who played a prominent role in the Institute of Maritime Law when he took up the appointment as its Director. The 1980s was also a decade when the Faculty developed fully a wide range of well recognised specialisms such as maritime law and criminal justice – something that had begun in the late 1970s. Indeed in 1985 the Faculty established a new Institute of Criminal Justice, championed by Professor Rutherford, and this was followed by a new MA (Criminal Justice) degree in 1990. It was during the 1980s that the Faculty really made the transition to being research-led and postgraduate numbers continued to rise significantly.

With threats of more government funding cuts, the Faculty attempted to boost student numbers and to encourage the external sponsorship of lecturers in a bid to maintain the quality of teaching. This proved successful and, during the 1990s, six sponsored lectureships were secured. Over this decade the three main research areas remained maritime law, socio-legal problems and environmental law. A further area was added in 1992–3 – international law and human rights. The most significant achievement was the RAE award of a research rating of 5 in 1996 and of 5* in 2001.

Links with the profession have been a continuing focus in the Faculty. This could be seen in the 1960s by the range of conferences offered for magistrates and refresher lectures for solicitors. That emphasis has continued and many

highly successful conferences over the past decade have helped boost finances and reinforce the contribution that Law can make to current legal issues. Additionally, individual Faculty members have been appointed to positions where they have been able to contribute to law reforms. They have included Andrew Martin, who was awarded a Chair in 1963 and was a Law Commissioner for five years; Professor Heuston who was a member of the Lord Chancellor's Law Reform Committee; Professor Dworkin (the successor to Phillips as Professor of Law and Dean of the Faculty in 1968) who served on

The Law Faculty, with the Steel Forms *sculpture to the right.*

the Committee of Justice which produced a report on privacy and the law; and Vice-Chancellor Professor Jim Gower who served with Martin as a Law Commissioner. The Faculty now houses a number of influential research centres, such as the Institute of Maritime Law, the Institute of Criminal Justice, the Centre for Environmental Law and the Behavioural Sciences and Law Network. On a broader level the Faculty has an ongoing relationship with national and international bodies such as the European Court and the United Nations.

The ability to influence legal developments in this way has been achieved as a result of the Faculty's research performance. The importance given to research can be seen in the balance of student numbers: according to recent figures undergraduate students number around 160 a year, while postgraduate students account for about 100 students and PhD students around 25. Students are able to study at both undergraduate and postgraduate level, in subjects as diverse as maritime law, health care law, commercial law, European law and international law.

The Faculty was awarded the highest possible rating of 5* in the most recent National Research Assessment Exercise. For a small Faculty, Law has also been successful in securing the essential funding needed for research projects. The current Dean, Professor Andrew Rutherford, points out that the Faculty has recently been awarded funds for two research projects from the Arts and Humanities Research Board and he believes it can succeed in attracting further such funding.

The Faculty places great importance on the link between research and teaching: members of staff are involved at both national and international level in the development of law, whether it be company law or criminal justice, shipping law or social security, all of which feeds back into teaching. Key appointments in recent years include a Research Professor in Commercial Law – Robert Merkin – along with a new lecturer in human rights law and another in intellectual property law. Europe has also been a feature of new developments within the Faculty, demonstrated by the recent appointment of the first Professor of European Law – Takis Tridimas – who has written *Principles of European Community Law*. In recent years, the Faculty has greatly enhanced its expertise in European law. In addition to the compulsory undergraduate course on EU law, there are now two new LLM courses focusing on EU commercial law and the European Court of Justice, and a number of research students studying for doctorate degrees in various areas of EU law and human rights. The Law Faculty has recently organised two major Euro-events – His Honour Judge Melchior Wathelet, judge at the European Court of Justice, presented a seminar on 'Taxation and free movement in the EU', and Professor Tridimas delivered his inaugural lecture, 'The European Court of Justice: a Supreme Court for the Union?'

A new degree in Law (International Legal Studies) was launched in September 2000. This was created following a student exchange agreement between the Faculty and the Faculty of Law, Hong Kong University, which provides the opportunity for a small number of Law students to spend a year studying at Hong Kong University. Plans are also being considered to extend the exchange programme to other international destinations. One of the main changes to take place since the Faculty's beginnings is an increasing international emphasis – a growing number of foreign students, links with other European universities and a growing focus on the teaching of European law. The University of Oslo, for example, regularly sends undergraduates to Southampton as a result of strong, established links between the two institutions. At postgraduate level, the presence of overseas graduates is high – out of some 100 LLM students, 60 are from overseas, including China, South America and the Middle East.

Another inevitable change has been the introduction of information technology and many courses are now available on-line. The Faculty has its own Computer Laboratory which comprises 25 workstations from which students have access to a wide range of on-line legal resources. The Information Technology Law course has recently been made available in an on-line format. Dr Steve Saxby, who has been teaching the course since 1981, said, 'The course is the longest-running undergraduate IT law course in the UK and it needed to make this breakthrough.' In this way, the Faculty has successfully managed to combine tradition with modernity.

The Institute of Maritime Law

The Institute is the largest centre in the UK for the study of maritime law and for teaching, research and consultancy in the subject. It has also built up an international reputation and is one of the most respected bodies of its kind in the world. Founded in 1982, its aim was to give focus to a decade-long interest in maritime and shipping law at Southampton. A large number of courses, seminars and lectures are given, both in the UK and overseas. These range in length from the annual established three-week residential course to the Donald O'May lecture, given by a leading figure in the maritime world. Courses and seminars are offered both to lawyers and other people whose work is connected with shipping or international trade. Consultancy is another service offered by the Institute and a large number of bodies, associations, corporations and law firms have enlisted its help on UK, foreign, public international and convention law.

One of the most important publications to emerge from the Institute is perhaps *The Ratification of Maritime Conventions*, published with Lloyd's of London Press. This contains the full text of all international conventions that are relevant to maritime and shipping affairs. The Institute has an impressive specialised library which contains material from all major maritime jurisdictions and a wide range of texts and papers. These sit alongside several electronic databases which have been developed within the Institute. Close connections are maintained with leading maritime lawyers throughout the world and with other maritime law centres in Antwerp, Dalian and Shanghai in the People's Republic of China, Durban, Gdansk, Hamburg, New Orleans and Oslo.

The Institute of Criminal Justice

The Institute was established in 1986 to conduct research and to examine issues relating to the balance between control of crime on one hand and the protection of civil liberties on the other. As one of the leading centres of excellence in legal and socio-legal research in the UK, the Institute offers the opportunity to undertake research in a wide range of criminal justice and legal specialities. At MA level, courses cover a variety of subjects relevant to modern-day society, including police governance and accountability; youth justice; criminal responsibility; punishment in the community; and race, politics and society.

The Behavioural Sciences and Law Network

The Network has three principal objectives: the design and provision of courses on existing topics at the interface between the behavioural sciences and law; the organisation of conferences on emerging inter-disciplinary issues; and the support of practical research and co-operation between the many professions concerned. Since its inception in 1994 the BS&L Network has established an international reputation for its courses and conferences which included 'Restorative and Community Justice: Inspiring the Future' in March 2001. Another major conference will be the 'Psychology and Law: International Interdisciplinary Conference' in July 2003. The BS&L Network has tackled some weighty and topical subjects in its past programme of conferences. These included in 1995 'The Cross-examination of Children' which considered whether the practice was desirable and possible, while in 1997 'Behavioural Syndrome Evidence in the Courts' considered the scientific status, and admissibility as expert evidence, of rape trauma syndrome, child abuse accommodation and battered wives syndromes, both in the USA and the UK. In 1999 the Network organised 'Psychology and Law' which was the first joint conference of the American and European psychology and law associations. It attracted a record number of participants – 560.

Proposals are being developed and considered for an inter-institutional and interdisciplinary instructional postgraduate degree in law, psychiatry and psychology. Research links and joint working have been developed also with the Department of Psychiatry and the Professorial Unit at Broadmoor Hospital. Particular staff interests and strengths lie in risk analysis, the admission and assessment of expert testimony, and therapeutic jurisprudence (TJ). An ESRC research award was gained in 1996 for a TJ analysis of domestic violence laws.

As a strong and well-respected, research-led Faculty, Law has managed successfully to influence and contribute to legal thinking at the highest level. The Faculty has established solid connections with the legal profession through a regular series of joint projects, conferences and seminars. At the same time, the Faculty has adopted a pioneering and flexible stance towards teaching and research in a bid to keep pace with ever-changing developments in law.

4. Mathematical Studies

Soon after the end of the Second World War two Professors joined the Department of Mathematics (as it then was) who were to influence its development for more than 20 years. In 1946, E. T. (Ianto) Davies arrived from King's College, London, to be Professor of Mathematics and Head of Department. He remained in that position until 1967, two years before his retirement, and also served as Deputy Vice-Chancellor (1954–7) and Dean of the Faculty of Science (1965–7). At a time when Oxbridge graduates dominated academic mathematics in England, Davies's appointment was unusual in that he had studied at Aberystwyth and Swansea (his first language was Welsh). He had then continued his studies in Rome (defending his doctoral thesis in Italian) and elsewhere on the Continent. On the research side, Davies' interest was differential geometry, the geometry of curved spaces. This topic was to prove of practical importance from the 1950s to the 1990s in work within the Department on designing the precise shapes of reflective dishes for satellites and other applications.

The Mathematics Tower (left) with the Zepler Building to the right.

Two years after Davies arrived in Southampton, he was joined by Hermann Jahn (English despite his name). Jahn became the first Professor of Applied Mathematics (Davies's title was then changed to Professor of Pure Mathematics). Jahn had taken his first degree in chemistry at Southampton and then a doctorate in mathematics at Leipzig. Soon after he came to Southampton, he secured a grant of £2,500, a large sum at the time, from the Royal Society for research with Professor Eric Zepler of Electronics into microwave absorption and molecular structure. Renowned internationally for his work on the foundations of the theory of elementary particles, his name is best remembered today for the Jahn-Teller theorem, which predicts the unexpected behaviour of transition elements in the way they form chemical compounds. His research apart, Jahn was Dean of the Faculty of Science in 1963–5 and Chairman of the Mathematics Department in 1968–9. He is remembered by many for his sense of humour, warmth and extreme generosity towards younger mathematicians.

In the 1950s, the Department widened its teaching by launching combined degrees with other subjects – for example, a special honours degree, Mathematics with Aeronautics, in 1956. Mathematics with Electronics followed. Until 1974, these were the only such degrees in the Faculty of Science, although a few students combined with Arts subjects.

Although the Mathematics Department had had serious research interests since Howland's professorship in the 1930s, the momentum which led to today's strong research Faculty really began with Davies and Jahn. The appointment in 1958 of a third professor, Bryan Thwaites, led to a contrasting interest: the teaching of mathematics in schools.

Thwaites was appointed as Professor of Theoretical Mechanics (he had made his name as editor of *Modern developments in fluid dynamics* and by designing the 'Thwaites flap' for aircraft). Part of his brief was to attend to the mathematical needs of the engineers, but his best-remembered contribution was originating and promoting the School Mathematics Project (SMP), for which he was adept at getting publicity.

School Mathematics Project

SMP was a new way of teaching mathematics in schools, intended to make it more fun and more relevant to contemporary needs, as well as bridging the gulf which had developed between mathematics as it was studied in schools and universities. The project was run from Southampton, with Thwaites as its director, and began with a number of schools of different types.

SMP's strength, compared to other projects of the time, was that its mathematics was in the hands of its teaching members. In 1963–4, it received a grant of £10,000 from the Industrial Fund for the Advancement of Science. By the end of the following year, its third, the creators were able to report that it was 'exerting an influence on secondary school mathematical teaching which greatly surpassed the original hopes of the University.' Three pupil texts together with teacher guides had been published, the first SMP O-level examinations had been held and the first SMP A-levels were planned for 1966. There had also been much overseas interest. In the next year, the University estimated that many thousands of children were learning SMP mathematics; now, however, Thwaites left Southampton to become Principal of Westfield College, London, taking with him the part which Southampton had played in SMP. Partly as a result of the interest aroused by SMP, but also because of the Department's involvement in other educational projects and in sixth-form conferences, Southampton by then had one of the largest mathematics departments in the UK in terms of student numbers.

At the same time as Thwaites left, Dr Geoffrey Howson, who had joined the Mathematics Department as a lecturer in 1962 in order to develop SMP and who was then SMP's editor-in-chief, was seconded to the Centre for Curriculum Renewal and Educational Development Overseas. In 1978, Howson returned to Southampton as Director of a newly-formed Centre for Mathematical Education. In the following year, he was rewarded with a personal Chair in Mathematical Curriculum Studies, and in 1985 oversight of the SMP project returned to Southampton.

By the time Thwaites moved to London, the Department had two more Professors. Brian Griffiths, a pure mathematician, had been appointed as the Department's fourth Professor in 1964, while Maurice Quenouille arrived in 1965. Quenouille was an eminent statistician and, during the eight years he was at Southampton, he developed both research and teaching of statistics (as well as playing an important role in the reorganisation of the Royal Statistical Society). Quenouille was a man of great entrepreneurial energy. He established the Operational Research Group, an important function of which was to promote contact with industry. He was also instrumental in separating the academic side of computing (which was then a sub-department of Mathematics) from the service provider side. He died in 1973 and his Chair went to Fred Smith, who was already a lecturer in the Department.

Although SMP had gone, the Department demonstrated its continuing concerns with education in 1967 when Griffiths introduced into the new options system a course in Mathematical Curriculum Studies, partly to produce graduates with enough knowledge to write the kind of material needed by projects like SMP. Eventually, a four-year Mathematics with Education course followed, unprecedented in Britain and highly commended by the external examiners. Education lecturers participated and students who graduated became qualified teachers. After the first students finished, however, the course was closed because economic conditions made it difficult to recruit students. Nevertheless, the Faculty did not give up its efforts to help produce good recruits to the teaching profession and, as an alternative, from 1974 offered a four-year Mathematics with Education course as one option in the combined honours programme. By this time also the Department's innovations in new courses and modes of assessment had attracted the attention of other universities which adapted the system to their local conditions. Some of these changes were based on a well-received study by Ron McLone, a lecturer in the Department, on the needs of employers of mathematics graduates, who had found a lack of communication skills in their recruits.

In 1967, J. V. (Jim) Craggs came from a Chair in Melbourne to join the Department as Professor of Engineering Mathematics. A very friendly and open character, he restored good relationships with the Engineering Faculty, which had deteriorated as a result of Thwaites's preoccupation with SMP. Engineering mathematics was also strengthened when David Barron was appointed the first Professor of Computation in the same year. The variety of interests of the Department's Professors then led to named degrees, such as Mathematics with Statistics. An innovation of the mid-1970s was a self-paced course in mathematics for first-year engineering students. The students worked on their own and only after mastering one stage of the course would they proceed to the next.

Craggs became Head of the Department (and, when Mathematics became a Faculty in 1976, its first Dean), but took early retirement in 1978. He went on to manage a Methodist chapel. When Davies and Jahn retired – in 1969 and 1972 respectively – they were succeeded by Stewart Robertson and Peter Landsberg. During his 27 years as Professor of Pure Mathematics, Robertson was a central figure in both the Faculty and the University. Like his predecessor, he pursued research in geometry and 16 out of a total of 19 of his PhD students went on to academic careers in the UK and abroad. He was a founder member of the European Mathematical Society, for many years Chairman of the University's Arts Committee and, for four years, a Deputy Vice-Chancellor. Peter Landsberg came from University College, Cardiff, where he had been Deputy Principal, to take the Chair of Applied Mathematics. He had research interests in both solid-state physics and cosmology and helped to build the thriving research school in these areas which continues today. He introduced some new undergraduate courses (for example, on statistical mechanics) and arranged research contracts, notably with the European Union.

Faculty Status

During the early 1970s, the Mathematics Department was in conflict with a number of other Departments over its desire to be raised to Faculty status. In 1952, the Department had been a full member of the Faculties of Arts, Science and Engineering. However, changes in administrative and financial structures had led to it becoming a member of the Science Faculty only, although it still had strong academic links with other Faculties, by that time increasingly with Social Science. Mathematics wanted Faculty status because of its teaching and research links with other Faculties, and because its research work was so unlike the laboratory work of other science Departments. The Science Faculty, on the other hand, wanted to retain Mathematics as a subsidiary, because its large number of students reduced overall unit costs while maintaining the importance given by large student numbers. It claimed that relinquishing Mathematics would cause unnecessary fragmentation. After seven years' debate, Science gave way and Mathematics achieved Faculty status in 1976.

In 1979, the increased importance of the Operational Research group, which

The steps to the Mathematics building.

Quenouille had founded, was recognised by the creation of a Chair of Operational Research. The first Professor, K. D. Tocher, came to the University from British Steel, but died after less than two years in the post. He was succeeded by Paul Williams, who developed this side of the Faculty's work considerably over the remaining decades of the century. Important research themes which developed early in the Operational Research group's life related to mathematical programming, scheduling, game theory, manufacturing systems, and modelling for health sciences and diseases.

By the beginning of the 1980s, the importance of computing to society at large was becoming increasingly apparent. The Faculty started a single honours degree in Computer Studies in 1982 and decided in the following year to form a new Department of Computer Studies. This was closely followed by the establishment of a new degree in Language Sciences, offered jointly by the Department and the School of Modern Languages in the Arts Faculty. According to Professor Griffiths, at that time Dean of the Faculty, 'The course contains equal proportions of modern language, linguistics and computing; and students will spend a year in placement with a European computer company.' Not long afterwards, however, the University decided to join electronics and computing into a single Department of Electronics and Computer Science, under the auspices of the Faculty of Engineering.

Although the late 1970s and early 1980s was a period of great restraint in university spending (see Part II, Chapters 3 and 4), the Faculty continued to make significant appointments. In 1982, Michael Howe arrived to take up the Chair of Engineering Mathematics, bringing with him research in aero- and hydroacoustics to add to the applied mathematicians' portfolio of interests. Nevertheless, in 1984, Fred Smith, in his Dean's report, commented unfavourably on the cuts that were being imposed. At the beginning of the 1983–4 session, the UGC's Mathematical sub-committee had reported favourably on the Faculty, but the UGC's promised level of funding in practice meant cuts of at least 1 per cent per annum and in fact, for 1984–5, the University imposed a cut of 3 per cent. The real culprit, Smith wrote, 'is not the University or the UGC, but a government which pays lip service to the need for qualified manpower and then proceeds to continue to cut expenditure on University education even after the savage cuts of 1981.'

In the following years, the Faculty put increasing effort into research, partly in response to University policy, partly to earn financial awards, and partly to improve its rating in the periodic Research Assessment Exercises (RAEs). In 1988–9, it had been reasonably satisfied with this, the Statistics group under Professor Smith being classed as 'outstanding'.

By the early 1990s, collaborative work on the use of operational research in health was flourishing. Joint studies, involving clinicians, general practitioners and others were looking at a range of diseases as well as organisational problems in the Health Service. Advisory groups for research on breast cancer, diabetes and maternity care were set up during the 1993–4 session. A key academic in the development of this interest was Dr Arjan Shahani, who was also responsible for building up the flagship MSc course in Operational Research.

Burgeoning Research

As a decade, the 1990s was one of burgeoning research interest for the Faculty, with the appointment of a number of new Professors and the creation of a great many links with other academic bodies, industry and governmental organisations. Professorial appointments included the appointment of Martin Dunwoody to the Chair of Pure Mathematics in 1992, in succession to Professor Griffiths, and Adam Wheeler to the Chair of Industrial Applied Mathematics two years later.

In the 1996 Research Assessment Exercise, the Faculty set itself the target of a rating of 4 in each of the four submissions it made. Pure Mathematics was the only group not to achieve this target, although the other groups either achieved the target or, in the case of Operational Research, exceeded it. During the following year, the Faculty put in place a strategic plan to take it into the new millennium. This led to new staffing initiatives geared towards higher research aspirations for the next RAE. In 1998 Professor Vic Snaith took up the Chair in Pure Mathematics and broadened the research base, until then predominantly in geometric group theory, to include algebraic K-theory, number theory, algebraic geometry, representation theory and algebraic topology. In the following year, Professor Russell Cheng, whose research interests encompassed simulation methodology and analysis, was appointed to a second Chair in Operational Research group.

In 1995, as part of the Faculty's long-standing commitment to postgraduate training, the Faculty formed a Graduate School to organise and promote the interests of its growing body of postgraduate students. This followed on the success of the Faculty's two MSc courses in Operational Research and Statistics with Applications in Medicine in attracting substantial funding and students as well as a growing number of PhD students.

Today, the Faculty of Mathematical Studies is one of the largest in the country, conducting research across a wide range of mathematics at international level. The high quality of its burgeoning research activity was publicly acknowledged when all its groups received a 5 rating in the 2001 Research Assessment Exercise. The Applied, Statistics and OR groups pursue the application of mathematics over an unusually wide range of inter-disciplinary areas in concert with a strong pure mathematics group at the heart of the discipline. In recent years the appointment of a cadre of young talented staff, complemented by world leading researchers at professorial level, has cultivated a thriving research ethos. The Faculty plays host to a large number of academics from across the globe to pursue research collaboration, as well as a wide range of seminar programmes. In turn, its academic staff travel widely on collaborative research visits, and sabbaticals, or to participate in international conferences, often as invited speakers. Further testament to the Faculty's high research reputation comes from the University's recognition of its staff's achievements through a burgeoning number of personal Chairs, as well as an impressive array of prestigious research awards from such bodies as the Leverhulme Trust, London Mathematical Society, and the Royal Statistical Society.

In Applied Mathematics Southampton is a leading centre of research in general relativity, industrial applied mathematics and mainstream applied mathematics. The general relativity group is now playing a key role in a new EU network on sources of gravitational radiation. One of its younger members, Dr Nils Andersson, was awarded a highly prestigious Philip Leverhulme prize in 2001 for his research. The Applied Mathematics group is also involved in a range of inter-disciplinary work with growing interests in mathematical biology and medicine, such as fluid flow in human eyes and models of tumour growth, to research on flat-panel loudspeakers, liquid crystals and crystal growth, and models of the migration of early civilisations. A major focus continues to be participation in Industrial Study Groups in which mathematical modelling and problem-solving are brought to bear on problems companies bring to these meetings. Staff from the group have frequently organised and participated in study groups across the world including Southampton, Oxbridge, Australia, USA, Mexico, China and Brazil.

The Operational Research group has recently strengthened and broadened its research interests. Industrial collaborations continue to be an important feature of the group's research. For example, a recent research contract won by Professor Russell Cheng and Dr Owen Jones concerns the analysis of real-time trials for investigating the efficiency of air-traffic controller operational procedures for National Air Traffic Services. Other interests include financial risk management, scheduling in supply chains and the modelling of health care and health services. A main focus of the teaching effort of the group is the MSc in Operational Research which has been very successful in giving mathematics graduates the skills necessary to contribute to business and industry, partly by including in the programme a number of relevant management and non-mathematical topics. The MSc attracts a wide range of companies, such as Pirelli, Shell and Tesco, to provide three-month work placements over the summer where the students work on practical problems of importance to them. In addition, EPSRC has provided a substantial tranche of Masters Training Package funding (jointly with the School of Management) in recognition of the excellence of the course and the preparedness of its graduates to enter industry.

The Pure Mathematics group has a wide range of interests which can be grouped roughly into those concerning the interface between geometry and group theory, and those related to algebraic K-theory. Numerous members of the group have been recognised recently for the excellence of their research. Professor Brian Bowditch won a London Mathematical Society Junior Whitehead Prize for his work in geometric group theory, and Professor David Singerman won a Silver

A lecture on the third-year unit Viscous Flow and Environmental Fluid Dynamics, 2002.

Medal for Research from the University of Madrid for his work on discrete groups and Riemann surfaces. Dr Bernhard Koeck was awarded a Heisenberg Research Fellowship for his work on the Riemann-Roch theorem in algebraic geometry, while Dr Jacek Brodzki and Professor Vic Snaith were awarded Leverhulme Research Fellowships for their work in algebraic K-theory. In addition, Dr Keith Hirst became one of the first to win a National Teaching Fellowship in recognition of his high achievement in the teaching of mathematics.

The Statistics group has consistently achieved high research ratings and undertakes a considerable amount of collaborative research with other Departments. Fred Smith retired and in 2000 Professor Alan Welsh, from Australian National University, succeeded him in the Chair of Statistics. One of its members, Dr Jon Forster, was recognised for his outstanding research achievements, jointly with Dr Smith in the Department of Social Statistics, who were awarded the Royal Statistical Society's Guy Medal in Bronze. The group's main research strengths lie in the design of experiments, sample surveys, the statistical theory of multiple comparisons, extreme values, sequential methods, Bayesian methods and model comparison. The work has direct applications to medical research and industrial quality improvement. A major focus in teaching for the group is the MSc in Statistics with Applications to Medicine, which attracts around 20 students each year and has been very successful in attracting support from companies such as GSK, Astra Zeneca, Pfizer, Quintiles and Amgen. This MSc also been recognised by EPSRC for its excellence and relevance to the needs of industry by the award of a large amount of Master Training Package funds.

The breadth and depth of the Faculty's research and teaching, along with the high quality and commitment of its staff, place it in a strong position as it progresses into the twenty-first century.

5. Medicine, Health and Biological Sciences

Southampton has been involved in medically related biological studies from the year it became a University with the appointment in 1952 of Kenneth Munday as a lecturer in comparative physiology within the Department of Zoology. Two years later, a second lecturer, Gerald Kerkut, was appointed and a sub-Department of Physiology and Biochemistry formed, which admitted its first group of eight undergraduates in 1956. The sub-Department subsequently separated from Zoology to become an independent Department in 1958. From the early 1960s members of the Department undertook research in collaboration with hospital staff in the Wessex Region.

In 1962 Munday was appointed to the first Chair of Physiology and Biochemistry. The title of his inaugural lecture was 'Physiology and Biochemistry – Science, Art or Medicine?' The same year the Department acquired a second house in University Road where it was able to install the University's first effective electron microscope, and space was made alongside Engineering's Faraday building for a new animal house. In 1968–9 plans for a Pre-clinical Sciences building at Boldrewood were agreed. Physiology and Biochemistry would move there when it opened, it was hoped, in 1972.

Whether or not Munday worked from his arrival towards the establishment of a Medical School at Southampton, the strength of his Department and the links he had established with Wessex Regional Hospital Board were important arguments in Southampton's favour when it had to compete with other universities to be awarded a Medical School. Meanwhile there had been various developments, some encouraging, some the reverse. Discouraging, indeed as it turned out plain wrong, was the report of the Willink Committee in 1957 which recommended a 10 per cent *reduction* in the country's intake of medical students. Two years later the University and Wessex Regional Hospital Board submitted a plan for a Medical School at Southampton but this failed, partly because the Government saw no reason for rejecting the Willink Committee's conclusions, partly because the Vice-Chancellor, Gwilym James, had little enthusiasm for the idea.

There, on the surface, matters rested for some six years until the setting up of a Royal Commission was announced. On 23 July 1965, almost precisely the day on which James retired, a Medical School Committee first met at the University, with John Raymont, founding Professor of Oceanography, in the chair. Its most important decision was to go again to the Wessex Regional Hospital Board and to form with it a Joint Committee. Two months later, in September 1965, the Royal Commission on Medical Education (commonly called the Todd Commission after its Chairman, Lord Todd) met for the first time. During the next nine months these two bodies were working in parallel. At its first meeting, on 14 December 1965, the Joint Committee for the

Development of a Medical School in Southampton (its full title) elected Kenneth Mather, the new Vice-Chancellor, as Chairman, and set out to make recommendations to the University and the Hospital Board on anything which related to its own name. At the same time it prepared evidence for submission to the Todd Commission specifically relating to medical education. This it submitted in March 1966.

On 15 June 1966, however, the Todd Commission took the unusual step of issuing an interim memorandum on a subject which was not strictly its concern and which first officially admitted how mistaken Willink had been. Its initial enquiries, the Todd Commission declared, had led it to 'form a conviction that a substantial increase in output [of doctors] is required without delay.' The memorandum suggested ways in which this could be achieved. The following March (1967) the Government asked the Commission to give advice about the different suggestions it had made for training more doctors, so for the first time bringing this question officially to the Commission's attention. Existing schools might be expanded, Todd had suggested, and one new school was already being established at Nottingham, but this would not be sufficient and more were needed. Success came for Southampton on 17 August 1967 when the government announced the Commission's opinion that 'the case for establishing a new medical school in Southampton is so strong that we advise the Government to authorise this development without waiting for our final recommendations.' Nottingham, Leicester (subsequently recommended) and Southampton were the first new schools of medicine to be founded in this country since the beginning of the twentieth century.

There were several reasons for Southampton's success. The Joint Committee had suggested two of them: the Wessex region was the only region without a medical school, and the University already took part in postgraduate medical teaching. The Todd Commission gave others: Southampton already had a well-established Department of Physiology and Biochemistry under Professor Munday which would be a strong nucleus for a Medical School; the Board was rebuilding the main Southampton Hospital on lines which could well be adapted for use as a School; and the University already had strong links with local hospitals and with the Wessex Regional Hospital Board (WRHB), which served a growing population of two million. The strongest reason was thus suggested but not precisely stated: that co-operation between the University and the Board would produce a school of a new character, combining the training of doctors with both service to the local community and research.

Success was in part the result of the character and drive of Dr John Revans – a former civil servant who was Senior Administrative Medical Officer of the Wessex Board, and determined to have a medical school in his region – but also in part to Mather's enthusiastic support for the project. Both of them had to face opposition. At the hospital Dr Goodbody, a consultant pathologist, was strongly against the idea. He had come to Southampton because it was *not* a teaching hospital. At the University, Professor David Rowan, Deputy Vice-Chancellor, believed that a Medical School would harm other Faculties by attracting funds away from them, since it could always argue that those it needed were for preserving life. There was also jealousy among the medical fraternity at Portsmouth. When Professor Donald Acheson arrived in October 1968 to be the foundation Dean, Mather told him to go to Portsmouth next day, 'because there were problems'. Later, Dr Dolph Polak, Director of the WRHB's renal unit at Portsmouth, accepted a personal Chair and an invitation to establish an academic renal unit at Portsmouth.

The new School demonstrated its intention to contribute quickly to increasing the country's output of doctors by proposing to take its first students in 1971 even if this meant 'improvisation on a grand scale' (Acheson), and to increase its annual intake within a few years to 130. A curriculum was therefore urgently needed. In devising this the School showed its determination to be not just another medical school but one of a different kind. The Joint Committee had started to work on a proposed curriculum before Southampton had been chosen. A curriculum working party which it had set up in May 1966, with Kenneth Munday as chairman, had produced a draft curriculum which had been included with the Joint Committee's submission to the UGC. When the founding of the Medical School had been approved, however, and Acheson had been followed a year later by four more Professors – David Millar, James Fraser, David Bulmer and Jack Howell – they and subsequent Professors formed a new Curriculum Committee, with Acheson as its Chairman. And this began afresh the devising of a curriculum.

There was widespread discontent with the curricula of existing medical schools (hence the Todd Commission), but imposing a radically new one on an existing one had so far proved impossible except to an extent at Newcastle. As a new school, Southampton had great advantages: no existing staff to provide conservative opposition and no problems of conversion from old curriculum to new. The new curriculum made full use of this opportunity. It was radical in many ways. Probably the most important of these concerned the fourth year of the five-year course (the main item adopted from the proposals of the first curriculum working party). In this year a student would undertake a study in depth, usually including a piece of research on his or her own in an honours-type course. Other medical schools offered certain students, usually the brightest, the chance to take an intercalated degree at the end of their preclinical course. Southampton was unique in making its study in depth an integral part of the training of every student.

The underlying aim went beyond emphasising that all medical knowledge and practice is based on science. The fourth year was meant to rectify the student's teaching so far, much of which would necessarily have consisted of learning generally accepted knowledge, and teach him or her that all such knowledge is hypothetical, to be confirmed or refuted by experiment, always liable to be replaced by a new hypothesis. Put another way, such a study in depth was meant to be a contrast with the sort of 'study in width', of which much medical education necessarily consisted and in which 'the sheer volume of facts to be learned means that they are often presented as oversimplified half truths and the uncertainty surrounding much accepted knowledge remains concealed' (Acheson). The student would be free to suggest his or her own

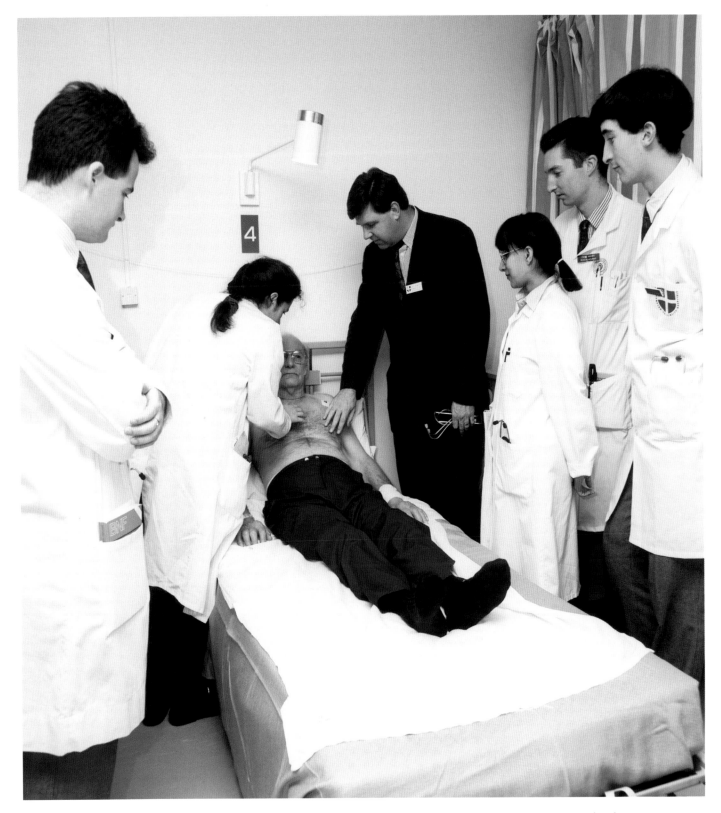

Medical training.

subject to a supervisor who would oversee his or her work throughout the year. It would be on some aspect of biological, social or clinical science, but this could be widely interpreted. It might verge on sociology and, for example, ask why some women who have early symptoms of breast cancer seek and receive treatment sooner than others. The students would be encouraged to pursue any of the many questions which occur to them each day, to which they could not find satisfactory answers.

Southampton's curriculum was also radical for the early years of the course. Traditionally medical students began their education with parallel or consecutive courses, each concerned with different areas of medicine: anatomy, pharmacology, physiology, pathology, epidemiology and so on. It was left mainly to students to recognise how any or all of them related to particular illnesses or functions of the body. Too often these courses crushed the students' early enthusiasm by seeming too academic and remote from the actual practice of doctoring which they were keen to start. The Southampton curriculum was to be based on system courses. Such courses allowed a student to learn about the anatomy, physiology and mechanism of disease in each system of the body, with the advantage that study of the abnormal would illuminate the normal. However, because some of the committee feared that new students would not have the background knowledge for systems, only one system course, Human Reproduction, was introduced in the first year with a further eight to follow in the second. And as a further compromise the first year retained 'introductory' courses on anatomy, biochemistry and general pathology. Only when the curriculum was revised in 1989–90 were system courses extended across the first two years as originally intended.

From 1971 the first year also included another new feature: students were quickly introduced to live patients. For example, they would attend an antenatal clinic and meet a woman in early pregnancy, then if possible attend the delivery of her child and visit the family later in the home. They would make similar visits to patients with chronically disabling illnesses. Professor Millar strongly promoted such early contact with patients. He had seen it in practice at Cleveland, Ohio. It was a serious loss to the School when Millar died in March 1971, aged 38. A memorial prize was established for the best essay on human reproduction by a first-year student, and a bust of Millar by Cecile Epstein was placed outside the lecture theatre in the South Academic Block at the Southampton General Hospital. By the final term of their second year students would be beginning to learn the techniques of history-taking and examination, and in their third year would be spending more than half their time doing clinical work in medicine, surgery, obstetrics, gynaecology, geriatric medicine, psychiatry and child health.

The fifth year of the course would be exclusively clinical. It differed from the practice in established medical schools of teaching hospitals, where groups of students, often large, would follow consultants around the wards. All medical schools gave initial clinical experience in the third year, more in the fourth and yet more in the final year. The problem was that many students from different years would be attached to wards at the same time, making it difficult for final-year students to gain 'hands on' experience and be closely supervised. To avoid this, Southampton decided to have no formal teaching in the fifth year in the form of lectures, and instead to invite consultants in hospitals across the Wessex region, from Portsmouth to Bath, Dorchester, Bournemouth, Basingstoke and the Isle of Wight, to take one, or at most two students on to their 'firms' and encourage them to learn directly as 'apprentices'. They would then be assessed *in situ* by the consultant and a visiting academic and the results would contribute to their final degrees.

The curriculum apart, those planning the Medical School – in particular Professor Acheson – were keen to educate students in the way environment, both material and social, caused diseases and the influence the environment could have on the way these could be managed – a concept commonly ignored in medical schools. The most obvious example was the way in which smoking caused lung cancer. But diet's connection with heart disease and cancers was another, and poverty or bad housing had a more general connection with illness.

While the Curriculum Committee worked on the curriculum the University tackled the difficult problem of providing space in which it could be studied. By 1969 a start had been made on the Preclinical Science Building at Boldrewood and a start was expected soon on rebuilding Southampton General Hospital, the town's largest. Some in-patient and the majority of outpatient facilities were also available at the Royal South Hampshire Hospital, the original voluntary hospital of the town. Misfortune followed in 1970 when the contractor for the rebuilding of the General Hospital went into liquidation. He was replaced and the delay was not expected to exceed a few months. Meanwhile there had been no shortage of applications from prospective students – evidence that they liked the proposed programme – and the first 40 had been chosen. Southampton was radical again in its method of selection. It held no interviews for school-leavers, believing that these gave unreliable indications of a candidate's suitability, and instead relied (except for mature applicants) on school reports and predictions of A-level grades. School reports might not be strictly impartial but they were likely to be realistic because schools would not want a reputation for being untrustworthy.

As regards accommodation, the University proved to have been optimistic. When the chosen 40 arrived in October 1971 neither the work at the General Hospital nor at Boldrewood on what was called the Medical and Biological Sciences Building had been completed. As a result the students had to be taught for their first two terms in buildings all over the Highfield Campus and for anatomy at the General Hospital.

Nevertheless 1971 was a year of celebration. The School was formally opened in October by Sir Keith Joseph, Secretary of State for Health and Social Services, and *The Times* published a special supplement on the University which included several articles on the Medical School. In December the University Grants Medical sub-committee visited the School and was impressed. Sixty-five students were accepted for admission in October 1972.

During 1972–3 the School of Medicine suffered further problems, though it

The School of Nursing and Midwifery viewed from the Social Sciences Graduate Centre.

eventually began to emerge from what the Dean described as 'a continuing state of flux'. Throughout the session students again had to be taught in borrowed classrooms and lecture halls, the main block of the Medical and Biological Sciences Building at Boldrewood being handed over only in July 1973. Work on the General Hospital was held back not only by a builders' strike but by a fire in the incomplete East Ward Block. The South Academic Block, however, had been occupied at Easter, so creating 'a focal point for the

194

University's presence' at the hospital. Here there were now lecture theatres, a library, a postgraduate centre and centres of Community Medicine and Teaching Media. Meanwhile the number of students admitted each year continued to increase.

In 1976 the first intake of students completed their course, all but one being successful in their final examination. That year the School had fulfilled one of its ambitions by accepting 130 new students. Meanwhile students had been asked to comment on each part of the curriculum following each of the systems courses, when they were given a 25-part, true-or-false, multiple-choice questionnaire, as well as being asked to complete anonymously a general questionnaire about the course.

Many clinical staff had been concerned that a fourth year of study in depth would mean that too much had to be crammed into the other years. They were also afraid that in future the larger numbers of students might make it impossible for staff to identify sufficient topics and provide sufficient fourth-year supervision. Nevertheless, after understandable worry by students in their first year, most became enthusiastic. Students themselves, at the end of each fourth year, arranged a day at which each would present a summary of his or her results at a day-long conference – to be followed by a ferry-boat trip to the Isle of Wight, music and drink. The systems courses of the early years had also been generally popular. Debate about all parts of the curriculum would continue, the Dean wrote. He hoped this would 'attract people to the School who enjoy innovation,' and would 'most important of all, generate enthusiasm.'

The same year Sir George Pickering, Regius Professor of Medicine at Oxford, wrote, 'The boldest and in many ways the most successful new curriculum is that of the University of Southampton,' and added about the fourth year, 'I would like to hazard the opinion that this venture of Southampton's is the most important experiment in medical education in my lifetime. It should provide the young graduate with the discipline and habits of mind of the scholar, and thus fit him for the opportunities of self-education which he will enjoy . . . for the rest of his life' (*Quest for Excellence in Medical Education*, 1976).

Ten Years On

On 27 and 28 May 1981 the Faculty celebrated (a few months early) the tenth anniversary of the opening of the Medical School. It had reached no final verdict on the new curriculum, but had already in 1977–8 decided that its main features should be retained. Meanwhile what Southampton had done was still arousing much interest. In 1979, when the Association for the Study of Medical Education met at the University, it devoted its first day to the Southampton curriculum. Now sessions on the afternoons of both 27 and 28 May 1981 were devoted to the curriculum and were attended by visitors from a number of other UK medical schools.

By July 1982, 597 students had graduated. If a verdict on the School were to depend on their view of the Southampton experience it would certainly have been favourable. Not only had fourth-year students continued to organise an annual conference at which each described the results of his or her study in depth, but others were planning an Association of Alumni, the May Ball had become an annual celebration and later that summer a group calling itself BOSOMS (Best of Southampton Old Medical Shows) was to stage a revue entitled *Beyond the Syringe* at the Edinburgh Fringe.

During 1977 the Faculty put into practice a new venture, which at first thrived, for enabling students who had had little or no science education to qualify for entry to the school. To be prepared for this they would have to take a year's foundation course. That October twelve candidates, five of them mature students, began this course, taught largely by staff from Chemistry, Physics and Biology, and next June all passed. The success of the scheme owed much to the enthusiasm of its co-ordinator, Professor Trevor Shelley. Unfortunately such students had increasing difficulty in obtaining financial support and the scheme was eventually abandoned.

Two other ventures followed. In 1976–7 the University approved the launching of a degree course in nursing. It was another five years, however – by which time a senior lecturer, Lyn Martin, had been appointed and the curriculum was ready – before October 1982 was set as the date for the first intake to arrive. This course produced its first ten graduates in 1986. Its annual intake was increased to 15 in 1989, to 20 in 1990 and to between 40 and 50 by 2000. Equally successful was a postgraduate course in Rehabilitation Studies, launched in 1978–9; eight of the first twelve students were awarded Master's Degrees, the rest diplomas.

From 1977 the Faculty, like the rest of the University, suffered increasingly from government underfunding. In 1977–8 for the first time its UGC grant ceased to be separately earmarked. At first the School used its reserves to maintain its activities, but the 1981–2 cut imposed by B & D 2 (see Part II, Chapter 4), of 10 per cent was potentially disastrous. The UGC eventually agreed that clinical departments should suffer slightly less than non-clinical but a freeze on new staff appointments remained. This was so much more devastating for Medicine than other Faculties – since all its lecturers in clinical subjects were on short-term contracts – that the University was forced to make exceptions.

A major change occurred in the Faculty when, in 1978, Professor Acheson, foundation Dean, gave up that post. He remained Professor of Clinical Epidemiology, becoming Head of the Medical Research Council's (MRC) new Environmental Epidemiology Unit when this was established at Southampton General Hospital; and in 1981–2, when the four Area Health Authorities were divided into ten District Authorities, he became Chairman of Southampton and South-West Hampshire Health Authority. In 1985, however, he left Southampton to become the Government's Chief Medical Officer. He had been succeeded as Dean by Professor Jack Howell, another of the Faculty's first five professors and, like Acheson, one of the principal architects of the School's curriculum. Howell was also by coincidence to succeed Acheson as Chairman of the District Health Authority. In 1989 he was to be President of the BMA.

If the 1970s was the decade of the curriculum, the 1980s and 1990s were those in which research gained its own high reputation. Already by 1981–2 research was being undertaken in 23 areas. To choose (doubtless invidiously) a small selection of then current projects, the Biochemical and Physiological Sciences group was continuing its study of the role of diet in thrombosis, in the development of arterial disease and in the regulating of the concentration of cholesterol in plasma. Dr Wailoo of Child Health had obtained substantial grants for his study of factors contributing to unexpected infant deaths. Community Medicine was investigating the connection between smoking and road accidents.

The MRC Environmental Epidemiology Unit had studied 12 million death certificates to enable it to identify towns with above-average incidence of certain diseases. It planned an atlas showing these, and was investigating explanations – local diet, water, occupations, housing, etc. Human Reproduction and Obstetrics was studying male infertility and the risks of pregnancy for obese women. A group in Medicine 1 had undertaken a study of the epidemiology of respiratory symptoms in Southampton, from which it had devised an operational definition of asthma – something not achieved before. In Medicine 2 the Professorial Medical Unit was researching gastro-intestinal and liver immunology. Microbiology was studying gonorrhoea and assessing the possibility of developing a vaccine, but meeting the problem that the organism could change its surface coat during an investigation.

Michelle Ferris, Young Microbiologist of the Year, and Robert Broadbridge, Young Investigator Award, 1997.

Orthopaedic Surgery had completed a study of wound infection and as a result modified its aseptic techniques at Southampton General Hospital, so reducing the occurrence there to less than 5 per cent. Primary Medical Care made an important contribution to teaching in the Medical School, using the Aldermoor Health Centre for the purpose. There Dr David Jewell had noted the coincidence that its GPs spent *above average* time counselling their patients while the centre's drugs bill was £41,000 *below average* for its practice of 8,200 patients.

A study of the burden on a family of having a schizophrenic member at home was undertaken in Psychiatry, and in Rehabilitation a parallel study of the effects on a family of having a disabled person at home. Renal Medicine was playing a part in developing a promising new drug, cyclosporin, for preventing the rejection of transplanted kidneys. And the Surgical Unit, where another foundation Professor, Sir James Fraser, had just been succeeded by Professor Irving Taylor, was assessing the use of lasers in cancer surgery.

Soon the research of certain groups began to be recognised as of special originality. One of these was the MRC's Environmental Epidemiology Unit. At first under Acheson its most interesting investigations had been into childhood leukaemia and lymphoma around the nuclear-waste reprocessing plant at Sellafield. By 1987 it had shown that it was only children *born* in the area who were at above-average risk of contracting these diseases. Under Acheson's successor, Professor David Barker, it turned its attention to the links of adult diseases like strokes and coronary heart disease with events in childhood perhaps 60 years earlier. In 1987–8 it demonstrated a link of this sort with motor neurone disease and suggested that this resulted from childhood infection with the poliomyelitis virus. Next year the Unit concluded from a study of 5,000 men in Hertfordshire born between 1911 and 1930 that those with the lowest weights at birth and at one year had the highest death rate from coronary heart disease.

There was an important development in the early 1990s. Professor Barker began to work closely with Professor Jackson of the Institute of Human Nutrition, and with staff in the Departments of Child Health and Obstetrics (an example of the way research throughout the University was becoming multi-disciplinary), and the combined group's investigations now included the possible connection of the experiences of a foetus with adult diseases. Meanwhile the Environmental Epidemiology Unit was also investigating a connection between Alzheimer's disease and aluminium, with drinking water a possible source.

A distinguished member of the Faculty at this time was Barbara Clayton, appointed Professor of Chemical Pathology and Human Metabolism in 1979. In 1983 she was to be awarded the CBE and in the New Year Honours of 1988 to be made a Dame. She was unlucky to be Dean of the Faculty during another period of exceptional financial gloom (1983–6), as was her successor, Professor Charles George (1986–90). Staff were reduced, new appointments being frozen or left temporarily unfilled as an economy. It was inevitable that teaching, research and patient care would suffer.

There were compensations. The Faculty was awarded a total of five of the UGC's new-blood staff appointments. The Medical School prospered, taking about 130 new students each year, as originally promised. The seven-week elective visit to study health care anywhere in the world at the beginning of the fourth year was proving particularly popular, though difficult for some students to afford. And research on a broad front continued. But it was only at the end of Professor George's first year as Dean (1986–7) that he was able to report the Faculty's finances to be 'virtually in balance'. To this rare and happy state of affairs research grants, contracts and consultancies were making an important contribution. By 1991–2 they totalled £6.7m. – exceeding the University Funding Council's grant.

In 1989–90 a committee chaired by Alan Thomas undertook the second review of the Medical School's curriculum. Far from reversing its novel features, they confirmed most of them and made changes to the first and second years which extended their most important feature. The more didactic introductory courses, most of which had been left in the first year, were now incorporated into the systems courses which were spread over the first two years. Professor Jack Howell was able to experience the consequences, since in the year of the change he taught the Respiratory Systems course both to first-year students under the new arrangement and to second-year students under the old arrangement. He found that 'the difference in the enthusiasm of the students was striking.' Other staff also welcomed the change.

In 1990–1, one of the first acts of the new Dean, Professor Colin Normand (1990–3), was to set up a Research Strategy Committee. This was chaired initially by Professor David Barker, later by Professor Eric Thomas, to give advice on the areas of research to which priority should be given – essentially those which already had a national or international reputation. The MRC Environmental Epidemiology Unit's work, often in co-operation with other groups, remained foremost of these. The Unit had been rated alpha plus in MRC's quinquennial research assessment. Essentially it continued to make connections between adult diseases or conditions and pre-natal or early childhood experiences. By 1993 it confirmed, from a search of many archives, a connection between men and women who had low weights in the womb or early childhood, and their liability to develop high blood pressure, diabetes and raised serum cholesterol and plasma fibrinogen concentrations. The *British Medical Journal* had (unusually) published a book describing the Unit's studies in Hertfordshire, Preston and Sheffield.

In 1993–4 it collaborated in a study of the later medical history of children born at the time of the Dutch hunger winter of 1944–5. Results suggested a link between the poor diet of mothers at this time and an increased incidence of obesity in their children at the age of 19. The unit was carrying out similar studies in other countries and these had been spectacularly successful in India,

Seyyare Beyzade running DNA samples on an acrylamide gel.

where the average birth weight was 2.5 kg. They provided more evidence to support what was becoming known as the 'Barker hypothesis'. Ahead for the unit was research to discover how size and nutrition in the womb initiated adult diseases, and how a mother's diet affected her ability to feed her unborn baby. In attempting to answer this last question the unit began in 1998 a three-year study of 20,000 Southampton women in order to relate the size, health and diet of the 3,000 of them who would probably become pregnant to their babies' size and development in the womb.

Immunopharmacology's work on asthma (and other allergies like eczema) was another research area acquiring an international reputation. In 1991 it had been awarded a £1m., five-year, MRC grant to pursue its asthma research. Stephen Holgate, head of Immunopharmacology, was also awarded an MRC Clinical Chair, of the sort which could be held wherever he chose. Holgate chose Southampton. Its asthma research was based, not on treatment of the symptoms, as was common practice, but on controlling the cause, now recognised to be inflammation of the airways. Dr Jill Warner of the Unit had discovered a specific test for potential allergy sufferers, based on T-cell responses at birth. She was also researching the effectiveness of vacuum cleaners, bed covers, dust mite sprays and dehumidifiers in protecting asthma sufferers at home. Like other research, that on asthma now involved or was influenced by the work of staff in different groups. Professor Michael Arthur of Medicine (one of the Faculty's own graduates) had made discoveries in researching cirrhosis of the liver which suggested that similar mechanisms might cause chronic inflammation of the airways. Professor John Warner of Child Health was researching the connection between asthma and the immune system. At the same time Child Health was extending its allergy research to peanuts.

The Faculty's third area of outstanding research was cancer, in particular leukaemia and lymphoma. In this field Dennis Wright, Professor of Pathology had been awarded, soon after he came to Southampton, a major international cancer prize for his work on the pathology of Burkitt's lymphoma in Uganda. Similarly, Professor George Stevenson, director of the Tenovus Cancer Research Laboratory, was co-recipient of the first Armand Hammer award for his work on the immunology treatment of lymphoma. Professor Freda Stevenson, also of the Tenovus Laboratory, was testing a unique genetic cancer vaccine using the DNA of cancer tumours. 'In theory tumour cells should be killed by the immune system,' she explained, 'because it is programmed to destroy anything which is not a normal healthy cell. However, tumour cells are cunning. Though clearly labelled, they have developed ways of switching off the immune system to their presence. Our vaccine puts the immune system back on the scent. We reproduce in the patient those same tumour labels but this time the immune system is able to recognise them. It is then able to mount an attack on the tumour cells.'

Since cancer research depended on the management of patients with lymphomas and testicular cancers, and thus on collaboration between laboratory scientists and clinicians, it was a great help that the Cancer Research

Campaign Medical Oncology group was based at Southampton.

During the 1990s a decision was made to broaden the portfolio of health professions as part of the University's expansion. On 1 August 1995 the Faculty of Medicine became the Faculty of Medicine, Health and Biological Sciences. This now contained four schools: Medicine, Nursing and Midwifery, Occupational Therapy and Physiotherapy, and Biological Sciences. (Non-medical aspects of Biological Sciences are discussed in Part III, Chapter 7.) The new Faculty employed 800 staff and was the largest budgetary group in the University.

The School of Occupational Therapy and Physiotherapy was a new venture, which from the outset integrated education of the two professions wherever possible. The School soon developed research and postgraduate teaching across a wide field of rehabilitation, and was joined by Podiatry to form the School of Health Professions and Rehabilitation Sciences. The School of Nursing and Midwifery amalgamated the small degree course in nursing with the education previously provided through the NHS. The School was based in Southampton, but with sub-campuses in Basingstoke, Portsmouth and the Isle of Wight. The main aim of research was the promotion of effective nursing by the collection and assessment of evidence about current practice.

Within the School of Biological Sciences the Institute of Human Nutrition (which had received a 5* rating in the 1996 Research Assessment Exercise) was researching the part played by the bacteria of the lower bowel in providing the body with essential amino acids. Their ability to do this, it had found, could be enhanced by a correctly balanced diet. This was a discovery which could transform ideas about enabling the world's 850 million starving people to obtain adequate protein. The School of Biological Sciences now covered the whole range of biology in its teaching and research, from the chemistry of enzymes at one extreme to (theoretical) studies of why sex is a good thing at the other. Undergraduate numbers had increased enormously from just eight in 1956 to over 700. Academic staff numbers had also increased, from one in 1952 to 40, and a Graduate School with about 100 research students.

Alongside the Professors and scientists of the Faculty, one administrator, Sheila Mooney, must be mentioned. Her contribution to the Faculty's success over some 25 years was out of all proportion to her position as Senior Assistant Registrar. Her competence was outstanding. 'Members of the Medical Faculty would always perform better,' others remembered, 'if they came with a brief from Sheila.' What made Sheila unusual was that she combined this with an enormous enjoyment of everything she did, from her work to her sailing. Sir Charles George remembered above all her 'fairness, loyalty and fun – she always enjoyed a good laugh,' a frequent sound at both the Hospital and Boldrewood.

The School of Medicine earned itself a notable expansion of its research capabilities when, in 1997, it won a £3m. Wellcome Trust Millennial Clinical Research Facility award. Professor Eric Thomas, Head of the School of Medicine, and Professor Michael Arthur had been largely responsible for Southampton's application for one of these awards, which had been made

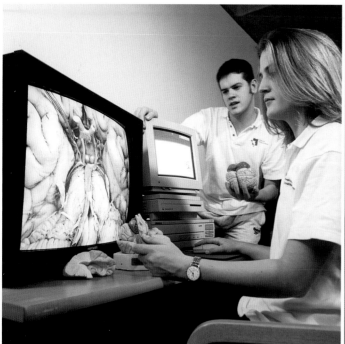

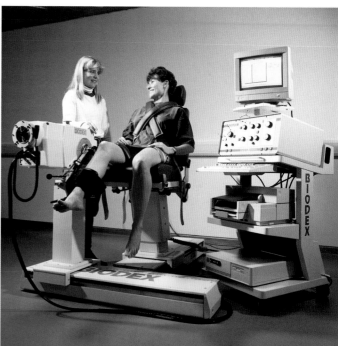

The School of Health Professions and Rehabilitation Sciences.

Above left: *learning through multi-media facilities.*

Above right: *muscle performance testing in the bio-mechanices laboratory, using 'Biodex Isokinetic' testing equipment.*

Right: *anatomy put into practice in a splinting session.*

jointly with the Southampton University Hospital Trust. Sir Charles George, Dean for a second spell, described the award as the School's 'peak of research for the year'. There had been 31 applications and Southampton had been one of five to be successful. The money would pay for a 1,000 sq. m. building at Southampton General Hospital with a room for 12 in-patient beds, another for eight out-patients and a fully equipped clinical investigation area.

By the mid-1990s, 2,000 doctors had graduated from the School. It was receiving 157 new students a year when in 1999 it was asked to take an additional 24, to be followed by further expansion – a deserved recognition of 28 years of original teaching, producing what the members of the Faculty like to think is a recognisable Southampton doctor.

In December 1999 the School was independently reviewed for its teaching – especially the way in which this was implemented and evaluated. It received the maximum grade. This exercise is continuing nationally and to date only a very small number of schools have received such a score. Its founding fathers had good reason to be pleased.

6. Research and Graduate School of Education

In September 1999 the remaining Department of the Faculty of Education – the Research and Graduate School of Education – merged with the Faculty of Social Sciences, bringing to an end more than fifty years of faculty status. The training of teachers at the Hartley College had begun 100 years earlier in the 1890s. The chapter glances back at those times but is mainly about teacher training and other educational activities, carried on under various names, since the Second World War.

At latest by 1896–7 the College was running courses for pupil teachers (who might be as young as 14, but were vital at this time for teaching in elementary schools). Three years later the Day Training Department was formed with the support of the Department of Education to train adult teachers. From then onwards the Department of Education was as important a funder (and critic) of the College as was the Treasury, and trainee teachers, until the start of the Second World War, almost always formed a majority of the College's students. Even between the Wars, when Joe Cock, most fondly remembered of staff of these years, was Professor of Education as well as Philosophy, and when student numbers as a whole fell from about 500 to reach 269 by 1939, trainee teachers still numbered 156. During the War their number did indeed fall, as well as their proportion of total numbers, since potential teachers (unlike scientists and engineers) were not allowed to postpone their military service. They rose quickly again to 168 in 1947–8, with many men and women back from the War. These ex-servicemen, in the words of Dudley, now the Professor of Education, 'set an example of zeal, industry and interest in all that pertains to teaching which had . . . been a source of inspiration to the tutors.' Some students were taking a four-year course, some a one-year course, these both leading to a Cambridge Certificate in Education.

By the time the College became a University there had been several changes. Most of the ex-servicemen had gone (the last two left in 1955); the Ministry had closed the four-year course, a move widely favoured – Dudley describing it as a parallel means of entering the universities for less qualified scholars who were 'good enough to teach'; and a new body interested in education had arrived on campus, the Institute of Education, with its own building.

Though the College's Faculty of Education shared this building, formed part of the Institute and provided Dudley to be its Director, the Institute was not exclusively a University body. It had been formed in response to the McNair Report of 1944 which recommended that teacher-training colleges be linked to their local universities, and Southampton's six local training colleges as well as the local education authority were represented in the Institute. It did, however, affect the Faculty, most immediately by creating its own Certificate in Education. Thereafter the Faculty's students worked for this instead of the Cambridge certificate. So did the trainee teachers of the local training colleges. In 1954 a total of 534 were examined by the Institute for its Certificate and all except 16 were successful. The Institute soon extended its activities, running courses and conferences, and from 1953–4 awarding Diplomas of Education to practising teachers who took part-time courses. In 1950 Professor F. W. Wagner came from Oxford University's Department of Education to succeed Dudley, as both head of the Faculty and Director of the Institute. Wagner was an Australian, educated in England at Christ's Hospital and at Oxford where he was a Rhodes Scholar. He was hard-working, competent and in many ways effective.

By 1954–5 the Faculty's make-up and activities had settled into a pattern which they were to follow for almost 15 years. Virtually all its students were graduates taking a one-year course leading to a certificate in education. The majority had graduated at Southampton, but sometimes almost half at other universities. About twice as many were Arts graduates as Science or Economics graduates. Women graduates in the Arts outnumbered men, but men graduates in Science and Economics outnumbered women, so producing roughly equal numbers. Over 95 per cent of students were usually awarded certificates. Most then went to teach at secondary rather than junior schools.

There were regular reforms of the course, an early one giving new trainees two weeks' teaching experience at the start of their first term. Also successful was the substitution in 1962 of essays for three-hour, final examination papers. Numbers rose steadily, starting at 70 a year. In 1957 the Ministry realised that the country would need many more teachers and began to encourage teacher-training colleges and universities to train more. In response, the Faculty planned to raise its intake to 120 a year by 1961–2 and was given more staff and an enlarged building. For the first time this included a laboratory-workshop to enable trainees to prepare themselves for teaching practical science.

Numbers did not rise quite so much (to 108 by 1961–2), chiefly because schools were increasingly employing graduates who had no training in teaching, this in turn a consequence of the Ministry's failure to give a date at which a teacher-training qualification would be compulsory. But the new accommodation was fully occupied because it was also being used by some 30 bursars from Commonwealth countries taking Institute of Education courses.

This account of a Faculty functioning effectively, improving its teaching and expanding in numbers, is unfortunately only part of the truth. It was not a happy Faculty and for this Wagner's authoritarian style of management was responsible. Matters became worse from October 1963 when it was given a second Chair, and Professor Jack Wrigley came, to be responsible for research. A research unit was set up 'to investigate problems in education of fundamental and great practical importance.' 'I had always thought I could get along with people,' Wrigley remembered. Wagner proved an exception.

Wrigley's position was in part the trouble. It gave him responsibility but not power. Wagner had supported Wrigley's appointment because in theory he wanted the Faculty and Institute to undertake research – till now it had done little, staff only publishing an occasional book – but in practice he resented Wrigley, criticising and interfering with his work. An open rift occurred when

Wrigley proposed support for a project by one of his research assistants, Fred Inglis, on the teaching of English. Wagner wanted to reject this project and there was an open row in committee. Wagner lost the vote and Fred Inglis subsequently published *The Englishness of English Teaching*.

Thereafter members of the Faculty, indeed of the University, aligned themselves with Wrigley, or (in smaller numbers) with Wagner. A group of newly appointed young professors (Sims, Hills, Griffiths) 'rather egged me on,' Wrigley remembered. He admitted that Wagner knew his job. What he did not know was how to treat his staff. 'He couldn't harm me, but others he could and did harm.' This was in contrast to the University as a whole which Wrigley considered 'very democratic, with long meetings of Senate at which real issues were discussed'.

Vice-Chancellor James 'had little time for Wagner,' according to Wrigley. James's successor, Mather, on the other hand, 'had a high opinion of Wagner and his Faculty. I didn't complain to him. It meant more staff for education.' When Wrigley resigned in 1967 to become Professor of Education at Reading, Mather was astonished. The only time Wrigley regretted leaving Southampton was years later when he returned on a visit and found Professor Peter Kelly, 'so confident, in charge of such a good Department'.

When Wagner died in 1979 Paul Fordham wrote of him that 'work with teachers and students came first, and in his Department a long list of publications was . . . evidence of time misspent.' This was the essence of his quarrel with Wrigley. He did not favour research, let alone a research professor.

Meanwhile, Institute and Faculty became more closely involved with each other in the summer of 1964 when the Institute began to frame proposals for a BEd degree. Next year working parties proposed syllabuses for the degree and schemes for assessment and the examination of candidates. The course would be run at the six training colleges and last four years, the first leading to a certificate in education, the other three consisting of degree work. Those judged fit to undertake these (only a small proportion) would be selected by panels, to include a staff member of the student's college and of the University department in which the candidate wished to specialise. The first course was held in 1967–8 and in 1969 42 of those who took it were awarded a BEd.

That year the Faculty and Institute were united as the School of Education. Within this the Institute would continue to be responsible for awarding Certificates in Education, but the Faculty would take responsibility for the BEd. The Faculty Board as well as the Institute Board would have representatives from the training colleges.

By 1970 over 200 graduates were taking one-year teacher-training courses at the University. The Board of the Faculty was also awarding BEd degrees to more than 50 students at the six training colleges, while the Board of the Institute was awarding teacher certificates to more than 1,300 students from the training colleges.

In the next few years these arrangements were to be demolished. Warning that something was about to happen came when the (Eric) James report, *Teacher Education and Training*, was published in January 1972. That

December came the White Paper, *Education, a Framework for Expansion*, which proposed changes quite other than those suggested by James. 'For the University,' Professor Robin Pedley, Dean of the School, wrote, 'this means not expansion but a major contraction of its responsibility for the education and training of teachers.' The White Paper removed from Southampton (as from other universities) the control which it had exercised over the training colleges in its area. Other proposals were based on the Government's intention to reduce drastically the number of teachers the country needed, thereby allowing class sizes in state schools, which would have fallen, to rise instead. A number of teacher-training colleges would close, and those which survived would be required to have at least 1,000 students.

Early in 1973 Vice-Chancellor Gower commented on the Government's proposals in a 'personal paper'. Among the various roles which Departments of Education might undertake, he believed that the University was best qualified for two: the continued training of experienced teachers and research. The role which was now its principal one, courses for graduates leading to a certificate in education, it could only continue to undertake if it expanded to reach the Government's minimum size. The vast enlargement that would require was impossible and the University should therefore abandon this activity.

There was, however, an alternative possibility: to amalgamate with one of the training colleges and establish a college of education of adequate size as part of the University. The colleges might welcome such an arrangement since they, too, were anxious about their future. Only three of them came close to the minimum size required, and were considering amalgamation. This was probably the development which Gower favoured and though he mentioned King Alfred's College, Winchester, as a possible partner, his preference was the Roman Catholic College of La Sainte Union, situated less than a mile from the Highfield Campus. By the end of the year both these possibilities had been eliminated, the first because the Department of Education and Science did not favour a new campus ten miles away at Winchester, the second because of incompatibilities between the statutes of the University and the Catholic ones of La Sainte Union. Perhaps there was also some incompatibility between Gower, an agnostic, and the devout Sister Imelda Marie, Principal of the College (though they were good friends).

In consequence the School of Education at first adopted what were in essence Gower's other suggestions. Though it did not abandon the one-year graduate course leading to a Certificate in Education, it planned to reduce the numbers accepted for this course (in the event from over 200 to 114 by 1979) and spend the time and money saved on more in-service courses for practising teachers and more research. The demand for the former was great, the Dean wrote, but without more money 'the limits of what can be expected of even the most devoted and hard-working staff must be near.'

In 1975 there was a more radical reorganisation. From August that year a newly named Faculty of Educational Studies replaced the School of Education, and both the Board of the old Faculty and the Board of the Institute ceased to exist. In Pedley's opinion the Institute had been doomed ever since the introduction of BEd degrees because universities were not willing to give institutes – which included such non-academics as schoolteachers and officers of local education authorities – responsibility for awarding degrees. This university attitude he considered 'gravely mistaken'. It was 'the reluctance of universities to embrace as truly equal partners people outside the walls . . . which today leaves us perilously alone, short not only of money and friends but – in the end most important of all – of information and ideas.' The Board of the new Faculty would, however, retain the old Board's responsibility for the teaching of graduate trainees on campus and for its research. Now again under its original name as the Department of Education, it was also soon extending its in-service teaching, in particular with a part-time MA (Ed). At the same time a Board of Collegiate Studies was created, to include representatives of the associated colleges, which would oversee all courses run by these colleges.

More fundamentally, the new Faculty would include three previously separate Departments: Adult Education, Physical Education and Teaching Media. At this time Adult Education had some 5,000 enrolments (and could have had more with more money). For many years one of its activities had been Service Education, including the training of army officers and 'defence studies'. As part of the latter it regularly took part in conferences, often at the Royal Naval College, Greenwich. Physical Education was a small Department (14 in 1975–6), partly because students had to prove themselves physically fit for it, partly because the amount of a student's time it took made it difficult to combine with a main course. In 1979, however, it launched a new course for graduate trainee teachers, designed to qualify them for teaching all manner of games and sports, from rugby and netball to athletics.

Fastest growing of the added Departments was Teaching Media, founded in 1971. Ten years later it had a staff of 30, mainly involved in providing audio-visual material to support the teaching of other Departments and associated bodies. Its largest clients were the Wessex Regional Health Authority and the Area Health Authorities within the region. It also served the Faculties of Medicine, Engineering and Science and other Faculties. And it provided material for internal university communications, public relations and fund-raising. In 1985 it made more than 100,000 photographic transparencies and 60,000 prints. Meanwhile it had developed an introductory course on the uses of media in teaching for probationary lecturers.

The new Faculty aimed to be 'a major channel of communication between the University and its region' (Paul Fordham, Dean from 1975 to 1979). This did not prevent it establishing a Centre for International Studies in Education, and cultivating an increasing number of foreign links, for example with the Universities of Frankfurt and Dar es Salaam.

Fordham had been, and was again to be, an effective Dean, considered by colleagues a skilful university politician and sharp but not abrasive. He was succeeded as Dean by Peter Kelly, from Chelsea College. Professor Kelly brought with him a new (if somewhat desperate) vitality. 'When you are up to your butt in alligators,' he quoted at the start of his 1979–80 report, 'it is difficult to remember that you are supposed to be draining the swamp.' The alligators were, of course, the Government and its agent, the UGC. Clearing the swamp was spreading the message that 'educational innovation is of fundamental importance to the life of the country and its economic recovery' – a message which, as far as it concerned Higher Education, the Government had still not understood. Besides enthusiasm, Kelly's most important contribution to the Faculty was the promotion of research. His own research, mainly into health education, he had mostly already done, but he now encouraged others.

In 1981–2 the Faculty attempted 'to look at the future as positively as it could,' Kelly wrote. The events of October and November 1981 had led to the most dramatic split of the century in the University when B & D 1 proposed the way in which each Faculty would suffer. Education's funding was to be cut by 30 per cent, far more than any other Faculty's, almost four times as much as the cuts imposed on Science, Medicine and Engineering. B & D 2 reduced Education's suffering to 14.7 per cent. Painful as this was, what was not generally realised, Kelly wrote, was the serious effect it would have on people outside the University. In-service and adult education courses would both suffer. So would University Faculties served by the Faculty of Educational Studies.

The funding in the form of research grants and contracts which the Faculty was now receiving helped it to recover. On the other hand it faced new problems. The reduction in staff which had followed meant that those who taught had no time for research. Researchers thus became separated from teachers and could not benefit from each other's experiences. Furthermore the Faculty had to decide in which activity it should invest more heavily. Relentlessly, driven by University policy and the fact that a large proportion of government funding was related directly to a faculty's research rating, this grew in importance. Between 1973 and 1983 research students increased from 10 to 42, and part-time postgraduates from 32 to 176. Teaching, as represented by the number of higher degrees awarded each year (87 Masters degrees in 1983) also rose but not to the same extent.

During the last 15 years of the century the Faculty of Educational Studies underwent a succession of further changes which culminated in its dismemberment. In 1987 came the establishment of a School of Education within the Faculty, which brought together the research group of the Department of Adult Education and the Education Department. An underlying aim of this amalgamation was to unify the research which both Departments had been undertaking and allow Adult Education to concentrate on extra-mural teaching.

The following year was a successful one. The number of students taking what was now known as the Postgraduate Certificate in Education course rose, and recruitment of mature students to the two-year mathematics course, also leading to a Certificate in Education, was particularly successful. This encouraged the Faculty to bid successfully for a further increase in numbers for such courses of 40 per cent.

At the same time the 1989 Research Assessment Exercise judged the Faculty above average. Its research activities were soon falling into three areas: research into the nature and effectiveness of the teaching and research of other

Faculties or Departments; the teaching of research students how to undertake research, a new development in 1990–1; and general research into teaching and education.

The latter in turn fell into various categories, among them health education, for example a study of children's attitudes to smoking and to puberty; language education, for example into the consequences of the introduction of the National Curriculum for bilingual children, but more generally into the processes of language teaching; information technology and so-called distance education, this with European Community funding; assessment and evaluation, for example into the nature and effectiveness of school-governor training; and environmental education, this being supported by UNESCO and by industry, and concerning among other things developing training materials for environmental education in schools and industry. These other projects gained the Faculty a rating of 4 in the 1992 Research Assessment Exercise.

Meanwhile, among many changes to which the Faculty had to adjust was the Government's requirement that in-service courses should provide individual schools with what *they* wanted rather than what Local Education Authorities considered they ought to want. In 1994 it also stipulated that students taking Postgraduate Certificate in Education courses should spend much more time practising teaching in schools and less studying their specialist subjects at a university.

Although the University retained responsibility for awarding certificates, the result of this change was that the schools took on much of the actual training. This should have reduced the work of the University's staff, but in practice it did not, and the Faculty had in addition to pay the schools for the extra training they were providing, thus severely straining its budget. Changes of these sorts, imposed by central government, made teaching educators feel, as Gordon Bloomer wrote in his short history of education at Southampton, 'increasingly to be no longer in control of their own destiny.'

In 1992 the Department of Teaching Media left the Faculty, to become a non-academic provider of services. But it was not until the University acquired the (bankrupt) College of La Sainte Union in 1997 that the Faculty was fully dismembered. Adult Education then moved to the La Sainte Union Campus, renamed the University's New College, and became independent of the Faculty. The Department of Physical Education, though it had undertaken a fair amount of research since it became part of the Faculty, was reduced like Teaching Media to a non-academic provider of services. The Faculty thus would have consisted of the single School of Education, but since this was considered too small to be a Faculty, it merged with the Faculty of Social Sciences. In the 1996 Research Assessment Exercise these had again earned a rating of 4.

7. Science

'The past session in this Faculty has been very prosperous,' Professor Neil Adam, the Dean, began his 1952 report. By the year 2002 many of the Departments on which he was reporting had left the Faculty. Mathematics had become a Faculty of its own; Zoology and Botany (united as Biology) and Physiology (launched in 1952–3) had joined the Faculty of Medicine; while one other Department, Oceanography, did not yet exist. Chemistry, Geography and Physics, however, were core Departments of the Faculty as they still are today. So is Geology, as part of the School of Ocean and Earth Science.

Throughout the 1950s and early 1960s the Science Faculty grew steadily, its students in 1958–9 totalling 517, of whom 65 were postgraduates. It could have grown more quickly if it had had more staff, funds and accommodation, and had been allowed to do so. For admission in October 1960 it had 1,522 applicants – half as many again as in the previous year – but was only permitted to take 160. Meanwhile it steadily increased its research. 'Nothing can do more,' Adam wrote, 'to establish our reputation throughout the world as a vigorous young university.'

In 1961–2 the Faculty took an important step towards enhancing the standing of its undergraduate degrees. In future, all undergraduates would start on an honours degree and only those who were not up to honours standard would continue in the second and third years to work for an ordinary degree. The new arrangement was a success. Of the 292 students who completed their first year in 1965, 240 were judged fit to continue to work for an honours degree.

Two other significant changes, foretastes of what was to follow, were occurring in these years. The proportion of postgraduate research students grew. In 1960–1 they had numbered 107 out of a total of 594 undergraduate and postgraduate students. Next year they increased to 147, while only four additional undergraduates were allowed. The Faculty was also gaining increasing outside support for research. In 1958–9 it had 22 research funders, ranging from the Admiralty and the US Army to the British Empire Cancer Campaign.

In 1963, the Robbins report seemed to give recognition to what all science-based universities had long been saying: that for the good of the country they must expand. Southampton was allowed to bring forward the date by which it would reach 4,000 students from 1980 to 1967–8. The Science Faculty's share in this expansion would be to more than double undergraduate and postgraduate research student numbers from 730 to 1,485. To provide the senior staff these additional students would need, the University appointed 11 Professors to the Faculty, four to arrive in 1967–8, the other seven the following year. Among these, the one to become most distinguished in his field, and the first Southampton alumnus to become an FRS, was Alan Carrington of Chemistry; the one to have most influence on the University's expansion was Henry Charnock of Oceanography.

The 1967–72 quinquennium was a period of consolidation with numbers rising only slightly, but already by 1971 it seemed likely that in the subsequent quinquennium there would be a further increase of around 30 per cent in the Faculty's student numbers. It therefore set about reorganising itself with the general aims of encouraging growth in specific areas rather than uniform expansion, and of encouraging inter-disciplinary courses and research. Both these would produce economies and would make the Faculty more attractive to students. Two concrete results were the launch of a new undergraduate degree in Environmental Sciences and the combining of Botany and Zoology into a single Department of Biology from the start of the 1972 session.

The Environmental Sciences course became possible as part of a long-planned change in course structure in the Faculty. The unit course scheme, developed by a working party under the Chairmanship of Professor Graham Hills of Chemistry, enabled students to 'build' their degrees from a number of units provided by different departments. According to the Faculty report in 1972, 'The flexibility inherent in a unit course scheme could have many advantages for the undergraduate; it reflects the Faculty's increasing inter-disciplinary co-operation.' In the following year, the scheme was described as 'one of the most far-reaching changes agreed by the Faculty in its teaching for many years. A noteworthy feature of the unit course structure is that it has been found possible to allow students in certain cases to take two subjects to degree level, whereas previously only a small number of joint Honours degrees were available.' The common basis for the provision of units led to more radical and challenging degree programmes – for example, the full Honours programme in two subjects was completed in four-year Double Honours programmes, leading to degrees with a separate classification in each subject.

One of the Government's most remarkable suggestions, contradicting almost all previous and subsequent advice, formed part of the UGC's 1972–7 quinquennial settlement: that universities should save money by taking a smaller proportion of postgraduate students. 'Applied nationally,' Professor Frank Hodson, the Dean, wrote, 'the deleterious effect of discouraging research might not become apparent for a decade and could take another decade to rectify.' Five years later, when the UGC replaced quinquennial settlements with forecasts of government funding for only a year ahead, it showed an even more remarkable ignorance of the time needed to plan and carry out research or to launch new courses.

In practice, the Science Faculty survived well. It welcomed and took advantage of budgetary devolution – the new arrangement introduced in April 1974 which gave each Faculty its own budget to spend at its discretion. Alongside good financial management, the Faculty helped itself by devising more courses or course programmes which would attract students – vital when direct government funding was based largely on numbers. Southampton was able to do this and still choose good students because its reputation in schools was improving and the number of applications it received each year was increasing rather than paralleling the national decline.

In 1976, Mathematics was finally allowed to become a Faculty in its own right and Physiology and Biochemistry became financially part of the Faculty of Medicine. Physics also lost Cryogenics, which became a separate Institute within the Faculty of Engineering and Applied Sciences. Despite the financial difficulties which universities experienced in the late 1970s and early 1980s, the different departments within the Faculty managed to maintain and enhance their research reputations. In addition, the undergraduate courses continued to attract well-qualified students. The later years of the 1980s began with excellent results in the 1985–6 Research Assessment Exercise. Chemistry was judged one of the five outstanding departments in the country, while Geography, Geology, Oceanography and Physics were all above average. Forty-three per cent of the University's postgraduate research students now worked in the Faculty.

The 1990s began with more of the same. The Government continued to reduce its direct funding, partly by cutting the unit of resource (payment per student), partly by transferring monies from direct support to research councils. The effective cut in 1993–4, for example, was 10 per cent. The Faculty responded by putting yet more emphasis on research, concentrating more emphatically on what it did best and making still greater efforts to win grants, contracts and consultancies. As the following sections on individual departments indicate, that emphasis continues today. At the same time, the Faculty continued to review and respond to the needs of undergraduates and their employers. In the early 1990s, following the lead shown by Engineering and Applied Sciences, it introduced new four-year full-time programmes of study which contained a significant element of professional education and which led, initially, to the degrees of MChem and MPhys in the Chemistry and Physics Departments respectively, but was subsequently extended to include MGeog, MGeol, MOcean and MEnvSci. All departments within the Faculty were judged 'excellent' (with 22 or more points out of 24) in the national assessment of teaching quality over the period 1993–2000, a singular achievement.

In the late 1990s, the Faculty's undergraduate numbers stabilised at around 1,400, while the number of postgraduate instructional students, postgraduate research students and research grant income continued to increase at a rate of around 10 per cent per year. Following further growth in key research areas and buoyed by strong departmental performances in both research and teaching, the Faculty felt confident enough to take a longer view. It articulated a collective vision for its future 'to be one of the UK's leading centres for scientific research and teaching' and a strategy to achieve this vision – 'maintain an unwavering commitment to excellence in research and research-led teaching' – that was supported by a bold strategic plan. 'It is this commitment to international levels of excellence coupled with tight financial control that will ensure the success of each and every component of the Science Faculty in the years to come,' wrote Professor Paul Curran, the Dean, in 2001. In the Research Assessment Exercise of 2001 all parts of the Faculy were graded 5/5* – the highest level of research performance.

Biological Sciences

When Southampton achieved University status, the Science Faculty included separate Departments of Botany and Zoology. Within a few years, autonomous Departments of Physiology and of Oceanography had emerged from Zoology. During the 1950s, the Zoology Department carried out a range of research into plankton, some of this in collaboration with the Harbour Board and the electricity authorities, with respect to the industrialisation of the Southampton Water neighbourhood. Botany research at this time was concerned with topics such as the decline of *Spartia townsendii* in the Lymington estuary, larch canker, the effect of x-rays on chromosomes and the metabolism of fats in oil seeds.

In 1959, Physiology became an autonomous Department and, three years later, Kenneth Munday was appointed its first Professor. When Oceanography became a separate Department in October 1964, John Raymont became Professor of Biological Oceanography. His successor as Professor of Zoology was L. Brent, who brought with him a research group in tissue transplantation immunology and reorientated the Department's interests towards cell and developmental biology.

On 1 August 1972, the new Department of Biology came into existence, bringing together Botany and Zoology. Its research interests fell into six major categories: cell biology, developmental studies, genetics, ecology, behavioural studies, plant diseases. Research in Physiology and Biochemistry (as it was now called) included: biochemical elucidation of metabolic pathways in mammals and bacteria; nutrition, including the aetiology of diabetes, cardio-vascular disorders and obesity; and physiological mechanisms by which the renin-angiotensin system regulates sodium ion and fluid transport processes in the kidney and intestines. With the medical emphasis of much of the research, it was not surprising that these Departments became more closely associated with the emergent Faculty of Medicine (see Part III, Chapter 5). However, the research interests were not entirely medical. In the late 1970s, there were still strong agricultural interests, such as fungal diseases of cereals, parasites of farm animals, plant breeding and the farming of deer. The breadth of research is indicated by the fact that, in the early 1980s, the Department of Biology was in receipt of major research awards from all four of the Science Research Councils – Agriculture and Food, Medical, Science and Engineering, and Natural Environment. During the 1980s considerable activity developed in the Department on the impact of pesticides on the environment and ways of improving the environment for beneficial insects.

In 1988, the Southwood report on the future of biological sciences in the UK was published. Its major conclusions had already been foreshadowed by the University's own working party on the biological sciences, which recommended the creation of a new School, bringing together the Department of Biology and the School of Biological and Physiological Science. The new School came into being on 1 August 1990 with John Hall as the first Head of School. At its inception, it had four Departments: Biochemistry, Biology,

The Botanical Laboratories today, now home to the Careers Advisory Service.

Human Nutrition, and Physiology and Pharmacology.

In the early 1990s, the School continued to expand its research in non-medical areas. Under the direction of Dr John Bradshaw, a new Anthrozoology Institute was established in 1993 to focus on interactions between humans and other animals. In the same year, Biology was undertaking research on crops in Ghana, on the effects of pollutants on soil ecosystems, and on fish genetics. A year later, Steven Hawkins was appointed to the Chair of Environmental Biology, with special interests in marine biodiversity and ecology, while the University Centre for Bioelectrostatics was set up in conjunction with the Department of Electrical Engineering.

On 1 August 1995, the Faculty of Medicine, Health and Biological Sciences came into being and biological sciences ceased formally to be a part of the Faculty of Science.

Chemistry

Chemistry started its life as a University Department with new buildings, which had opened in stages between 1948 and 1952. 'The new Chemistry block was ready for use by the beginning of the session, and has proved very satisfactory,' wrote Professor Adam, in his Dean's report for 1952–3. 'There is ample provision for expansion when this becomes necessary; but unless unexpected developments occur, the present building should suffice for a good many years.'

Adam, who was already a Fellow of the Royal Society when he came to Southampton as Head of Department in 1937, was distinguished for his studies on surface films. Others in the Department in the early 1950s worked on a variety of organic chemical reactions, organometallic chemistry and spectroscopy, some of the latter in collaboration with a group in the Physics Department which was to become the nucleus of the Electronics Department – an early example of the cross-disciplinary research which is now an enormously important feature in the University's research portfolio. Also presaging future interests were syntheses of molecules which were then studied for their pharmacological activity.

When Professor Adam retired in 1957, he was succeeded as Head of Department by Richard Cookson. Cookson, who came to Southampton from a Readership at Birkbeck College, London, was primarily an organic chemist. His special interest was synthesis, including routes to perfumes. In the early 1960s, a second Chair (in Physical Chemistry) was created in the Department; this went to Graham Hills whose particular research interest was in electrochemistry. Perhaps more importantly, he was a brilliant university politician and eventually left Southampton in 1980 to become Principal and Vice-Chancellor of Strathclyde University. Hills and Cookson shared a determination that the Department should grow and prosper. This ambition made Chemistry the grade 5 Department it had become by the 1990s – one of only four chemistry departments (with Oxford, Cambridge and Imperial College, London) to have been rated 5 or 5* in all Research Assessment Exercises to date.

Good appointments were an essential feature of Cookson and Hills's policy. They believed, as their successors do today, that outstanding individuals can often be identified at the outset of their careers and then supported. However, they also appointed distinguished chemists from outside. Hills persuaded Martin Fleischmann, possibly the most brilliant electrochemist in the country at that time, to come to Southampton, and the Central Electricity Generating Board to sponsor the Electricity Council Faraday Professorship for him. In the common room, if Fleischmann saw an empty chair beside another member of staff or student, he would take it and instantly start to tell him, whether scientist or not, about his latest idea. These 'bubbled from him, one a day at least. You never knew what was coming next,' recalls Geoffrey Luckhurst.

Shortly after his retirement in the mid-1980s, Fleischmann became briefly world-famous for one idea, the validity of which many questioned: cold fusion. Together with Professor Stanley Pons of Utah, Fleischmann claimed to have demonstrated the fusion of atomic nuclei – the process which powers the Sun – in a small electrochemical cell at room temperature. If true, this might have led to virtually inexhaustible supplies of energy at low cost. Unfortunately, few of Fleischmann's fellow scientists believed him and the number who did has dwindled, although not completely vanished. The future will determine whether cold fusion was indeed achieved or whether their claim was erroneous.

Coincident with Fleischmann's arrival at Southampton, Ian Beattie joined the Department as Professor of Inorganic Chemistry. Soon afterwards, Alan Carrington, who had taken both his BSc and PhD at Southampton, was appointed to a further Professorship, with the needs of theoretical chemistry in mind. With this group of five Professors, the Department's research effort expanded rapidly. As in many chemistry departments, academic staff pursued a range of individual interests; nevertheless, certain key themes emerged, such as advanced forms of spectroscopy, electrochemistry and synthetic methods. The use of lasers in chemistry was developing at this time and, as a result of Beattie's interests in structural chemistry, Southampton became the first university in the UK to have equipment for laser Raman spectroscopy.

A decade after Adam had talked about the 'ample provision for expansion' in the Chemistry building, the Robbins report provided the 'unexpected development' which led to shortage of space. A new building came into use in 1962–3, but the Department was still short of space until part of the physical chemistry section was able to transfer to the old Physics building in 1967 to provide temporary relief.

The Department's strength in electrochemistry led to the introduction of an international summer school in the subject in 1969. This continues today, when it not only draws participants to Southampton from Europe and further afield, but also has been successfully repeated in both North and South America. The establishment of the Wolfson Centre for Electrochemical Science reflected the interest in applied electrochemistry and the Department's strong links with industry. Another innovation of the late 1960s was the introduction of lecture

*The Chemistry Department: efficient,
modern 2 m. fume cupboards.*

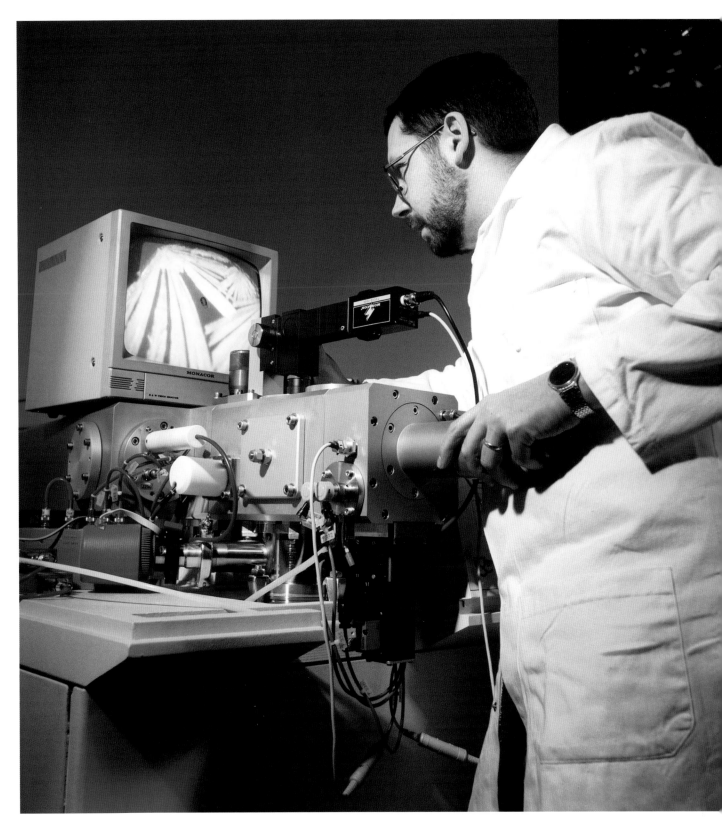

*The Chemistry Department: modern
mass spectrometry.*

courses as part of the Graduate Training Programme. At the time, it was uncommon for postgraduate research students in British universities to have to attend any lectures, but these lecture courses have remained an important part of graduate training to the present day. They also led to the development of MSc programmes (see below) and, in the 1990s, to a five-year pilot programme in conjunction with EPSRC to develop the MRes degree, offering an MRes in Chemistry.

In 1971, the Department initiated an MSc degree in Photochemistry. This was followed later in the decade by MScs in Electrochemical Science and, with Biology, in Insect Control Research Methods. Involvement in chemical entomology emerged from the research interests of Ray Baker, who had joined the Department as a lecturer in 1964 and was promoted to a personal Chair in 1977. Baker collaborated with the biologists and the end result of this work was the formation of the Institute of Chemical Entomology. Baker left Southampton in the mid-1980s for a post in the pharmaceutical industry and the Department's interest in chemical entomology has now waned, although the School of Biological Sciences continues to have both academic and commercial interests in applied entomology.

The first personal Chair in the Department had been awarded in 1973 to Neville Jonathan, who took over responsibility for physical chemistry as Graham Hills became more concerned with University affairs as Deputy Vice-Chancellor. Jonathan, who subsequently became Dean of the Faculty in the early 1980s, undertook research on gas-phase chemiluminescent reactions, infra-red emission and dynamics of simple atom–molecule reactions with particular application to the design of gas-phase chemical lasers, and new methods of production of semiconductor materials by chemical vapour deposition.

From the late 1970s to the present day, Professor Geoffrey Luckhurst and his team have carried out significant fundamental research into the fascinating behaviour of liquid crystals: substances which flow as liquids, but show some of the characteristics of crystals. The importance of liquid crystals and their technological applications, especially in the field of flat-panel displays, has increased enormously in the past 20 years. In 1997, the Southampton Liquid Crystal Institute was inaugurated. This multi-disciplinary centre, involving chemists, mathematicians and physicists, is now under the directorship of Professor Harry Coles of the Department of Physics and Astronomy.

Following Richard Cookson's retirement in 1985, Professor Philip Kocienski became Professor of Organic Chemistry. He expanded the Department's interest in pharmaceutical and medicinal chemistry. The synthesis in the mid-1990s of mycalamide, an immunosuppressant 1,000 times more active than those then in use, is an example of the successful research which his group undertook in this field.

1986–7 saw another major cross-Departmental development: the formation of the Institute of Biomolecular Science. The aim of this was to encourage collaborative research and the sharing of expertise at the interfaces of chemistry, biochemistry and medicine. In Chemistry, the Laboratory for Bio-organic Chemistry was opened in 1993, with joint funding from the University and the Wolfson Foundation.

In the early 1990s, a number of Professors were appointed, some continuing the Department's traditional interests, others broadening and strengthening the research spectrum. In 1991, Professor Roger Parsons, who had succeeded Fleischmann as Professor of Electrochemistry, retired, to be succeeded in turn by Philip Bartlett. One of Bartlett's research interests has been the development of an 'electronic nose' to identify specific odours. This research, which involves participation from electronic engineering, information technology and biology, has been widely supported by external grants because of its potential applications in animal health, environmental monitoring and the food and beverage industry. At about the same time, Tom Brown joined the Department as Professor of Bio-organic Chemistry and established strong links with Biochemistry with work on genetic analysis and studies of DNA repair. On the inorganic side, John Evans became Professor of Inorganic Chemistry with research interests in studies of inorganic materials, notably industrial catalysts, using synchrotron radiation. Professor Evans is currently Chair of the Users' Group of the Diamond Project which is establishing a new high-energy radiation facility near Oxford.

The level of instrumentation available within the Department increased significantly during the 1990s. There are now 13 high-field NMR spectrometers and nine mass spectrometers, and the Department gained significantly in instrumentation and expertise with the move of the EPSRC National Crystallographic Service to Southampton following the appointment of Professor Mike Hursthouse to the Chair of Structural Chemistry in 1997.

As early as 1991–2 the Department was again drawing attention to the severe deficiencies in both quality and size of its accommodation. Vice-Chancellor Gordon Higginson, when showing round visitors from the Universities' Funding Council, would begin, 'Here you have a grade-five department in a grade-three building.' For health and safety reasons, almost all synthetic chemistry research work was by now being done in fume cupboards rather than on the open bench, but the Department had an acute shortage of these. At last, seven years later (in May 1999) a state-of-the-art new Synthetic Chemistry Building, costing £12 million, was officially opened by Science Minister, Lord Sainsbury. It is attached to the existing chemistry buildings, has five floors and contains 17 eight-person modules for research particularly concerned with pharmaceutical and medicinal chemistry, together with facilities for materials chemistry and x-ray crystallography. This building was only the first phase of a plan to provide modern laboratories for the whole Department. The Chemistry Tower, originally built in 1962, has been refurbished and renamed the Graham Hills Building, while another building is being refurbished to provide homes for large instrumentation and much of physical chemistry, with support from the Wolfson Foundation, for research in surface science and laser spectroscopy.

The most recent development on the building front is a major research centre in combinatorial chemistry to be built alongside the Synthetic Chemistry Building. Combinatorial chemistry uses novel approaches for the rapid identi-

The opening of the Synthetic Chemistry Building in 1999.

A spectroscopic experiment using a spectrometer designed and built in the new Physical Chemistry Teaching Laboratory.

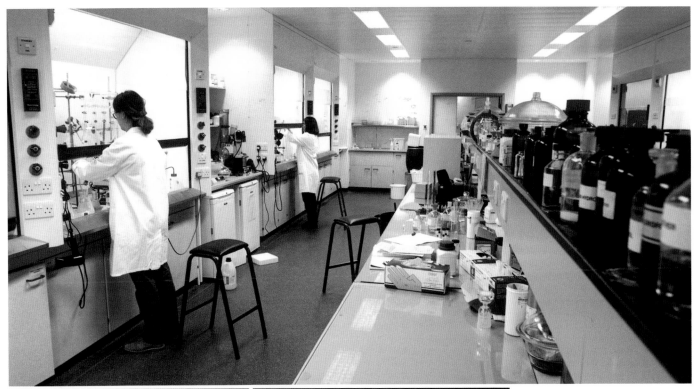

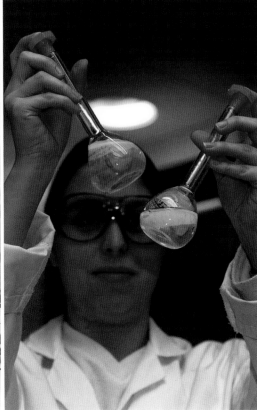

Laboratories in the new Synthetic Chemistry Building.

fication of compounds with optimal properties and is already widely used within the pharmaceutical industry to identify active components for drugs. The new centre, led by Professor Mark Bradley, currently receives support from a consortium of nine pharmaceutical companies. In parallel, a consortium of companies to support materials combinatorial chemistry has been formed, covering topics such as fuel cell catalysts and novel battery materials.

At the end of the 1990s, the Department continued to have one of the largest graduate schools outside Oxford and Cambridge. Its increasing annual research income from grants and contracts reached £4m. in 2000–1 and it secured a grade 5 in the 2001 Research Assessment Exercise.

Geography

The appointment of W. H. Barker, the first Professor of Geography in the then University College of Southampton, was on 1 October 1921. In many ways, this date represents the birth of the modern Department, which enjoyed its seventy-fifth birthday celebrations in 1996. It was to be many years, however, before Geography emerged as a separate Department with a distinct and continuous identity. At the time when Southampton was awarded University status, Geography had only recently joined the Science Faculty, after 14 years in the Economics Department. During these years, and until 1953, Florence (Flo) Miller, who had joined the Geography Department in the early 1920s, was the acting Head of Geography. Teaching was her *métier*, rather than research. 'Weeks and whole terms seemed to be spent on analysing single one-inch Ordnance Survey sheets in exhaustive detail,' recalls one of her students.

In 1954, the Department appointed its first Professor since 1936, Frank Monkhouse. Remembered as 'a great enthusiast, a congenial colleague and a wise counsellor,' he was a traditional geographer, described by a friend and former colleague as 'essentially a craftsman in the art of regional description. To him this meant a detailed analysis of the physical geography of an area, the detailed reconstruction of its economic development and a picture of the accompanying changes of landscape and settlement pattern . . . He was uncompromising in his view of the subject and had little time for theory in geography or for new developments, unless these were seen to bear fruit in a regional context.' By the time he retired in 1967, the Department had expanded from six to twelve full-time academic staff, but had not established a significant research school.

Monkhouse was succeeded by Jim Bird, a post-war Southampton alumnus and, briefly, an assistant lecturer in the Department. He had then worked in London, eventually in University College's large geography department, where he became an authority on the geography of ports. Under Professor Bird, teaching continued to be the Department's central activity, partly because of the broad coverage of the undergraduate curriculum. Gradually, however, research became more important. Staff were encouraged to teach from their own research rather than from the research of others.

Fieldwork in the 1920s.

The Geography Society Rag float, 1952.

In the late 1960s, Geography moved from its former space in the library building and two houses in University Road, to the Arts 2 building. Besides the obvious lecture rooms, this provided a cartographic studio and laboratories, one of which was used by Keith Barber for his palaeoecological research which was to acquire an international reputation.

Despite the many changes and expansions of Bird's time, he later wrote that if he had known he would have to wait nine years for a second Professor, he might have thought twice about returning to Southampton. The second Professor, who eventually arrived in 1976, was Ken Gregory, whose special interest was water resources. Gregory succeeded Bird as Head – or Chairman, as he preferred it – of Department in 1979.

During his four years as Departmental Chairman, Professor Gregory strengthened the research base. Staff, together with their research students, were grouped into a limited number of research themes: cold regions research; dynamics of industrial change; environmental management; European development processes and planning; fluvial geomorphology and hydrology; history and patterns of British settlement in prairie states of the USA during the nineteenth century; metropolitan growth; Middle and Near East; palaeoenvironments; and rural planning.

Ken Gregory and some of his colleagues were particularly interested in environmental management, and this led in the early 1980s to the idea of carrying out applied research on a contract basis. In 1984 a GeoData Unit (later the GeoData Institute) was created on an inter-disciplinary basis within the Faculty of Science and, in the following year, an Urban Policy Unit was established. The formation of these units led to considerable debate within the

Arolla, Switzerland, 2001.

Department about the balance between teaching and research, and whether the commercial pressures associated with contract research would detract from both 'pure' research and teaching. This debate took a new twist in 1986, when the results of the first Research Assessment Exercise (RAE) became available. The Geography Department emerged as 'average' overall but 'above average' in physical geography. Although the staff were pleased with the outcome, they realised that research activity had to increase.

Gregory went on to become a Deputy Vice-Chancellor at Southampton and subsequently Warden of Goldsmiths' College, University of London. In 1993 the Department instituted an annual Gregory lecture in his honour, the first of these being given by Professor Peter Haggett of the University of Bristol. The lecture series has brought the world's leading geographers to Southampton and acts as a showcase for the discipline within the University and locality.

A number of steps were taken in 1986–7 to improve the research rating and, in the second RAE in 1989, the Department scored a rating of 4 on a five-point scale. However, during the 1990s, the Department underwent a truly remarkable transformation from being generally regarded as 'middle-ranking' to become one of the UK's leading centres for geographical research. The catalyst for change was the appointment in 1990 of Professor Neil Wrigley who brought an international reputation in the fields of both quantitative social science and economic geography, having begun his academic career as a lecturer in the Department between 1973 and 1976.

Building on the foundations of a reinvigorated research culture left by Professor Gregory, Wrigley instigated a series of key changes at Southampton

Undergraduate fieldwork, 2001.

– in particular the development of a research-led Department that rewarded initiative, effort and enterprise. An expansion of student numbers provided funds for the recruitment of a group of highly talented staff, both established Professors with international reputations and young researchers just beginning their academic careers. Key academics in the former category included Professor Paul Curran, one of the world's leading figures in the rapidly evolving field of remote sensing (and the youngest ever recipient of the Remote Sensing Society's Gold Medal).

Curran maintained the pace of change during his term as Head of Department in the mid-1990s. He was the prime mover behind the formulation of a visionary Departmental strategy which involved explicit and quantifiable goals in the fields of research, teaching and administration. Research was focused on three internationally recognised research themes. As a consequence of these initiatives the indicators of Departmental research status – Research Council income, numbers of international refereed journal articles published, the number of times staff publications were cited by others and the numbers of international awards and prizes – all showed remarkable increases throughout the 1990s.

The three research themes are economy, culture and space; environmental processes and change; and remote sensing and applied spatial analysis. Economy, culture and space explores the interconnections between geographies of economic restructuring, cultural practices and the production of space. It includes one of the largest groups of economic geographers in the UK, while the presence in the group of strong cultural and urban geographers continues to enhance the ability of members to contribute to innovative thinking in theoretical debates in human geography. Environmental processes and change analyses and attempts to understand past, present and future variability in fluvial, glacial and terrestrial environments, and uses this knowledge together with advanced field, modelling and computer techniques to inform environmental management decisions. Its three foci are hydrology and fluvial geomorphology, polar and alpine environments, and palaeo-ecology. Remote sensing and spatial analysis aims to understand and inform the management of physical and human environments through remote sensing and GIS. The remote-sensing foci include information extraction and 'scaling up', with particular attention to forested environments. Spatial analysis interests include census and health analysis, urban modelling and geocomputation.

The long-established traditions of excellent teaching were not neglected, however, and by 1996 the Department was one of the small band of UK geography departments which were judged to be both 'excellent' for teaching by the TQA and grade 5A for research by the UK Research Assessment Exercise. The same year the Department moved into new accommodation in the refurbished and newly named Shackleton Building (the former geology building). The new accommodation included a suite of physical and computing research facilities comprising the prestigious Global Environmental Change Laboratory, established with funding from the Wolfson Foundation and the University. By 2002 the reputation of the Department was manifest in the presence of no less than nine Chairs. In the same year, it was on course to join the elite band of geography departments in the world with an annual research income in excess of £1 million.

Physics and Astronomy

As we enter the third millennium much of the vision for Physics and Astronomy at Southampton is coming into full bloom in a Department that now has 17 Professors. Fifty years ago, the then University College was recovering from the immense effort of wartime teaching and training. The Department had one of the first purpose-built laboratories in the country and, by the onset of the 1960s under Professor Maurice Taylor, had begun expanding research. Macromolecular research, led by 'Jerry' Jerrard, was a significant activity during the 1950s. Many of his PhD students found key positions in the chemical industry. Similarly Sydney Weintroub's students spread his expertise in the growing of single crystals of soft metals. In 1958 Ralph Scurlock initiated low-temperature research which later spawned the Institute of Cryogenics, and Brian Hopkins set up surface physics, which became the largest single activity during the 1960s.

In 1960, Gwilym James, the Vice-Chancellor, strengthened Physics with the appointment of George Hutchinson to the second Chair. It is in Hutchinson's vision that we can see many of the roots of the present Department. In some ways, he had a prescient view of the important fundamental lines of inquiry into the immense and the minute in physics. He installed the beginnings of experimental high-energy physics both at the sub-nuclear level and in astronomy; some say he was the founding father of gamma-ray astronomy.

It was during this period too that another strand of the modern Department took shape in the form of Pamela Rothwell and her work in solar-terrestrial physics. The 1960s were an exciting time because of the national mood to invest in universities. A new building, intended then to be only phase one, was completed in 1966 with a projected intake of 90 undergraduates a year. Physics gained another two Chairs – Eric Lee brought fundamental solid-state studies in magnetism and John Taylor came with an established reputation in theoretical particle physics. Taylor left after only three years to take up the prestigious Bondi Chair of Mathematics at King's College, London, and was replaced by Ken Barnes who proceeded to forge a strong group of the most able people at the frontiers of understanding in elementary particle physics. Fifteen posts were created during the decade in support of the new research interests.

The 1970s were a more astringent period. Funding was going to large national or international facilities and the Department was fortunate to attract, from Imperial College London, Brian Rainford, a leading researcher in neutron scattering and magnetic materials. He brought with him a track record at the major European research centres for neutron scattering. With budgetary constraints increasing, it was possible to appoint only eight staff in this decade. Within the Department the development of the core technology for gamma-ray astronomy was actively pursued and is currently reaching fruition with the international gamma-ray imaging satellite sensor (INTEGRAL) due to be launched in 2002, and with many spin-off applications in medicine and industry. A start was made on complementing the instrumental programme with the appointment of observational astronomers with interests in high-energy compact objects such as neutron stars and black holes. This was the beginning of a new era in which astronomers worked with data from a large range of ground-based telescopes and satellite sensors, with emphasis being placed on key astrophysical questions. Both astronomy and cryogenics made large demands on mechanical and electronic techniques with the consequence that by the early 1980s the Department had established well-staffed and effective technical workshops. In experimental laboratory physics, the decade saw magnetism research overtake surface physics as the largest activity.

In the 1980s new opportunities in experimental physics were seized with the transfer from the Electronics Department of David Hanna and the appointment of Allister Ferguson to create a laser science group. Through Hanna a nexus was formed between Physics and the Optical Fibre Group in the Electronics Department, which was expert at purifying fibres. This connection was soon developed by Anne Tropper, at that time a new appointment in Laser Physics, who stimulated interest in spectroscopic studies of doped fibres. This led to the development of fibre lasers, and eventually to the fibre amplifier, which is a key component in optical fibre communications networks worldwide.

The interest in the physics of miniature structures of smaller and smaller sizes, exhibiting new wave and quantum phenomena, grew throughout the following decade. The synergy between the various groups working with fibres and lasers chimed with government policy in the late 1980s to create inter-disciplinary research centres. The Departments of Physics and Electronics jointly formed the first such centre at Southampton, the Optoelectronics Research Centre (see p.165), which came to be the umbrella for nearly all the physics staff working with lasers.

Twelve new staff were appointed during this decade. In addition the Department gained from the secondment of a senior researcher in solar terrestrial physics, Henry Rishbeth from the Rutherford Appleton Laboratory (RAL), who was using the greatly increased mainframe computing power then available to formulate accurate models of ionospheric winds. This was also the decade in which the desktop computer began to make a major contribution to data analysis and more sophisticated modelling in all areas of physics. Massive computational power was also of central importance in the particle physics field and the Department, through Chris Sachrajda, was a founder member of the UK Quantum ChromoDynamics collaboration for supercomputer simulations of the strong nuclear force. Through the 1990s, the focus shifted to theoretical and numerical efforts to perform non-perturbative calculations on the one hand, and on studies of new physics beyond the 'standard model', including the most recent developments in string and now M-theory, on the other.

At the beginning of the 1990s, when national funding models squeezed Physics, investment strategies relied on offering permanent positions to people who had already won five-year senior Research Fellowships from the national science research councils. Astronomy was successful in gaining six staff over this period, while 12 new staff were spread among the other groups. The importance of astronomy was recognised formally in 1996 when the Department changed its name from simply Physics to Physics and Astronomy.

Two notable developments occurred in the last half of the decade: Harry Coles brought liquid crystal device physics from Manchester University, and Jeremy Baumberg brought research in ultra-fast physics and nano-scale materials from the Hitachi Laboratory in Cambridge. The latter was a joint appointment between the Departments of Physics and Astronomy and Electronics and Computer Science. In some senses this brought the Department full circle, in that the Electronics Department had grown out of the Physics Department in the 1950s, and Coles's PhD supervisor was from Jerrard's macromolecules group. In the early 1990s the magnetism research was encompassing quantum coherence and vortex physics in studies of high-temperature superconductors, and magnetic superlattices on the nanometre scale were an important focus. There was a convergence of interest among the physicists working with small-scale structured matter which provided the momentum to form a larger umbrella group called Quantum and Functional Matter. This marries

The second astronomy dome comes on-line.

A physics lecture.

research into the fundamental properties of matter on the nanometre scale with the creation of new applications and devices.

At the end of the 1990s, the astronomy staff was augmented with three appointments. The Chair appointment to lead the astronomy group was Phil Charles from Oxford University, an established world leader in the study of black holes within our galaxy. Closer to Earth, solar-terrestrial physics gained another joint appointment with RAL, Mike Lockwood, an active user of large ground-based ionospheric radars and magnetospheric satellites. But perhaps the climax of the decade was the election to Fellowships of the Royal Society of Professors Sachrajda and Hanna, and just recently the inclusion of the Department among the top five in the country for research.

Throughout this period of research growth there had been parallel developments in the undergraduate curriculum. The Physics Department had pioneered unit courses in the Science Faculty and project work had been introduced for all final-year students. The greater flexibility of course structure allowed the creation of Physics with Another Subject degrees. The most successful of these were 'with astronomy', 'with space science', and 'with laser science'. An important component of the first was the astronomy field course run jointly with the University of La Laguna in Spain, which won an award for innovative teaching. The Department also made a major contribution to the Geophysical Sciences degree which contained a strong foundation of physics and mathematics. Many of its graduates are now in senior positions in companies which rely on geophysical expertise. More recently the Department was one of the earliest to create a new four-year MPhys degree course.

In the early 1990s the 'phase one' building had reached its design capacity of 90 students per year, but with pressure on space the building now housed two other Departments. The delivery of teaching material also changed from being solely dependent on lectures to support with tutorial workshops and problems classes. At the same time, the Department modernised and focused its teaching of laboratory physics, with the emphasis being put on quality of experience with modern equipment and on exemplary experiments in direct support of the lectures. Advanced undergraduate projects were supported with specialist quantum photonics experimental stations, and the installation of dedicated astronomical observatories. At this juncture the Department is well positioned to respond to the national concern for science education. Research is the driving force of the Department and this was rewarded with a rating of 5* in the 2001 Research Assesment Exercise.

Centre for Environmental Sciences

With the introduction of the unit course system in the early 1970s, and the proposal to amalgamate Botany and Zoology into a single Department of Biology (which took place in 1972), it was no longer possible to offer a joint botany/geography degree. Dr Joyce Lambert, a member of the Botany Department well known for her ecological work, especially in connection with the Norfolk Broads, proposed a new degree in Environmental Sciences. As there was no Environmental Sciences Department, a Board of Studies was appointed to administer this degree, and people in the contributing Departments – Geology, Geography and Biology – were appointed to the Board to administer it. 'The course replaces and represents an expansion of the successful combined honours degree in Botany and Geography, which has run for four sessions,' the Dean of Science reported in 1971.

At the time, 'environmental sciences' was nowhere near as common a phrase as it is today. 'Environmental Sciences at Southampton really was a pioneer,' recalls Professor Mike Clarke. 'It was set up alongside Environmental Sciences at the University of East Anglia and it created a sort of bipolar model in the UK of different ways to do the same thing. It was put together out of the combined Botany-Geography course and it represented a growing realisation that many of the big problems, global problems, could only be solved if you looked at them right across the subjects – but at that stage, much more than nowadays, it was totally unfashionable.' Since then, Environmental Sciences has grown substantially and currently has an undergraduate intake of around 50 students per year.

In its early years, the course grew slowly, not through lack of applicants, but because numbers were restricted by the University. Furthermore, while prospective students may have wanted to become environmental scientists, the world outside was not entirely ready for them. 'Students found huge difficulty in being accepted; it was not a subject people recognised. There were no adverts in the papers for environmental scientists. We had to let employers know that they were not just jacks of all trades and masters of none. That, of course, is where the concept of pathways came into the system, the idea that as an environmental scientist you could look across the sciences but nevertheless have a focus of a particular direction within them that would help employers see what it was they were buying . . . The concepts of integration, of holism, of globalism are so much part of national and international thinking today that one has difficulty in imagining what a big deal it was,' according to Professor Clarke.

In 1994, a taught MSc in Integrated Environmental Studies was introduced, followed in 1997 by a four-year MEnvSci degree, whose first five students graduated in 2001. The MSc course introduces students to environmental law and environmental impact assessments and comprises three pathways: Environmental Science, Environmental Engineering, and Environmental Communication and Management. The four-year MEnvSci, on the other hand, combines the three-year undergraduate course with a fourth-year research topic.

Part of the research in Environmental Sciences reflects Southampton's location and includes both freshwater, coastal and marine topics. However, social aspects of the environment are also studied. A recent PhD in Environmental Sciences was awarded for a study, sponsored by the retail chain B&Q, on the environmental impact of out-of-town shopping centres, while a current research project is looking at people's recycling behaviour. Current research themes in Environmental Sciences include: ecosystem function of chalk rivers; environmental impact of out-of-town shopping centres; impacts of marine pollutants on rocky shore ecosystems; designation and management of marine conservation areas; communities, habitat and restoration of streams and rivers; oil pollution of coastal marine waters; coastal community ecology and palaeo-ecological evaluation; and environmental management systems.

In 1996, the Centre became responsible for co-ordinating the Qing Dao University Institutional Development project (funded by DFID). This project has involved the Department of Civil and Environmental Engineering, the School of Ocean and Earth Sciences and the School of Biological Sciences in providing development of training and research in disposal of sewage in the coastal zone for China's Ocean University of Qing Dao.

Master of Geology students on a field trip to the Pyrenees studying deformed evaporites such as salts and gypsum.

Southampton Oceanography Centre

The Southampton Oceanography Centre, sited 'off campus' in Empress Dock, is a joint venture between the University and the Natural Environment Research Council (NERC). It comprises the academic School of Ocean and Earth Science, and NERC research divisions and support services all of which have their own history.

School of Ocean and Earth Science

The School of Ocean and Earth Science (SOES) came into being in 1998, as a consequence of the Natural Environment Research Council/University initiative which had led to the establishment of an Oceanography Centre on Southampton's waterfront. The new School brought together two of the Science Faculty's Departments, Geology and Oceanography, both of which, coincidentally, had emerged originally from the Department of Zoology.

Geology

Second-year Geology students studying sediments in the tectonically active region of Almeria Province in south-east Spain. These sediments were laid down between 2 and 5 million years ago.

Although geology had been taught at Southampton since the 1890s, it was not until 1946 that a separate Department was established, with Dorothy Wisden as lecturer in charge. Over the next decade the intake of Honours students remained very small, although the Department provided a popular subsidiary course for other Science Faculty students (especially geographers). In 1958 the Department was awarded its first Chair and appointed Frank Hodson, who remained Professor of Geology until 1981 (as well as being Dean of the Science Faculty in 1972–4 and again in 1977–8). Under Professor Hodson, the Department grew substantially. By 1967, when it moved into the Shackleton Building, it had sufficient capacity for an intake of 15 Honours Geology students, with space for 48 students in first-year courses. These provisions foreshadowed the Faculty's unit-course developments which came into operation in 1971–2, making possible the establishment of two inter-disciplinary courses: Environmental Sciences (see page 212) and Geophysical Sciences (see page 232).

At the same time, the Department had been expanding its research interests and, by the mid-1970s, was undertaking research in geochemistry, geophysics, clay mineralogy, micropalaeontology, stratigraphy, structural geology, sedimentology and mineral deposits. In 1978, the University approved a second Chair in Geology which was awarded to Bob Nesbitt, who joined the Department as its Head in 1982 and subsequently served as Dean of Science. He brought with him an interest in the geology of Japan, which he researched in collaboration with the University of Tokyo.

There followed a strengthening of the research interests in applied geology

Dr Ian West, the longest-serving member of staff (he started in 1957) shows Petroleum Geology students cross-sections of a petroleum bore hole.

giving the Department a distinctive international flavour. A contract was secured to train Saudi Arabian students in the 1980s and a succession of EC contracts (Rhodope, Greece; Iberia) building links with European institutions.

After these developments in the early 1980s, the next major expansion for Geology came when it was one of the few Geology Departments in the UK to emerge successfully from a major rationalisation exercise. Following this, Southampton's Department doubled in size, gaining additional Professors from two other Universities whose Geology Departments were closed: John Murray from Exeter and Michael House from Hull. At around the same time, as a result of support from the oil industry, David Sanderson joined the Department from Belfast as Professor of Geophysics. A collaboration with the Department of Civil and Environmental Engineering led to the establishment of a Geomechanics Research Group undertaking front line studies, modelling fractures and fluid flow through rock. The work of this unit has been strongly supported by the oil and gas industry. These initiatives were allied with a surge in postgraduate numbers. A highly successful MSc course in Micropalaeontology was established under the leadership of John Murray. It was shortly after this that a plan to move the Departments of Geology and Oceanography to a new dockside campus was formulated (see page 241). In 1995 the Department was awarded an 'Excellent' rating for its teaching.

In 1997, following the University's announcement of an initiative to allow Departments to recruit extra staff in preparation for the next Research Assessment Exercise, the senior staff in Geology and Oceanography decided to create an integrated School of Ocean and Earth Science. The Department of Geology ceased to exist as an entity on 1 August 1998.

Geophysical Sciences

At the inception in the early 1970s, the aim of the BSc course in Geophysical Sciences was to bring expertise from the Departments of Geology, Oceanography, and Physics together to offer an interdisciplinary degree programme focused on the physical aspects of the Earth and its environment. The course was and still is run by a Science Faculty Board of Studies the chairmanship of which has rotated between the principal contributing departments. Eight students were admitted as the first Geophysical Science's intake in October 1973.

Following Professor George Hutchinson (Physics) as first Chairman in 1972, the Geophysical Sciences Board has been ably led by a succession of Chairmen in particular, Professor Norman Hamilton and Dr Jon Bull from Geology, Dr Ernie Hailwood from Oceanography and Dr Geoff Daniell from Physics. Nowadays the Board of Studies includes representation from the Faculty of Mathematical Studies and the Department of Geography.

Geophysical Sciences has always maintained the focus of a relatively small intake which amongst the individual year entries has given a strong sense of corporate identity. As one of the 12 or so UK Universities offering geophysics as a first degree, Southampton has sustained on average the highest level of admissions entry over last 25 years. There are now over 350 Geophysical Sciences graduates who are pursuing a range of successful careers in hydrocarbons, mineral exploration and many other areas of commerce and industry.

Oceanography

Marine biology emerged as a component within the Department of Zoology in the 1950s as a result of the enthusiasm of Zoology's Professor, John Raymont, for the subject. In pursuit of this topic, the Department had acquired a boat: *Aurelia* was a ferryboat, probably built in the late 1800s, 'in a terrible state and, in a current, as likely to go backwards as forwards,' according to Bill Conway, who became the Department's boatman, and after whom the current SOES boat is named.

Professor Raymont proposed the formation of a Department of Oceanography in 1960. Four years later, it was created, as part of a combined Zoology and Oceanography Department. It officially became a separate Department within the Science Faculty in 1965 and, that September, moved into purpose-built accommodation on the site of an old market garden at the north end of University Road. The previous year, four students had arrived to take the first course, an MSc in Oceanography. That year, Raymont became Professor of Biological Oceanography and relinquished the Zoology Department to Professor Brent. In 1966, Henry Charnock came from the National Institute of Oceanography (later the Institute of Oceanographic Sciences) to be the Department's first Professor of Physical Oceanography.

In its early years, marine biology and chemistry were the areas in which the

Brain coral.

Sea through fish-eye lens.

Oreaster reticulatus.

RRS Discovery.

An aerial view of Southampton Oceanography Centre with RRS Discovery *and RRS* Challenger *in the dock while RRS* Charles Darwin *(foreground) comes into Southampton Water.*

Department principally taught and carried out research. In 1965, the biology group was studying the phytoplankton of Southampton Water and the metabolism of zooplankton, while the chemistry group was investigating the distributions of trace elements in sea water. Soon, however, the Department was broadening its activities. In the mid- to late 1960s, links with the University of Anamalai's marine laboratory led to a series of studies of waters near Porto Novo in south India. Similarly, collaboration with the University of Stockholm laboratory on the island of Askø, and with the Marine Biological Association at Plymouth, led respectively to work on the Arctic glacial relics of the Baltic and on the plankton of the English Channel.

To further the Department's interests in geophysics, Tony Rees was appointed in 1967; together with Henry Charnock, he formulated the proposal which led to the Department's first NERC-sponsored research cruise on the RRS *John Murray* in 1969. During the next decade or so, there was an expansion of ship-based activities, many involving more co-operative international programmes. Highlights included the geological-cum-physical cruise in the Mediterranean on which participants included Norman Hamilton, later to become Head of the Geology Department.

In 1970, Henry Charnock left Southampton (temporarily, as it turned out) to become Director of the NERC's Institute of Oceanographic Sciences. He was succeeded as Professor of Physical Oceanography by John Woods, who brought with him an interest in the then rapidly growing science of marine meteorology. Together with colleagues, Woods was engaged in an extensive international study aimed at developing a mathematical model of oceanic and atmospheric conditions. In his 1976 report as Dean of the Faculty of Science, Professor Graham Hills observed that 'Oceanography continues to weave its several disparate interests into a single subject. Thus, physical oceanographers simulating wind and tides live and work with those examining the composition of seas and sediments whilst yet others lay the foundations for fish culture and, we hope, fish farming.'

The 1970s ended, sadly, with the death of John Raymont, aged 58, when swimming off Townsville, Australia. He was a far-sighted and distinguished academic, known by his peers for his seminal books on plankton and by his staff for his benevolent guidance and support. Meanwhile, in 1977, Henry Charnock had returned to the University and his old Chair of Physical Oceanography, which had become vacant when Professor Woods moved to the Institut für Meereskunde at the University of Kiel. During the next 20 years, Oceanography was to undergo a transforming expansion, and Charnock, as much as any single person, engineered this. New staff included the appointment in 1980 of Dr Margaret Deacon to a Hartley Research Fellowship in the History of Science. Her studies over the next 20 years on the History of Oceanography have received wide international recognition.

During the 1980s, Oceanography's research continued to cover a wide range of topics. A number of these were undertaken in co-operation with the Institute of Oceanographic Sciences, for example the marine biology group's examination of the vertical distribution of hyperiids south of the Azores and, later, physiological studies of crustacea off Ascension Island (the latter coinciding with the Falklands War, but undisturbed by it). The chemistry group carried out a succession of studies of trace elements in the Atlantic and the Mediterranean, while the physical group used satellite observations of colour and temperature to study the sea-surface thermal skin layer. The geological group worked to develop an absolute time framework based on geomagnetic field reversals.

The 1984–5 session was the most important year for Oceanography since its foundation. The University Grants Committee's Physical Sciences Committee announced its proposals for the future of academic oceanography in the UK: of the four departments (Swansea, Liverpool, Bangor and Southampton) it recommended that only two should expand. Southampton, it reported, was in 'a clear leading position' judged by 'the standing of the existing staff and in particular their research'. In 1985, six new staff arrived together with the first undergraduates to take degree courses which combined Oceanography with either Biology, Chemistry, Geology, Physics or Mathematics. (The Department had been involved in undergraduate teaching before this; in 1974 a Combined Honours course in Chemistry with Oceanography had been the first formal recognition of Oceanography constituting part of a first-degree course.)

In 1989, four years after the Department had been chosen for expansion, its first undergraduates obtained their degrees. During these years, teaching had become a major Departmental activity alongside research. Under the successive headships of Professor Peter Lockwood and Professor Steve Thorpe, the Department grew steadily in size and reputation. By the early 1990s the first-year courses were attracting up to 200 students per lecture, and the Department was awarded an 'Excellent' rating for teaching to match its grade 5 for research. The 80 staff and many research students were outgrowing the new building erected in 1989. However, plans for the Southampton Oceanography Centre were now well developed, and the move to the new campus took place in 1995 under the direction of Dr Ian Robinson.

Southampton Oceanography Centre

In 1985, the House of Lords Select Committee on Science and Technology called for a general strengthening of contacts and collaboration between government-funded research institutes and higher education; and for strengthening in particular the links between the University and the NERC's Institute of Oceanographic Sciences, based in Wormley, Surrey. So the Southampton Oceanography Centre (SOC) was born as a joint venture between the NERC and the University, bringing together the NERC's IOS and Research Vessel Services (based at Barry), with the University's Departments of Oceanography and Geology. In May 1988, NERC submitted a restructuring bid to the Advisory Board for the Research Councils to fund the construction of a centre for deep-sea oceanography at a new dockside campus at Southampton University. Funding was approved in February 1989 and complementary funding secured

This squid, Onychia caribbaea, *emits a brillant blue light.*

An SOES diver (Jenny Mallinson) assesses the impact of large-scale fishing and climate changes such as El Nino on the rich Galapagos sea life. Counting the numbers of fish such as these Moorish Idols builds a picture of the current health of the marine reserve.

Lowering a conductivity, temperature, and depth (CTD) instrument into the Atlantic Ocean. The results provide scientists with information on the changes in salinity and density of water at different depths.

AUTOSUB prepares to dive. Designed, developed and built at Southampton Oceanography Centre by NERC, this autonomous underwater vehicle (AUV) can dive to depths of 1600 m. and can travel for distances of up to 100 km.

from the Universities' Funding Council in 1990.

A 13-acre site in Empress Dock was leased from Associated British Ports and planning the new Centre started at the beginning of 1989. Howard Roe, then of NERC and later Director of the Southampton Oceanography Centre, co-ordinated the planning process with Professor Norman Hamilton of Geology. Some 16 discipline-based committees were established to draw up ideas from the University and NERC scientists, academic staff and technicians. These reported to a Management Committee, chaired by the NERC Director of Marine Science, Professor John Woods, and thence to a Board chaired alternately by Vice-Chancellor Gordon Higginson and the Chief Executive of NERC, Hugh Fish.

Plans were developed over the next three years. Inevitably there were cuts to meet budgets both in research ambitions and in national profile. The high tower intended for experimental work on plankton was an early casualty, as were the International Conference Centre and combined bridge/display area intended to provide the public with easy, informed access to part of SOC. Despite such cuts a magnificent building was designed by the Culpin Partnership and built by Wimpey UK Ltd, bringing together the University and NERC components within a custom-built facility.

SOC was created to be a world-class centre and a national focus for all aspects of marine and earth sciences, for teaching and training in these areas, and for the development and transfer of appropriate technology. The Centre was also intended to serve the national marine science community by hosting national facilities, of which the fleet of NERC research vessels is by far the largest. The total cost of the project was about £50m., a huge commitment to science and a testament to the importance of marine research to the UK and to the vision of those individuals from NERC and the University who conceived and drove the project forward.

Because of its size and status, and because it was conceived as an experiment (can large-scale government-funded research facilities be successfully integrated with and managed by a university?), the project attracted great attention both nationally and internationally. Presentations were made to MPs, to members of the House of Lords, to visiting international scientists and dignitaries. A travelling roadshow, complete with model, toured the UK. The then Prime Minister, John Major, visited a very wet site one evening in February 1992 when a caravan housed display boards overlooking a sea of very muddy pile caps. The Minister for Science, William Waldegrave, visited in June 1993, burying a time capsule in the form of a model of AUTOSUB (the autonomous submarine developed at IOS and then at SOC) beneath the main entrance, and the Mayor of Southampton attended the topping out ceremony, hoisting the final part of the roof structure in place in June 1994.

The Centre was completed in the summer of 1995 and staff began to move into the new building in August and September, with the first intake of students arriving that October. The first Director, Professor John Shepherd, had been appointed in April 1994 and oversaw the setting up and establishment of the Centre as a complex and complicated fusion of different employees, staff and students, and a wealth of equipment and infrastructure. So successful was this initial 'bedding in' that the Centre was ready to be opened officially in April 1996 when HRH the Duke of Edinburgh performed the opening ceremony. Since then the Centre has developed markedly in its scientific vision and capabilities, in numbers of staff and students – there are currently some 1,100 people who can call SOC home, of whom more than 600 are students – and in its reputation. Management changes continued after the opening: the two University Departments, by then headed by Professors Mike Collins (Oceanography) and Bob Nesbitt (Geology) were merged under the leadership of Professor Patrick Holligan to become the School of Ocean and Earth Science in 1998, and Professor Howard Roe succeeded Professor Shepherd as Director in April 1999. In the following year, the NERC Research Vessel Services were separated into a ship component – the Research Ship Unit, managed by NERC and housed at the Centre – and a technical support group managed by SOC.

Oceanography is a multi-disciplinary science and from the outset SOC was intended to be an integrated centre, bringing together different communities of scientists and support staff, and also the different disciplines of biology, physics, chemistry, mathematics, geosciences, modelling, engineering and technology. The NERC scientists arrived grouped into four research divisions. The James Rennell Division for Ocean Circulation and Climate, headed by Trevor Guymer, carries out research into global-scale circulation, patterns of ocean currents, interactions between the sea and the atmosphere, satellite observations, and large-scale models of the world's oceans. The George Deacon Division for Ocean Processes, headed originally by Professor Howard Roe and now by Professor Peter Burkill, studies the interactions of biology and physics throughout the water column from the surface to the seabed, and once there, the relationships of the benthic communities with seabed geology and seabed ocean currents. The Challenger Division for Seafloor Processes, originally led by the ex-Director of IOS, Colin Summerhayes, and now by Professor Phil Weaver, researches into the geology, geophysics and geochemistry of the ocean floor, the ways continents form and move apart, underwater volcanoes, and formation and destruction processes on continental margins. The Ocean Engineering Division, headed by Professor Gwyn Griffiths, creates novel technology and engineering for the researchers, be these individual sensors or the world-beating autonomous underwater vehicle, AUTOSUB, which is capable of carrying out a variety of scientific missions from the seabed to beneath Antarctic ice.

The research of the Divisions comes together with that of the SOES in a mutually complementary way via the SOC Research Themes. These are a group of eight overlapping research areas developed to integrate the interests and expertise of all scientists and students at SOC. These themes encompass the overall research programme of SOC, namely: large-scale ocean circulation and the ocean interior; the upper ocean; coastal and shelf processes; sediments and the benthic boundary layer; plate boundaries and ocean margins; palaeo-oceanography and climate change; systems, platforms and sensors; and Earth systems science and modelling.

A box corer takes a sample of sediment from the ocean floor.

TOBI, Towed Ocean Bottom Instrument, produces acoustic images of the seafloor 6 km wide at depths of up to 6000 m. The images provide a view of the seafloor and can give details of the underlying sediments, particularly important in oil and gas exploration work.

These titles indicate the range of the Centre's research interests, which vary from the role of the oceans in global climate change, coastal processes which directly impact the 70 per cent or so of the world's population who live alongside the ocean, marine ecology and environmental impacts of man's activity on the sea and seabed, the development of technology to permit work in an extremely difficult environment, and the development of models both to understand processes and also to predict future events.

SOC is not just research – teaching and training are a very major part of its activity. Several hundred undergraduate and postgraduate students work at the Centre, studying alongside the academic staff and research scientists of both the SOES and the NERC divisions. Undergraduates study for a range of degrees in Oceanography, Marine Sciences, Geology and Geophysical Sciences, with the opportunity to add elements from other subject areas such as French. A range of Masters' courses is taught and the number of students for these is increasing rapidly, while the Graduate School hosts the PhD students who are recruited both nationally and internationally. The unique character of SOC is particularly manifested in the Graduate School, where senior NERC staff work with students alongside their University colleagues.

The Southampton Oceanography Centre is still very young, but already is recognised as an international centre of excellence. The original dream has been fulfilled: the Centre is a credit to the University and to the Natural Environment Research Council, and is a very considerable national asset.

8. Social Sciences

The Faculty of Social Sciences has built up a successful national and international reputation over the last four decades in a wide range of different areas: economics and econometric modelling; applied sociology, in particular social policy; psychology; politics and international relations; management; demography and social statistics.

On a research level, the Faculty has also made its mark by displaying its strong multi-disciplinary and international approach to a range of programmes – its ongoing global research on reproductive health is just one example. Quantitative methodology has been the bedrock to much of the Faculty's undergraduate and research-led programmes.

However, it is not just the academic side where the Faculty has stood out over the years. It has also been instrumental in changing the course of events both within the University and at government level where it has, for example, influenced thinking about student population forecasts.

So how did a Faculty that started small manage to achieve this worldwide reputation while maintaining a strong bond of collegiality among its staff (one of its defining characteristics) throughout its history?

Laying the Foundations

Social Sciences' current approach derives from the academic philosophies of the Faculty's early 'founding fathers'. Established Faculty members agree that a series of forward-thinking and influential figures have shaped the defining nature of the Faculty. At an early stage of the Faculty's history, the focus on quantitative methodology and the applied nature of social sciences had already been defined.

The roots of the Faculty rest in economics, with the appointment of a lecturer in economics in 1919. The arrival of Percy Ford in 1926 expanded the work beyond economics and into sociology. He also made the Faculty's first foray into local authority surveys.

The Faculty was small, with just 96 full-time students when the college became a university in 1952–3. It also had just one Faculty member in Politics and one in Psychology until David Rowan's appointment as Dean. However, although growth was slow in the 1950s, the Faculty was gradually getting a solid reputation for its research. Even in 1958, the Economics Department described research as 'first among the activities of the Faculty'.

Before 1960 there were already two Chairs in Economics – Percy Ford and Wallace Armstrong, who retired in 1961. Ford and Armstrong were the only Social Science professors before 1960. In the early 1960s the Faculty was taking an applied approach to sociology with key figures such as John Martin, John Smith and Gordon Trasler establishing a strong 'criminological and penological' emphasis to the programmes.

The 'key' founding father arrived in 1960. David Rowan, who was returning to the UK from Australia, not only had a huge impact on the Faculty both in terms of the Economics teaching and research at that time, but he also used his time as Dean to establish a multi-disciplinary approach to study and research – common now throughout universities but ahead of its time in the 1960s. Others included Ivor Pearce, appointed in 1962, who played a key role in steering the direction of the Faculty with the world-renowned Southampton Economic Model Building Unit. Kenneth Hilton was also directly involved in the econometric model. Other notable figures over that period included Joseph Frankel, who was appointed in 1964 as Professor of Politics and also Dean. Frankel focused heavily on international relations such as foreign policy. 'They were fabulous scholars but also out there in the real world, advising and having a real impact,' according to the Faculty's recent Dean, Professor Ian Diamond. They all had a particularly powerful influence on the Faculty's development, establishing a direction that is still being followed today.

John Smith, a Sociology Professor who was appointed in the early 1960s, is recognised today as a very 'powerful influence on the university,' said Diamond. Smith joined Southampton along with eight other new staff including Kenneth Hilton who went on to became Professor of Financial Control. The move was to cope with a massive explosion in size over the period 1963–8. In 1964–5 the Faculty gained another two figures who would have an influential role in developing its shape: Professor Gordon Trasler, for the Psychology Department, and Gordon Fisher (appointed in 1964) for Econometrics. A watershed development in the 1960s was the foundation of the Department of Econometrics and the appointment of the first Chair in Econometrics, which again reinforced the statistical, quantitative approach adopted by every department within the Faculty.

In fact 1962–4 could be considered defining years for the Faculty. This was when the Faculty of Economics renamed itself as the Faculty of Social Sciences (1962/3). At the time of the rebranding the Faculty was split into five Departments: Economics, Sociology, Politics, Commerce and Economic Statistics. With the new name 'Social Sciences' in 1962–3, the definition of the Faculty's approach was clear – the analytical, scientific and quantitative stance had shaped the Faculty's way of thinking. All these Faculty changes came hand in hand with a period of massive expansion at the end of 1960s when Social Sciences continued to develop and grow its multi-departmental approach. A growing reputation in the outside world helped the Faculty attract prestigious funding from the newly established Social Science Research Council which awarded grants to five Departments in its first year of operation in 1965–6. Funding from the Leverhulme Trust allowed the financing of two Professors (one of these was the aforementioned chair of Econometrics in 1964).

By 1964 there were seven Departments in Social Sciences: Economics and Economic Theory with two Professors, Rowan and Pearce; Commerce and Accountancy with no professors; Sociology and Social Studies with John Smith as Professor; Economic Statistics with no professor; Politics with Joseph

The Social Sciences Graduate Centre.

Frankel as Professor (Peter Calvert who is now a Professor was then a lecturer); Econometrics with a newly arrived Professor, Gordon Fisher; and Psychology where Gordon Trasler was about to be appointed.

Moving into the 1970s, other formidable academics joined the Faculty. David Rowan, Ivor Pearce and Gordon Fisher all had major roles in Economics while Graham Kalton, one of the most famous social statisticians of that time, led the new Department of Social Statistics and immediately gave it an emphasis on social surveys in which the Faculty was later to become a 'world leader'.

Right up until the end of the 1970s planned expenditure was agreed on a five-yearly, rolling basis. That contributed to some fractiousness within the Faculty because competition for resources became fiercer and it was necessary to plan on much shorter time horizons. The arrival of a Conservative Government in 1979 was followed fairly rapidly by the economic crisis in universities in 1981 which had a profound effect on the Faculty as it did elsewhere. Not only were there no more appointments but there were also attempts to get rid of some people. 'Nobody went but it wasn't a very nice occasion,' commented one member of the Faculty staff. In 1980–1 the University, along with many others, was asked to make major cutbacks. It imposed quite a high percentage cut on

Social Sciences – 16 per cent – compared with other Faculties. The amount of money asked to be cut equated to approximately a whole Department, that of Social Work Studies.

The Faculty closed ranks and insisted that it would not countenance the closure of one whole Department. 'It's something that has remained – there's a great collegiality across the different departments and schools help each other through any difficult times,' said Diamond. The then Dean, Tim Holt, put together a group of people who devised a series of money-saving recommendations for the University without having to resort to wide-scale compulsory redundancies. The group's report was called 'An Alternative Strategy for the 1980s' and in time a number of its recommendations were adopted by the University and some are still in use. Professor Diamond summed up, 'At a very difficult time for the University, forced perhaps by the potential closure of a Department, the Faculty got a group of wise people together. They produced a set of recommendations that had an impact on the University throughout the 1980s and 1990s in terms of how Southampton used its resources more efficiently.'

Although Diamond admitted that these were 'not easy times', he believes that a number of developments took the agenda of methodology and policy forward in a positive way. The main ones were: health policy coming into Sociology in the mid-1980s; changes in Economics, and expansion in Accounting and Management Science.

Politics

In Politics, the teaching of international relations began in 1964 and the first postgraduate degree was introduced a year later. Two of the major figures over the 1960s and 1970s were Peter Richards and Joseph Frankel. The latter, as Professor of Politics, focused on international relations and published a number of influential books on foreign policy. In 1979 a Chair of Political Theory was appointed – Professor Raymond Plant who, through a research-led approach, continued to have an important role. In the 1980s Plant received a grant from the SSRC which allowed Politics to set up a Centre for International Policy Studies.

Another key development was the eventual emergence of the Mountbatten Centre for International Studies – a separate organisation within the Department of Politics which engages in research principally in the field of nuclear non-proliferation.

The vital nature of the research undertaken at the Centre was acknowledged and rewarded; in the 1990s it became effectively the Secretariat to the United Nations Nuclear Non-proliferation Organisation. 'It's having a huge international role in that way,' commented Professor Diamond. Professor Lord Plant, who returned to the University in 1999 to a Research Chair, is involved in a wide range of research areas including rights, welfare, justice, modern political thought, political philosophy, Hegel, electoral systems and citizenship.

Comparative politics is another area being investigated. Faculty members point to an increasing European flavour to some of the political research being carried out.

Management Science

Originally there was a Department of Commerce and Accountancy, led by Barney Hart. When Gordon Fisher set up the Econometrics Department he brought operational research into the Social Sciences Faculty as part of his remit. When Fisher left, Econometrics was merged with Economics. In 1979, just after Kenneth Hilton was appointed Professor of Financial Managerial Control, his contract gave him an option to take Accounting out of Economics. The Department of Accounting and Management Science was then set up. It was one of the earliest business studies departments and was strongly focused on accounting and management science. Many joint degrees were offered with economics and also law and politics.

Hilton was an influential figure. He was a Dean of the Faculty and a Deputy Vice-Chancellor of the University. Faculty members point out that Hilton transferred from the model-building unit to economics and then on to management in a 'very organic' way, an interesting example of the way the Faculty's structure reflects the interests of the leading players.

The University set up a separate management school in the mid-to-late 1980s which limped along for a time and was not part of the Faculty. In 1995 the new Vice-Chancellor Professor Howard Newby commissioned a report which recommended its closure. However, the Department of Management decided to take on the students and have done so with massive success so that it is now a fast-expanding and soon-to-be major management school.

The School achieved a top 5 rating in the 1996 national Research Assessment Exercise (RAE). Not only that, but the School was recently graded as 'excellent' in the assessment of its teaching quality by the national Quality Assurance Agency for Higher Education. The School of Management has links with the Department of Aeronautics and Astronautics (MSc in Aviation Management), the School of Engineering Sciences more generally, and the Operational Research (OR) group in the Faculty of Mathematics (MSc in OR). As a result of the School's links with Engineering a new four-year MEng is about to come on stream.

Economics

Apart from David Rowan and Ivor Pearce, other notable figures in the early years included Alan Budd (who went on to become Chief Economic Adviser to HM Treasury) and Ken Hilton. In the 1980s there was a generational change as people who had been the dominating characters of the Department – Ivor Pearce, David Rowan and Ken Hilton either retired or moved into other departments. 'All these founding fathers suddenly retired or left,' said Diamond.

Other key Professors in Economics included Grayham Mizon and James Malcomson. A large group of young Faculty members arrived in the late 1970s and for many it was their first university appointment. This influx of new blood included the likes of Alistair Ulph, Professor and former Dean and Deputy Vice-Chancellor; Barry McCormick, Professor; Alan Hamlin, Professor and Dean; Paul Geroski, now Professor of the London Business School; Saul Estrin, now Professor of London Business School. These fresh appointees, who came just prior to the slowdown in the growth, had a fundamental effect on the Department. At the same time, the econometric model was beginning to be wound down because these sorts of models had 'had their day' in the UK at that time. However, the Department's great strength in econometrics continued and continues today with two Professors in that area.

Although growth has not been dramatic, there has been a continuing focus on an international perspective, and on quality. At the time of writing there were 14 different nationalities on the teaching staff. In terms of research, the study of economic and econometrics theory is ongoing, along with environmental economics and labour economics.

Psychology

The Department was built up by Gordon Trasler in the 1960s. He had been responsible for teaching a large part of the Social Sciences Faculty's degree programme, including social institutions, sociological theory and methodology. He was appointed Professor in 1964 and his reputation in the field of criminology grew steadily over the years. The Department still has a strong scientific and quantitative approach to undergraduate study with a heavy weighting towards statistics and both pure and applied psychology. Today, the Department's research organisation is built around research groups (RGs) and centres (RCs). These play distinct and complementary roles in relation to strategy. In 1997 the Department established five new RGs organised around major sub-disciplinary areas in psychology: Clinical and Health Psychology; Cognitive Psychology; Developmental Psychology; Learning and Behaviour Analysis; and Social Psychology.

Sociology and Social Policy

The Department's current applied stance can be traced back to the late 1940s when applied training was already in evidence. An emphasis on penology and criminology was also emerging at an early stage; John Martin was a leading figure in penological circles in advising Royal Commissions. Sociology and Social Administration has continued to reinforce the 'applied' dimension of sociology, i.e. how it can be applied in the real world.

Social Work Training and Health Visitor Training, jointly developed with St Thomas's Hospital, came on board, and Southampton was one of the first higher education institutions to offer degree courses to nurses. The efforts of John Smith and Jon Clark in the 1990s led to much health-related research. Today, Sociology and Social Policy is one of the leading Departments of its type in the UK. It has established its applied focus, concentrating on a joint approach where interests can be combined in two disciplines. Sociology and Social Policy achieved a score of 21 (out of 24) in the latest HEFCE Quality Assurance exercise, and was graded 5 in the most recent Research Assessment Exercise. The Department has particular research strengths in the areas of family, household and community; health (including both the sociology of health and illness and the history of health and social welfare); gender and work, and citizenship and social divisions.

In current Sociology research, the most notable development has been the establishment of a new technology research group which is looking into areas such as micro-electronics. This is a good example of a cross-discipline, collaborative project which combines the strengths and interests of Sociology with those of Electronics.

Social Work Studies

The Faculty offered a 'Certificate in Social Work' in 1937, before the Departments of Sociology and Social Policy, Politics, Psychology and Social Statistics existed. By the 1970s the then Department of Sociology and Social Administration was hosting a postgraduate (MSc/Dip) social work programme. In September 1981 all social work teaching groups in the University were combined to form the new Department of Social Work Studies, with its own Professor. The Social Work undergraduate degree started in October 1990, at the same time as Population Studies.

Social Statistics

The Department of Social Statistics, previously the Department of Econometrics and Social Statistics, was set up as a result of some fractiousness between Professors Fisher and Kalton.

The Department is unique in the UK and has been described (Raftery, *JASA* 2000) as 'the most successful effort of this kind to date'. This high international profile was a major factor in the £1.35m. award from the Joint Infrastructure Fund (JIF) for the establishment of a Social Statistics Research Centre at Southampton.

The main areas of focus are: sample survey theory and methods; statistical modelling of social science data; demography and actuarial studies. From its very beginning, the Department has been at the forefront of international research into methodology for the design and analysis of sample surveys. A major research contract with the ONS's Methods and Quality Division has led to a wide variety of methodological projects while collaborative research has developed with a number of European partners, including the national statistical institutes in the Netherlands, Sweden and Finland. In August 1999 the Department organised a major international conference on Analysis of Survey Data at Southampton.

Throughout the 1990s research centred on two areas: census statistics and reproductive health. Small area estimates and projections for local authorities in Britain came under the microscope. Another project, carried out jointly with the University of Manchester, looked at the accuracy of local authority estimates using data from the 1991 Census. Department members were also actively involved in developing the methodology to handle underenumeration in the 2001 UK Census.

Reproductive and sexual health is also an important area of research. The critical issues of family planning and reproductive health in developing countries are being tackled in two five-year research programmes funded by the Department for International Development. The first programme, 'Opportunities and Choices', based in the Department of Social Statistics, concentrates on an array of reproductive health issues such as maternal health, contraception, nutrition, sexual health, HIV/Aids and obstetric and gynaecology services. Countries where the research is being carried out include Yemen, Kenya, Pakistan, India and Zimbabwe. The second programme, 'Safe Passage to Adulthood', which is being spearheaded by the Department of Psychology, addresses the problems faced by young people. These include unplanned pregnancy, sexually transmitted infections and the lack of access to education, information and services.

The ongoing research interests of the various Departments demonstrate that the multi-disciplinary and quantitative approach that has been a defining characteristic of the Social Sciences Faculty is still very much in evidence.

9. Professional Support Services

The Library

In 1935, when the Turner Sims Library filled most of the gap between the two parts of the old main building, it was welcomed as a long overdue improvement on the single room in the south wing of the old building which it replaced. But within a year its shelves were full (30,000 volumes on the first floor, 5,000 in study rooms on part of the ground floor and 12,000 in the stacks). There were also problems which the Library's planners must have foreseen but found no way to avoid. At first much of the ground floor and some of the first were used by Departments of the Arts Faculty, waiting for a building of its own, and much of the rest was closed each year for six weeks in the summer during examinations. None of this prevented the new Library from being an enormous asset. The curators also reported 'a most marked improvement in the demeanour of those who used the place.'

The Library survived the war undamaged, but space remained a problem. In 1942 it disposed of a number of books of sub-university standard, giving 200 to Birkbeck College Library which had been bombed. When, in 1945, the College received a valuable collection of 3,000 volumes on agriculture from W. Frank Perkins, with the proviso that they should be made available to the public, it had no space to do this.

By now an extension was being planned, but in 1947 the curators admitted that there was no prospect of it being built for some time. Successive delays followed and it was ten years later that work began on a library extension, designed by Colonel Gutteridge, to be known as the Gurney-Dixon Building. Sir Samuel Gurney-Dixon, 21 years Chairman of Council, finally declared this open in December 1959. At the same time he added to the important Dante collection which he had already given the Library, six rare editions of the *Divina Commedia*, the first of these, the Brescia edition of 1487, becoming the Library's earliest printed book.

The Librarian till the start of the war had been Miss D. P. Powell, a formidable lady. 'Your purpose is to take the blame,' she told one junior assistant, referring to the faulty reshelving of books. She was succeeded, first as acting librarian then from 1941 as Librarian, by the even more formidable Marjorie Henderson. For 20 years Miss Henderson dominated the Library. She alone decided what books should be bought. Any she thought improper she either didn't buy or kept in her private room. Katy Hall (French lecturer) remembered her as 'a loveable Gorgon'. Maurice Line, a senior Assistant Librarian for her last six years, found her so impossible that they spoke only at monthly meetings, otherwise communicating by notes. Apart from her rudeness, which alienated most library users, it was her inability to delegate which infuriated him. She personally wrote out all library cards with a steel-nibbed pen when the Library was small and later insisted on staff doing the same. With a rubber

she would remove any pencil marks in books. Thirty years later books could still be found in which she had written 'All marks removed', with the date and her initials.

The Hartley Library, level five, in 1980.

When Miss Henderson announced in 1960 to her assembled staff that she was taking early retirement there was an amazed silence. Eventually Alexander Anderson, Line's fellow Assistant Librarian, stood and said, 'Miss Henderson, the Library will never be the same without you.' Line's relief was widely shared. At last those who worked for her were free to take initiatives of their own. 'She taught me one thing,' Line remembered. 'How *not* to motivate staff.' He was later (1974) to become one of the Directors-General of the British Library, in charge of its northern division with a staff of 1,100.

His criticism must be balanced against Miss Henderson's achievement in integrating the new and old libraries. It should also be said that many in

257

Southampton who knew her in private life found her a friendly and exceptionally generous person.

Line learned something else from Miss Henderson: that libraries were for people, not books. The old attitude had been, 'We've got it, you find it.' In 1962 (and again in 1965) he carried out surveys of students' attitudes to the Library, the first such surveys to be undertaken in the United Kingdom. The Library also developed a Reader Service department to help users, began to give courses in special kinds of library use – bibliographical searching, for example – and made a film to introduce freshers to the Library.

Miss Henderson was succeeded by B. M. Bland, a gentle man, who managed the Library with quiet efficiency for the next 16 years. Between 1966 and 1968 it was one of the first in the country to introduce a computer-based issue system, employing punched cards, thereby saving much staff time. Soon, however, it was suffering in exactly the way the Turner Sims Library had suffered, and in 1969, by which time it was housing over a quarter of a million books, Bland reported 'a critical space problem'.

That year an extension to the first floor for the Special Collections was completed, and he believed that taking over the remaining Administration accommodation between the two wings of the original main building would solve its problem for a couple more years. In October 1970 a north wing and mezzanine extension were ready and by the end of that session the Library had a new, 'attractive and welcoming entrance'. But the extra book space had already been almost filled by the Ford Collection of Parliamentary Papers. A more extensive enlargement was now included provisionally in the 1973–4 building programme. As time passed this retreated further into the future until, with the disappearance of the building programme in 1974–5, it vanished.

Southampton was not alone in having library space problems and in 1976 the University Grants Committee published an enquiry into 'Capital Provision for University Libraries', known as the Atkinson Report. It was not well received. 'For this library,' Bland wrote, 'to relegate a third of its stock, acquired mainly in the last 10 to 15 years, to store and disposal after five years, would require a complete disregard of the nature of a large part of this stock and of the needs of the University.'

Meanwhile the space problem became more acute and, to prevent the Library being full by 1978, 900 metres of new shelving were erected, though at the expense of space for readers. An application was also made for an extension to the mezzanine floor. This was still being considered in September 1977 when Bland retired. At the time of his appointment the Library had contained 150,000 volumes and had been spending £21,000 a year on books, binding, periodicals and administration. Now it held 550,000 volumes and was spending £343,000 annually. Bland had been, in the words of his successor, Bernard Naylor, 'the architect of the Library Service the University enjoys today'.

In 1978 the most serious attempt to deal with the space problem in 20 years was begun: the addition of a mezzanine floor to the old Turner Sims part of the Library, creating 500 sq. m. of new space. When this was opened in 1979 by Dr R. C. Tress, Director of the Leverhulme Trust, the Library presented him with a nineteenth-century pamphlet, having what Naylor described as an apt title: *A Remedy for the Relief of Our Present Embarrassment.*

The need for space by no means prevented the Library from modernising the service it provided. In 1979–80 the Telepen-based circulation system replaced the punched card system and made possible a completely up-to-date loan file at all times, not just at the end of a day. In 1984 the on-line circulating system was introduced, eventually entirely to replace the off-line system.

The Library also revised its acquisition policy – a move delayed until the Academic Goals working party set up by Vice-Chancellor Roberts should give a clearer indication of the University's future make-up. The financial crisis of 1981 soon followed, depriving the Library of money, forcing it to accept voluntary retirements, to make cuts in opening times of some of its counters and to buy fewer books. Interestingly, it protected periodicals, only closing one subscription in order to be able to afford a more needed one. By 1982–3 it was spending more on periodicals than on books.

Probably the most significant event since the Library opened its Gurney-Dixon extension in 1959 was the arrival on 17 March 1983 of the correspondence of the first Duke of Wellington. The Library had been collecting rare and valuable books and manuscripts for many years, including the 4,500 volumes of Dr Montefiore's library on theology and Judaism, the Ford Parliamentary Papers, Frank Perkins's collection of books on agriculture, Sir Samuel Gurney-Dixon's Dante collection and the James Parkes Library of Jewish/non-Jewish relations. The Wellington Archive was in another category, both for size and historical importance.

In a sense it had been long coming. In 1953 the seventh Duke of Wellington, while Chancellor of the University, had given the University the first Duke's 236 volumes of printed Sessional Papers of the House of Lords. In 1975 the eighth Duke had given the first Duke's 3,300 pamphlets (published between 1814 and 1841). As significant for the future, in 1956 the seventh Duke had written privately to Vice-Chancellor James, about the possibility that the first Duke's Archive should come to Southampton.

Early in 1979 it was announced that the whole of the first Duke's archive (100,000 documents) had been accepted by the Treasury in lieu of death duties on the seventh Duke's estate. Naylor was keen to bid for this, in part because, if it went elsewhere, the Duke's printed material which the University already held might follow it. He soon had the support of John Roberts, a historian who specialised in French Revolutionary and Napoleonic times, who had succeeded Gower as Vice-Chancellor in October 1979. But it was the Minister for the Arts who had to decide (with the advice of the Royal Commission on Historical Manuscripts) where the archive should be held. It helped Southampton's case that the new Minister, Norman St John Stevas (who had once taught at Southampton in the embryonic Department of Law) soon announced that he favoured the holding of some of the National Heritage outside London. The University became aware, however, that though the Minister favoured Southampton, the Commission did not. It also knew that its accommodation for the archive was below the required standard. When, after three years' anxious negotiation, St John Stevas's successor, Paul Channon, announced in February 1982 that Southampton had been chosen, the University urgently set about making the needed improvements. By the following March all was ready for the archive's arrival.

Three months later Naylor first learned that the University might be offered the equally important Broadlands Archive, including the Palmerston and Mountbatten papers. Negotiations were again prolonged, this time involving the Cabinet Office which had an interest in the uses to be made of the Mountbatten papers. However, the University had no space for this even larger collection. Fortunately it was now discussing with the UGC the first substantial extension of the Library since the Gurney-Dixon extension of 1959, and a major new suite to accommodate the University's Special Collections was incorporated in the building plans. By February 1987 the new suite was ready to accept the Broadlands Archive.

As a result of these major acquisitions the Library developed an additional role, becoming an important centre for primary historical research. The Leverhulme Trust gave it grants for cataloguing the Wellington Papers, and the Library put this on to the Internet as it was being compiled, the first university library to do such a thing. The Special Collections have continued to grow, acquiring, among many other items, 'the Anglo-Jewish Archive' in 1990, and subsequently two smaller collections which combine rescue with research importance. One was of historical music recordings, the other of knitting (as a result of the Winchester School of Art's interest in clothes and fashion).

The rebuilding of the renamed Hartley Library, which amounted in effect to the creation of a new library, coincided with the coldest winter for many years. Thanking the staff for their hard work in such conditions (when 'the revised heating system had not yet reached the stage where it could cope'), Naylor wrote that 'the conventional expressions of appreciation were quite inadequate.' It was finally opened on 25 March 1988 by Countess Mountbatten, daughter of Earl Mountbatten of Burma.

At the same time developments were taking place which would transform the way in which the University provided, and its members received, information. In 1992 the Library made use of SIGNET, the University's new campus-wide network, to enable staff and students to access its catalogue from any computer terminal on campus and also to access the library catalogues of other university libraries which had done the same. From 1993, when the World-Wide Web emerged, the Library made increasing amounts of information available on websites. By the year 2000, its website contained over 4,000 pages of information.

At the end of the century the Library was again full as well as having to serve a vastly increased number of students. Once more it was desperately in need of a major increase of accommodation.

The Special Collections room in the Hartley Library.

Computing Services

Throughout its existence the activities of the Computing Services often overlapped those of the Library, but the history of its development remains a separate one. This began in October 1956 when the University acquired its first computer, a Ferranti Pegasus, and installed it in a new building (later to become the Student Health Centre).

At that time Southampton was one of only five universities to be funded by the University Grants Committee to buy computers. Godfrey Lance, Director of Computing at Southampton for its first three years, compared features of the Pegasus with those of an average computer of 30 years later. By then there had been 'an improvement by a factor of 163 in the cost, 1,000 in the speed, 1,000 in the backing store and 4,000 in the direct access memory. So it seems no exaggeration,' he continued, ' to deduce that the power of the Pegasus was only a little over one-millionth that of a typical PC of 1987.' Even so, Professor Coulson, who officially opened the new computer lab in 1958, calculated that the Pegasus could do in 13fi minutes a calculation which would have taken 100 years using hand calculators. The Pegasus was such a rare possession that outsiders, from for example the Gas Board, as well as staff from other universities were eager to use it. One academic from Cardiff, who could only be given time at night, came with his campbed and set the Pegasus to wake him when it needed help.

Within the University, Civil Engineering was one of the first Departments to use the Pegasus. Others soon followed. But it was only in 1967 that the Computing Services was set up as a service operation outside the Mathematics Department. It now had a managing committee to devise policy, not for research into computing as a science, but for serving the University. At the same time Professor David Barron arrived from Cambridge where he had been a lecturer in the Mathematical Laboratory, first to become the University's Professor of Computation, a year later to be also made Director of the Computing Services.

Meanwhile the Pegasus was proving increasingly unreliable, as a result, in the opinion of Margaret Davis, of an upgrading in 1962–3. Miss Davis had come to Southampton in 1961 with no computer training and had had to learn from the manufacturer's reference book. Forty years later, still a member of Computing Services, she considered that Southampton's computer troubles had mostly resulted from its attempts to be at the forefront of the technology.

The Pegasus was replaced temporarily in 1967 by an ICL 1909; this was in turn replaced a year later with an ICL 1907, both of these, like the Pegasus, paid for by the UGC. The 1907 was not only capable

An Automation Collectadata machine for computer issue, installed in the Library with anti-noise hood, 1975.

of faster numerical calculations, but provided a time-sharing system with 16 remote terminals in academic departments. It was expected to last ten years but in practice was needed for twelve. Now the number of staff, and particularly of students, using the computer increased to such an extent that by 1971–2 time had to be allocated ('polite word for rationed,' the director wrote). The same year Southampton was linked to the more powerful University of London Computer Centre's CDC 7600, and allowed time with this for some of its more demanding work. The following year a tentative start was made on installing more terminals around the campus.

In 1974 a new full-time director of the Computer Service, Morley Sage, was appointed. That year the Computer Board promised the University a new ICL 2970, though not the new building originally proposed by the UGC, with the result that it had to be installed in the basement of the Mathematics Building. The new computer commenced service in October 1976. Two years of frustration followed since the ICL 2970 did not meet expectations.

It had also proved unable to meet the University's increasing demands and for these a PDP 11/45 was bought in 1975 to run in parallel with it. From the start this provided two teaching labs (later many more) for interactive BASIC programming and early CBT (Computer-Based Teaching) material, making Southampton one of the first universities to initiate interactive terminal-based teaching. Meanwhile the Computer Board had given the University funds to buy a Honeywell 6080 to compensate for the failures of the ICL 2970. The Honeywell proved satisfactory and more terminals were now installed, some in the Library and some in the Murray Building, where Mathematics and Social Sciences needed them for teaching. And the ICL 2970 proved less unreliable in its later years. Nevertheless in 1987 the Computer Board replaced both it and the Honeywell with an IBM 3090, probably the most powerful system IBM

The spiral staircase in the Turner Sims Building (later renamed the Hartley Library). It was built in 1979 (top left).

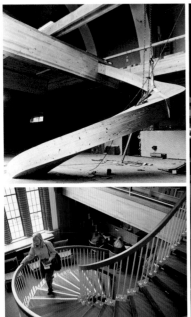

Installation art in the Hartley Library.

had installed in any UK university. Sage described the year of its opening as the Computing Service's most important. Much use was at once made of its vector processor facility (enabling it to make certain types of mathematical calculation at much increased speed), and work done by the London and other computer centres began to come back to Southampton. Its importance and the Government's new recognition of the importance of computing was demonstrated when Kenneth Baker, Secretary of State for Education, formally opened the IBM 3090 service.

In 1989 Computing Services (as it was renamed shortly after the appointment of its new Director, Dr Kenneth Heard) became part of a new group, the University Information Group, working alongside the Library and Teaching Media. Bernard Naylor became the first Information Services Co-ordinator. In 1993 the co-ordinated activities were relabelled Academic Support Services, and Heard succeeded Naylor for a term of office lasting to September 1998. The New Information/Academic Support Services group produced useful co-ordination and forward planning within the group. Nevertheless, its three components remained separately managed on a day-to-day operational level.

The transition from mainframe to a distributed computing architecture was confirmed in December 1993 when the University decided to replace its ageing IBM 3090 with a 'quartet' of multi-processor Sun computer systems and a complementary cluster of 'graphic' workstations. The large Sun systems were to act as separate servers for computation, for data storage and, subsequently, for web services and e-mail, while the cluster of more than 30 workstations would have their own local servers to supply software and local storage. The IBM 3090 was finally carried away 'on the back of a lorry' shortly after it was switched off at 4.16 p.m. on 16 August 1994, destined for recycling to recover what gold remained on its circuit board contacts.

The University telephone service had come under Computing Services management in mid-1992 and at Easter 1994 a new Ericsson-based service was brought into service connecting just over 3,000 handsets. During the next six years this same University telephone system was extended, still within Computing Services management, to service over 5,300 extensions at nine geographically separate University locations.

Computing Services' participation in multi-processor, high-performance computing had begun as far back as 1989, at first helping to make it easier to use the (at that time) revolutionary transputer chip, then had progressed through commissioning and development of services on a Meiko CS2 delivered in April 1993, to installation and exploitation of a 23-processor IBM SP2 system installed in November 1994, and enhanced in January 1996. That facility was partly funded under IBM's Shared University Research programme, Southampton being the first European university to benefit under this programme. In 1995–6 the Southampton SP2 was rated in the top 500 most powerful computers in the world (not counting classified military/government machines).

In the summer of 1997, a powerful new Silicon Graphics multiprocessor, Origin2000, was acquired to relieve the ageing IBM SP2 of its burden in shouldering computational support for research, together with a number of smaller but still significant Silicon Graphics Challenge systems. The Origin2000 was commissioned alongside a whole raft of new computationally intensive Unix workstations used for both teaching and research and a new 'quartet' (central servers have somehow often gone in fours) of SG 0200 server systems to relieve the older Sun servers. By the beginning of 1998 the computer suite which had earlier housed just the one IBM 3090 mainframe computer was home to well over 40 server systems, ranging from the multi-processor computer engines, through massive (GigaByte) filestore management systems to a myriad of 'pizza box'-style computers which host e-mail and related services. All this, alongside management and support of the University telephone service, the ubiquitous data network and its connection to the national and international Internet, the 955 workstations situated in 54 different clusters on every academic and several residential campuses of the University, and assisting over 25,000 customers for its services would, in Heard's words, 'continue to keep Computing Services fairly busy in the third millennium.'

The Administration

Only eight people have ever assumed the highest administrative office at Southampton since the formation of the University College, even though the first Registrar was appointed in 1900. He was David Kiddle, who was promoted to the post of Registrar from his former office as Librarian, serving the University altogether for nearly 40 years. Even at the end of his period of office, the administration had just two clerks, with the secretary of Senate still a professor.

George Grant, appointed in 1923, began the process of building an administrative framework, with one of the clerks appointed as college accountant and the other as clerk of works. Grant became secretary of Senate and committees were established for the first time.

Grant was to serve for 18 years, before being succeeded by Ernest Dyson in 1941, who nine years later was succeeded by Bruce Chalmers. Although Chalmers was to serve for only four years, his influence on the future governance of the University was significant, for he was a key figure in the preparation of the University's Charter.

Robert Robertson succeeded Chalmers in 1954 and was to be the institution's last Registrar, with the administration's highest office becoming Secretary and Registrar at the end of his term. Robertson's period of office saw one important appointment to his staff, that of Derek Schofield, a former President of the Students' Union, destined to be a future Secretary and Registrar.

In 1966 Roderick Urquhart succeeded Roberston, building round him a particularly able team. Derek Schofield was appointed as Academic Registrar in 1969, in succession to the formidable Miss Price-White, with Phil Halliwell as Works and Buildings Officer, and John Dalby as Finance Officer. Halliwell was to be much involved in development of the University estate in the 1960s and

1970s whilst Dalby was one of the architects of the move to budgetary devolution which is still a hallmark of Southampton's financial management systems.

The long-awaited move of the Administration from the Library into its own purpose-built Administration Building also took place in 1969, although the building was already too small to match the growth in the number of administrative staff, even by the time it was occupied.

Derek Schofield was promoted to Secretary and Registrar in 1978 and was instrumental in creating a climate of trust between academics and administration, stemming from his ability to marry an insistence on professional commitment with a firm advocacy of the Administration's service role. Like his predecessors, he was the keeper of the conscience of the institution, concerned to ensure that its rules and procedures were carefully preserved.

Schofield was a distinguished Secretary and Registrar, intimately involved in the planning and development of the University and influential in helping to adjust to changing patterns of funding and management. He also had a concern for the development of the profession and of individuals. His period of office also saw increased importance placed on the interface with outside world.

The Hartley Library today.

John Lauwerys was appointed in 1992, at the start of Southampton's most sustained period of growth. Lauwerys took a different view to his predecessor of the role of the Administration and saw the job as no longer that of simply a servant of the academic staff but as a true partner in managing the institution. His period of office has seen many changes, the emergence of quality assurance as a major function, the imposition of unprecedented levels of legislation, particularly employment legislation, and the recognition of the importance of strategic planning. Departments have been fundamentally reorganised: the staffing office has become the Personnel Department, most latterly headed by a Director of Human Resources; the Centre for Enterprise and Innovation is the latest mutation of a function first started 20 years earlier as the Office of Industrial Affairs; a new Department of Business Services has been created, responsible for halls of residence, catering and other services; and public relations and development have been merged into External Relations.

Lauwerys reflects that the scale, diversity, complexity, pressure and demands on the administration have all grown hugely with, not before time, university administration beginning to have the characteristics of a true profession. The skills required of the administrative staff have also shifted, from the generalist, able to deal with different tasks in different departments, to highly professional specialists with business and financial expertise, often drawn from the outside world rather than from the ranks of career higher-education administrators.

10. Support of the Arts

A well-attended theatre, art gallery and concert hall, closely linked to the Arts Faculty though formally independent of it, play an essential role in linking the University to the local and regional communities: visitors to these facilities regularly come from Chichester, Bournemouth or further afield.

The Nuffield Theatre opened its doors in 1964 following a substantial grant from the Nuffield Foundation and was immediately regarded as the central venue for University dramatic and musical performance and also visiting amateur and professional performances. Part of its function has been to provide a theatrical experience for the community of Southampton. Early appearances included Britten chamber operas and the highlights of the 1970s included visits by the Royal Shakespeare Company and the National Theatre. In the early days the theatre also put on exhibitions of Fine Art in one of its galleries. The theatre has a solid reputation for its excellent and wide-ranging performances – anything from contemporary work to the revival of classics.

In October 1974 the Turner Sims Concert Hall was opened, providing the people of Southampton with what was then, and still is, one of the best concert venues in the country. The Concert Hall is named after Edward Turner Sims, a Southampton businessman whose legacy launched a fund-raising appeal for the £216,000 building costs. The official opening concert was given by Swedish soprano Elisabeth Söderström on 19 November 1974. Since that time some of the best musicians in the world have appeared at the Turner Sims, with the original emphasis on classical chamber music being supplemented from the 1990s by jazz and world music. The Concert Hall celebrated its 25th anniversary in 1999–2000 with visits from, among others, John Williams, Alfred Brendel and Evelyn Glennie. The 2000–1 season included such diverse artists as the London Mozart Players, Emma Kirkby, Julian Joseph, the South African Gospel Singers and East European folk band Szapora, as well as a visit from the BBC Radio 4 quiz programme *Just a Minute*. During term-time, evening concerts are supplemented by twice-weekly lunchtime concerts organised by the Department of Music and featuring both students and outside artists.

The development of the visual arts at the University of Southampton, particularly in its public provision and its attraction of public funding, has been a notable feature over the past 50 years. The University's first gallery was in the Nuffield Theatre complex designed by Sir Basil Spence in the early 1960s. From then until the late 1970s Professor Nigel Glendinning, Professor Morice, Dr John Sweetman and many others provided the impetus for a broad ranging programme of activities. Additionally in 1973 the Photographic Gallery was established, the only one in a British University and one of only four of its kind in the UK. Funded by the Regional Arts Board, Southern Arts, and the Arts Council of Great Britain, it pioneered the role of the gallery as a catalyst linking a broad spectrum of interests inside and outside the University and achieving a national reputation for the range of its outreach activities and its work in helping to establish photography as a creative medium in its own right.

Then in 1980 all strands of the University's visual arts development were brought together in the form of the John Hansard Gallery. The project was a partnership between the Arts Council of Great Britain and the University to create a regional centre for contemporary art. Through the breadth and quality of its programme it has firmly established its position as one of the major publicly subsidised galleries in the country. The gallery organises seven temporary exhibitions each year by artists from Britain and abroad, in painting, sculpture, installation, photography and crafts. In addition, the gallery puts on a programme of events related to the exhibitions including lectures, seminars and conferences. Its exhibitions regularly receive project funds from the Arts Council, Visiting Arts, the Henry Moore Sculpture Trust and the cultural departments of foreign governments. The gallery organises several major touring exhibitions each year, and these often tour internationally.

The period of the gallery's evolution has been one in which a rapidly changing society has had far-reaching effects on higher education. Universities have dramatically expanded and through their building programmes become major patrons of architecture. Southampton has been at the forefront of this process, first with its appointment of Sir Basil Spence and now Rick Mather as consultant architects, both achieving wide recognition for their work on public

The Queen views a sculpture in the Nuffield Theatre, 1966.

The Turner Sims Concert Hall at dusk.

commissions in their respective eras.

During this period also the gulf between universities and the community has slowly lessened and at Southampton the public provision of the arts has been an important factor in helping to achieve this. Likewise the work of the former Department of Adult Education, which under various identities has continued to pursue a pioneering role, latterly in its present form as the Faculty of Continuing Education and Lifelong Learning.

In the community at large, urban development has swept onward and gradually awareness has increased of the important role that architecture and the arts can play in social and cultural regeneration and development. The University of Southampton has made a particular and continuing contribution to this movement. Through its patronage of architecture and the arts, and through the impact of its wide ranging gallery and adult education programmes, which from an early date spawned a number of collaborations, it has kept pace and linked up with changing aspects of society. To draw attention to this and to show it within the context of what others are doing, in its Golden Jubilee Year two inter-linked public Open Lecture series are taking place in 2002 hosted by New College and the John Hansard Gallery.

Above: *the Nuffield Theatre's production of King Oedipus, 2001.*

Left: *Andy Sheppard and Steve Lodder with Southampton Youth Jazz Orchestra, playing at the Turner Sims Concert Hall.*

11. Building a Vision

The Physical Framework of the University

Other university campuses may have specimen buildings that are architectural or historical gems, set off by landscapes so large that students are barely noticed, but not Southampton. The Highfield Campus area has something very different to offer. At the focal crossing point in University Road, between the Hartley Library and the Union Building there is an exciting sense of vitality that is reminiscent of a small and busy market town.

The setting that is so conducive to this atmosphere is largely the legacy of one man, the architect Sir Basil Spence. Educated and previously spending most of his working life in Edinburgh, in 1956 Spence was commissioned by the far-sighted University to prepare a masterplan of the Highfield Campus that would serve for the then foreseeable future. The requirement was to accommodate the anticipated substantial increase in students in the years to come, in attractive conditions on a well and cohesively designed campus.

Spence found himself challenged by a cramped piece of land that seemed unsuitable for realistic expansion. Totally locked in by the residential development that had grown up during the previous generation, the 59-acre campus site was split in half by a busy feeder road. On one side of this road was a wide variance in level, the quarry of a former brickworks that itself was split by a stream.

The highly detailed brick buildings of the existing University, which had been designed by the local architects Gutteridge & Gutteridge, were redolent of a more genteel pre-war age. These occupied a small, central part of the land, on either side of the road. Pleasant but unremarkable buildings, they had to be taken into account but would contribute little to the new aesthetic.

In the context of his decision that the site could never accommodate more than 8,000 students, Spence produced a very workable masterplan that was to stand the test of time for the next forty years. Not being able to eliminate the divisive road he substantially ignored it. Perhaps the only major criticism of his work at Southampton is that the plan and all the buildings that he subsequently designed turned their backs to the road, leaving it as a singularly unresolved piece of streetscape. It was true that, at the time, most of the road as it ran through the Campus was taken up with private housing that did not belong to the University, but during the intervening years it has purchased all of these and more for redevelopment purposes.

Apart from the Administration Building and the original Oceanography Building, which were designed by the Sheppard Robson Partnership, all the major Campus buildings of the 1960s and 1970s were designed by Sir Basil Spence. A man of controversy for some of his contemporary designs, Spence chose to work in concrete, glass and mosaic for most of his Southampton structures and used them in a manner that complemented the existing brick

Sir Basil Spence inside Coventry Cathedral which he designed after the original building was bombed during World War II. He also designed many buildings for the Umiversity of Southampton and devised a master plan for the main campus.

buildings well. Compared to some of his buildings elsewhere none of these are outstanding in their own prerogative, but set into groups they have a remarkable visual quality. To stand today beside the trickling stream, in the beautifully landscaped basin of the West Campus and look up and around at the wonderful ring of perfectly positioned buildings that surround it, one must humbly acknowledge that, as a designer of the urban environment, Spence got it absolutely right.

After building at a frantic pace for many years Treasury money for building dried up and during more than a decade before 1988 the University built no capital projects, either academic or residential. Then things began to happen again on both fronts. Finance was forthcoming for a new building and a large clean room, for the increasingly significant Department of Electronics and Computer Science. The commissioned architects were the John Bonnington Partnership, successors to the practice of Sir Basil Spence, Bonnington and Collins.

Architectural style had changed over the years. Concrete and glass buildings were unfashionable and in many cases had been discredited. The Mountbatten Building, as it was eventually named, was built in a highly visible location and completed in 1991. Its bland aluminium-clad structure was either loved or hated, but never failed to provoke opinion for many years.

Away from the Highfield Campus other plans were evolving. In the late 1980s the University entered into a joint venture with the Natural Environment Research Council to establish an oceanographic centre in Southampton. Approached from the sea the Southampton Oceanography Centre, which houses the School of Ocean and Earth Science, is now a prominent feature on the city's skyline. Designed by the architects Culpin Partnership, it was completed in 1994.

Also off the Campus, two residential projects at South Hill and Wolfe House were commissioned from Gutteridge & Gutteridge in 1990. Providing nearly 300 units of self-contained accommodation, these were designed in the firm's tradition of highly detailed brickwork, albeit now in a modern idiom. Setting a high standard of quality in both design and accommodation, they were built to house mature postgraduate students in self-contained bed-sitting rooms, each with a kitchenette and shower room en suite.

Two buildings designed by Sir Basil Spence.

Top: *the Law Faculty.* Middle and above: *the staff social centre in the grounds of Highfield Campus today.*

In parallel, Gutteridges designed the University Health Centre on a site adjacent to Southampton Common. As a building it was particularly important, not for its design but because it was the first one to contravene the Spence masterplan in its location. It entirely blocked what Sir Basil had prescribed as the natural visual flow of the West Campus garden landscape into the grass and woodland of the Common. This was significant because now that its rules had been broken the masterplan began to fall into disregard.

At this time, the University again thought about its future expansion. Student numbers had already risen to 8,000, Spence's suggested maximum for Highfield. Consideration was given to the construction of a second campus on 500 acres of Forestry Commission land at Lords Wood, just outside the Southampton City boundary. This plan fell through and given the opportunity

Facing page: *the Mountbatten Building (left), completed in 1991, linked to the Zepler Building (right), completed in 1998, both for Electronics and Computer Science.*

Below: *'To stand today beside the trickling stream, in the beautifully landscaped basin of the West Campus and look up and around at the wonderful ring of perfectly positioned buildings that surround it, one must humbly acknowledge that Spence got it absolutely right.'*

to purchase two important additional pieces of land in Highfield, those of Richard Taunton's College in Highfield Road and Hampton Park School on a site adjacent to the main Campus, it was decided to re-examine the potential of the main Highfield Campus.

In 1991 a Highfield Planning Group was formed within the University under the chairmanship of a Deputy Vice-Chancellor, Professor Tim Holt, later to be succeeded by Professor Alistair Ulph. Under their strong leadership the group's remit was to evaluate the alternatives available for the future expansion of the Campus and to oversee the production of a physical development plan for the coming generation, which would be acceptable to both the University and Southampton City Council.

The following year the University engaged the specialist town-planning services of Chesterton Consulting. Chosen for their work on behalf of speculative developers it was hoped that their experience in maximising the development potential of commercial sites could be applied to the Highfield Campus. Given the premiss of a rise in student numbers to 15,000 within twenty-five years and using the Spence masterplan as a starting point, Chesterton were to produce a comprehensive strategic development plan for the Campus.

Two halls of residence.

Top: *Wolfe House.*
Above: *South Hill.*

A principal obstacle to viable expansion was the question of accessible car parking within the Campus area, for which there appeared to be an insatiable demand. Draconian planning laws insisted upon the addition of large numbers of car spaces for every new building constructed. Chesterton proposed to resolve this by the construction of three large multi-storey car parks within the Campus area. The divisive location of University Road was another problem addressed and alternative proposals for an underpass and for a major diversion of the northern half of the road were examined, although neither of these came to fruition. A further suggestion for reduction of pressure on available floor space was for the redevelopment of the Richard Taunton College site.

Chesterton's final strategic development plan identified that, using commercial norms, a very substantial amount of additional accommodation could be achieved within substantially the existing land area of the Highfield Campus. Their greater success, however, despite considerable opposition, was the negotiation unchanged of their strategic development plan into the then current revision of the Southampton City Council Local Development Plan. This was to ensure a substantially easier passage in obtaining many of the University's future Planning Consents.

With new opportunities for development this was also a time of new approaches in the briefing and commissioning of the University's buildings. Rather than utilising the services of just one or two practices repetitively a range of new architects were appointed for the projects that followed. In 1993 the London architects Allies & Morrison were appointed to design the new Students' Union Shop Building. The following year another London practice, Hawkins Brown, designed the refurbishment of and a major extension to the Richard Taunton's College, which was subsequently renamed as the Avenue Campus. Into this moved the whole of the Faculty of Arts, with the exception

The central courtyard at Avenue Campus.

The Textile Conservation Centre.

of the Department of Music.

Student residential building had not lapsed. A re-evaluation of the University's housing stock had revealed a shortfall of at least 1,000 study bedrooms in the coming years if the guarantee of a room for every first-year student was to be fulfilled. A Residential Project Committee was formed under the chairmanship of the Secretary and Registrar, Mr John Lauwerys, in order to tackle this problem and to oversee the design and construction of new accommodation projects. Students were fully involved in the decisions of this committee, being represented by the President of the Students' Union.

In 1992 a major residential project of over 600 student bedrooms was commenced as the third phase of development at Montefiore, one of the University's two largest residential campuses. This scheme marked an important change of direction in the way in which the University tried to provide accommodation to meet the current living patterns of its students.

Previous generations of students had lived in large blocks with individual bedrooms and communal sanitary facilities. Some had had self-catering facilities but the majority took their meals together in centrally catered dining halls. For Montefiore 3 a new type of accommodation was attempted. Individual bedrooms with en-suite shower rooms were grouped into apartment-style units of seven rooms, eight apartment units in each of eleven separate buildings, with each individual unit having its own self-catering kitchen/dining room.

Following on from the experience of Montefiore, the University decided to focus as closely as possible upon the real requirements of its students. The London architects DEGW were appointed to carry out an in-depth study of the way in which students chose and aspired to live, relating this to optimum forms of accommodation and economical forms of building. In 1994 the DEGW Report became a guide for the design and construction of the University's future accommodation projects.

The first of these was the New Terrace at Glen Eyre, the other large residential campus, completed in 1996 and comprising nearly 200 study-bedrooms. Whilst generally following the pattern of accommodation established at Montefiore 3 the number of study-bedrooms in each apartment unit were reduced to six, a number that balanced acceptability in social terms with economy of construction. This was also the University's first residential project to use a design-and-build form of construction. Another three buildings, comprising 400 study-bedrooms at Hartley Grove, Glen Eyre, followed it in 1998. These used the same form of accommodation as the New Terrace and were again constructed on a design-and-build basis.

Chesterton's strategic development plan had identified several of the existing major buildings on the Highfield Campus that could be radically altered internally, to provide additional useful floor area. With the Faculty of Arts moving off the Highfield Campus it was possible, in 1995, to commence a programme of refurbishing these buildings. Academic departments followed each other into new accommodation as each building was refurbished in turn. In the next three years substantial alteration work was carried out to the Shackleton Building to house Geography and Psychology, to provide improved space for Physics and Astronomy and Mathematics and to move Computing Services to the Murray Building. They were supplemented by the addition of a new Social Sciences

The Shackleton Building.

The Nightingale Building, opened on the main University site in September 2000 to house the School of Nursing and Midwifery.

Graduate Building. Other buildings that were refurbished later included the Students' Union Building and the original Oceanography Building, the latter housing further areas of Electronics and Computing Science.

At the same time funds had become available for the construction of a new Synthetic Chemistry Building, the first new major building on the Highfield Campus for eight years. Designed in 1996 by London Architects, the Wilson Mason Partnership, it was completed in 1998 and the extra space provided enabled the subsequent refurbishment of the whole of the existing Chemistry accommodation, some of the oldest and most dilapidated on the Campus, two years later. A major extension to the Synthetic Chemistry Building, to house the new discipline of Combinatorial Chemistry, was added in 2002.

Of major impact on the University's strategic development plan, in 1996 Southampton City Council adopted the principles of the Government's Planning Policy Guidance Note 13 on Transport, designed to replace traffic congestion by improved public transport services. The effect of this was that Planning Consents for new buildings would henceforth stipulate maximum numbers of parking spaces as opposed to minimum. The need to build multi-storey car parks on the Campus vanished, freeing up additional new development sites. In hindsight the development of Richard Taunton's College site had not after all been necessary, but the City's change in policy had come too late.

Following the publication of the Local Development Plan, incorporating Chesterton's strategic plan, it was decided in 1996 that an urban design consultant for the Highfield Campus should be appointed and retained. The brief for this consultant would be two-fold. The preparation of a phased implementation plan for future buildings was to be based upon the development potential identified by Chesterton and the establishment of a comprehensive visual identity for future buildings. This would ensure that, whichever way the Campus developed, its overall appearance would remain cohesive and co-ordinated.

A London practice, Rick Mather Architects, were commissioned as the urban design consultants. Mather, who had studied architecture in the USA and urban design at the Architectural Association in London, was an experienced master-planner. His implementation plan for the Campus, whilst recognising Spence's achievement in the development of its western side, firmly grasped the problem of its division by University Road. It proposed that the road should become a tree-lined boulevard, backed on either side by a line of similar white-rendered buildings.

Emphasising the road thus would make it a major attribute of the Campus and a linear feature leading from its 'gateway' on Burgess Road to an enhanced central 'square' between the Hartley Library and the Students' Union. Mather also stressed the importance of the places between buildings having their own sense of presence, identifying a set of squares each linking specific groups of structures. He was concerned that new buildings to be designed, whilst retaining an identity of their own, should harmonise with the two existing Campus styles, the early red-brick Gutteridge buildings and the later concrete

Spence buildings.

It was to this end that, in order to establish a precedent in style, the first two new buildings of the implementation plan were built to the designs of Rick Mather. In 1998 the Zepler Building was completed as an additional building for the Department of Electronics and Computer Science. The Gower Building was a commercial building, completed in 1999, to free up other development sites by housing the four banks that had branches on the Campus and the University's bookshop. The upper floor also provided self-contained residential accommodation for postgraduate students. The first building to commence the development of the new University Avenue followed next. Designed by the Wilson Mason Partnership to integrate with Rick Mather's masterplan, the Nightingale Building was built to accommodate the rapidly expanding School of Nursing and Midwifery and was completed in 2000.

A substantial programme of development is envisaged on the Highfield Campus for the decade to come. There are current plans to substantially revamp University Road to truly turn it into a University Avenue. Several new buildings are already in course of design. These include a new Indoor Sports Centre with a swimming pool, a major extension to the Hartley Library to house its special collections of national importance and a new Student Services Building, adjacent to the Administration Building.

There is no doubt that the vitality of the University, so evident over the past half-century, will be intensified as the Mather implementation plan comes to fruition and that the Highfield Campus will remain an exciting place for students, staff and public alike.

Afterword

Professor Bill Wakeham, Vice-Chancellor from 2001.

After seven years at the helm, during which the University doubled in size and grew in stature, Professor Sir Howard Newby (he was knighted in 2001) was persuaded to take up the position of Chief Executive of the Higher Education Funding Council for England. He left the University confident of its future: its physical surroundings were radically improved, and the ethos of the institution underwent a profound transformation, ensuring a focus on research excellence which paid dividends in the 2001 national Research Assessment Exercise (RAE).

Sir Howard's successor as Vice-Chancellor was Professor Bill Wakeham, a chemical engineer who had been Deputy Rector of Imperial College, London, where he had played a key role in its development as a world-class university institution of science, engineering and medicine.

A few months after Bill Wakeham took over, the RAE findings were announced. In his words they were, 'Spectacular by anybody's standard'. They put the University in the top ten of research-led universities in the UK, indicating also that the University had made one of the biggest improvements in research quality relative to other universities.

In particular, the Engineering Faculty now had more researchers at the top grade of 5* than any other university in the country. Such achievement was in fact mirrored across the board, with generally high grades in all faculties, and the number of top graded departments increased from two to eight.

The outstanding RAE performance was the backdrop to Wakeham's 'Vision and Strategic Direction for the University of Southampton to 2010', which had been prepared after widespread consultation and discussion around the University. The document acknowledged that Southampton was now in a position to compete internationally as an elite research-intensive institution, but that it needed a clearly defined strategic direction and purpose.

'We must set out to lead the world in some selected areas,' said the Vice-Chancellor. 'We must select them, and they will be partly shaped by ourselves and partly by the outside world.'

As the University deliberated about its future organisation and direction, it also looked back from a significant anniversary in its history. 2002 marked the University's Golden Jubilee, the fiftieth anniversary of the granting of its Royal Charter on 29 April 1952. 'Our celebrations this year enable us to pay tribute to all those who have contributed to the University's success and achievements over the last 50 years – from students and staff to collaborators and friends,' said the Vice-Chancellor. 'As we celebrate the past we also look forward to the twenty-first century, taking with us the best of what has been achieved since 1952, and committed to playing an enduring and substantial role at the forefront of higher education and research, nationally and globally.'

Index